Traits and stories of the Irish peasantry

William Carleton, William Henry Brooke

THE HEDGE SCHOOL.

...igned & Etched by W.H. Brooke A.R.H.A.

[illegible] well the Thre[illegible] [illegible]

TRAITS AND STORIES

OF

THE IRISH PEASANTRY.

WITH

SIX ETCHINGS, AND ENGRAVINGS ON WOOD, BY
W. H. BROOKE, ESQ. A. R. H. A.

VOL. II.

THIRD EDITION, CORRECTED.

DUBLIN:
WILLIAM FREDERICK WAKEMAN,
9, D'OLIER-STREET;
SIMPKIN AND MARSHALL, AND RICH. GROOMBRIDGE,
LONDON.

MDCCCXXXIV.

DUBLIN:
PRINTED BY P. DIXON HARDY, CECILIA-STREET.

CONTENTS OF VOL. II.

Page

THE PARTY FIGHT AND FUNERAL 1

THE HEDGE SCHOOL, and THE ABDUCTION OF MAT KAVANAGH 139

THE STATION 263

THE

PARTY FIGHT AND FUNERAL

THE

PARTY FIGHT AND FUNERAL.

[We ought, perhaps, to inform our readers that the connection between a party fight and funeral is sufficiently strong to justify the author in classing them under the title which is prefixed to this story. The one being usually the natural result of the other, is made to proceed from it, as is the custom in real life among the Irish. Such is the preface with which we deem it necessary to introduce the following sketch to those who shall honour us with a perusal.]

It has been long laid down as a universal principle, that self-preservation is the first law of nature. An Irishman, however, has nothing to do with this; he disposes of it as he does of the other laws, and washes his hands out of it altogether. But commend him to a fair, dance, funeral, or wedding, or to any other sport where there is a likelihood of getting his head or his bones broken, and if he survive, he will remember you with a kindness peculiar to himself, to the last day of his life—will drub you from head to heel if he finds that any misfortune has kept you out of a row beyond the usual period of three months—will render the same service to any of your friends that stand in need of it—or, in short, will go to the world's end, or fifty miles farther, as he himself would say, to serve you, provided you can procure him a bit of decent fighting. Now, in truth and soberness, it is difficult to account for this propensity ; especially when the task of ascertaining it is assigned to those of another country, or even to those Irishmen whose rank in life places them too far from the customs, prejudices, and domestic opinions of their native peasantry—none of which can be properly known without mingling with them. To my own knowledge, however, it proceeds in a great measure from *education*. And here I would beg leave to point out an omission of which the several boards of education have been guilty, and which, I believe, no one but myself has yet been sufficiently acute and philosophical to ascertain, as forming a *sine qua non* in the national instruction of the lower orders of Irishmen.

The cream of the matter is this:—a species of ambition prevails in the Green Isle, not known in any other country. It is an ambition of about three miles by four in extent; or, in other words is bounded by the limits of the parish in which the subject of it may reside. It puts itself forth early in the character, and a hardy perennial it is. In my own case, its first development was noticed in the hedge-school which I attended. I had not been long there, till I was forced to declare myself either for the Caseys or the Murphys, two tiny factions, that had split the school between them. The day on which the ceremony of my declaration took place was a solemn one. After school, we all went to the bottom of a deep valley, a short distance from the school-house; up to the moment of our assembling there, I had not taken my stand under either banner: that of the Caseys was a sod of turf, stuck on the end of a broken fishing-rod—the eagle of the Murphys was a Cork-red potato, hoisted in the same manner. The turf was borne by an urchin, who afterwards distinguished himself in fairs and markets as a *buílla batthah** of the first grade, and from this circumstance he was nicknamed *Parrah Rack han.*† The potato was borne by little Mickle M'Phauden Murphy, who afterwards took away Katty Bane Sheridan, without asking either her own consent or her father's. They were all then boys, it is true, but they gave a tolerable promise

* Cudgel Player. † Paddy Riot.

of that eminence which they subsequently attained.

When we arrived at the bottom of the glen, the Murphys and the Caseys, including their respective followers, ranged themselves on either side of a long line, which was drawn between the belligerent powers with the butt-end of one of the standards. Exactly on this line was I placed. The word was then put to me in full form—"Whether will you side with the dacent Caseys, or the blackguard Murphys?" "Whether will you side with the dacent Murphys, or the blackguard Caseys?" "The potato for ever!" said I, throwing up my caubeen, and running over to the Murphy standard. In the twinkling of an eye we were at it; and in a short time the deuce an eye some of us had to twinkle. A battle-royal succeeded, that lasted near half an hour, and it would probably have lasted about double the time, were it not for the appearance of the "master," who was seen by a little shrivelled *vidette*, who wanted an arm, and could take no part in the engagement. This was enough—we instantly radiated in all possible directions, so that by the time he had descended through the intricacies of the glen to the field of battle, neither victor nor vanquished was visible, except, perhaps, a straggler or two as they topped the brow of the declivity, looking back over their shoulders, to put themselves out of doubt as to their visibility by the master. They seldom looked in vain, however; for there he usually stood, shaking up his rod, silently prophetic of its application on the following day. This threat, for the most part, ended in smoke; for except he horsed about forty or fifty of us, the infliction of impartial justice was utterly out of his power.

But besides this, there never was a realm in which the evils of a divided cabinet were more visible: the truth is, the monarch himself was under the influence of female government—an influence which he felt it either contrary to his inclination, or beyond his power to throw off. "Poor Norah, long may *you reign*," we often used to exclaim, to the visible mortification of the "master," who felt the benevolence of the wish bottomed upon an indirect want of allegiance to himself. Well, it was a *touching* scene!—how we used to stand with the waistbands of our small-clothes cautiously grasped in our hands, with a timid show of resistance, our brave red faces slobbered over with tears, as we stood naked for execution! Never was there a finer specimen of deprecation in eloquence than we then exhibited—the supplicating look right up into the master's face—the touching modulation of the whine—the additional tightness and caution with which we grasped the waistbands with one hand, when it was necessary to use the other in wiping our eyes and noses with the polished sleeve-cuff—the sincerity and vehemence with which we promised never to be guilty again, still shrewdly including the condition of present impunity, for our offence:—"this—one—time—master, if ye plaise, Sir;" and the utter hopelessness and despair which were legible in the last groan, as we grasped the "master's" leg in utter recklessness of judgment, were all perfect in their way. Reader, have you ever got a reprieve from the gallows? I beg pardon, my dear Sir; I only meant to ask, are you capable of entering into what a personage of that description might be supposed to feel, on being informed, after the knot had been neatly tied under the left ear, and the cap drawn over his eyes, that his majesty had granted him a full pardon? But you remember your own schoolboy days, and that's enough.

The nice discrimination with which Norah used to time her interference was indeed surprising. God help us! limited was our experience, and shallow our little judgments, or we might with less trouble than Sir Humphry Davy deciphered the Herculaneum MSS. have known what the master meant, when with the upraised arm hung over us, his eye was fixed upon the door of the kitchen, waiting for Norah's appearance.

Long, my fair and virtuous countrywomen, I repeat it to you all, as I did to Norah—may you reign in the hearts and affections of your husbands, (but no where else,) the grace, ornaments, and happiness of their hearths and lives, you jewels, you! You are paragons of all that's good, and your feelings are highly creditable to yourselves and to humanity.

When Norah advanced, with her brawny uplifted arm, (for she was a powerful woman,) and forbidding aspect, to interpose between us and the avenging terrors of the birch, do you think that she did not reflect honour on her sex and the national character? I sink the base allusion to the *miscaum* of fresh butter, which we had placed in her hands that morning, or the dish of eggs, or of meal, which we had either begged or stolen at home, as a present for her; disclaiming, at the same time, the rascally idea of giving it from any motive beneath the most lofty-minded and disinterested generosity on our part.

Then again, never did a forbidding face shine with so winning and amicable an expression as did her's on that merciful occasion. The sun dancing an hornpipe on Easter Sunday morning, or the full moon sailing as proud as a peacock in a new halo-head-dress, was a very disrespectable sight, compared to Norah's red beaming face, shrouded in her dowd cap with long ears, that descended to her masculine and substantial neck. Owing to her influence, the whole economy of the school was good; for we were permitted to cuff one another, and do whatever we pleased, with impunity, *if* we brought the meal, eggs, or butter; except some scape-goat who was not able to accomplish this, and he generally received on his own miserable carcase what was due to us all.

Poor Jack Murray! His last words on the scaffold, for being concerned in the murder of Pierce, the gauger, were, that he got the first of his bad habits under Pat Mulligan and Norah—that he learned to steal by secreting at home, butter and meal to paste up the master's eyes to his bad conduct—and that his fondness for quarrelling arose from being permitted to head a faction at school; a most ungrateful return for the many acts of grace which the indulgence of Norah caused to be issued in his favour.

I was but a short time under Pat, when, after the general example, I had my cudgel, which I used to carry regularly to a certain furze bush within fifty perches of the "seminary," where I hid it till after "dismiss." I grant it does not look well in me to become my own panegyrist;

but I can at least declare, that there were few among the Caseys able to resist the prowess of this right arm, puny as it was at the period in question. Our battles were obstinate and frequent; but as the quarrels of the two families and their relations on each side were as bitter and pugnacious in fairs and markets as ours were in school, we hit upon the plan of holding our Lilliputian engagements upon the same days on which our fathers and brothers contested. According to this plan, it very often happened that the corresponding parties were successful, and as frequently, that whilst the Caseys were well drubbed in the fair, their sons were victorious at school, and *vice versa*.

For my part, I was early trained to cudgelling, and before I reached my fourteenth year, could pronounce as sage and accurate an opinion upon the merits of a *shillelagh*, as it is called, or cudgel, as a veterinary surgeon of sixty could upon a dead ass at first sight. Our plan of preparing is this:—we sallied out to any place where there was an underwood of blackthorn or oak, and, having surveyed the premises with the eye of a connoisseur, we selected the straightest root-growing piece which we could find: for if not root-growing, we did not consider it worth cutting, knowing from experience, that a branch, how straight and fair soever it might look, would snap in the twist and tug of war. Having cut it as close to the root as possible, we then lopped off the branches, and put it up in the chimney to season. When seasoned, we took it down, and wrapping it in brown paper, well steeped in hog's lard or oil, we buried it in a horse dunghill, paying it a daily visit for the purpose of making it straight by doubling back the bends or angles across the knee, in a direction contrary to their natural tendency. Having daily repeated this until we had made it straight, and renewed the oiled wrapping paper until the staff was perfectly saturated, we then rubbed it well with a woollen cloth, containing a little black-lead and grease, to give it a polish. This was the last process, except that if we thought it too light at the top, we used to bore a hole in the lower end with a red-hot iron spindle, into which we poured melted lead, for the purpose of giving it the knock-down weight.

There were very few of Paddy Mulligan's scholars without a choice collection of them, and scarcely one who had not, before his fifteenth year, a just claim to be called the hero of a hundred fights, and the heritor of as many bumps on the cranium as would strike both Gall and Spurzheim speechless.

Now this, be it known, was, and in some districts yet is, an integral part of an Irish peasant's *education.* In the northern parts of Ireland, where the population of the Catholics on the one side, and of Protestants and Dissenters on the other, is nearly equal, I have known the respective scholars of Catholic and Protestant schools to challenge each other, and meet half-way to do battle, in vindication of their respective creeds; or for the purpose of establishing the character of their respective masters as the more learned man; for if we were to judge by the nature of the education then received, we would be led to conclude that a more commercial nation than Ireland was not on the face of the earth, it being the indispensible part of every scholar's business to become acquainted with the *three sets of Book-keeping.*

The boy who was the handiest and the most daring with the cudgel at Paddy Mulligan's school was Denis Kelly, the son of a wealthy farmer in the neighbourhood. He was a rash, hot-tempered, good-natured lad, possessing a more than common share of this blackthorn ambition; on which account he was cherished by his relations as a boy that was likely at a future period to be able to walk over the course of the parish, in fair, market, or patron. He certainly grew up a stout, able, young fellow; and before he reached nineteen years, was unrivalled at the popular exercises of the peasantry. Shortly after that time he made his *debut* in a party-quarrel, which took place in one of the Christmas *Margamores*,* and fully sustained the anticipations which were formed of him by his relations. For a year or two afterwards no quarrel was fought without him; and his prowess rose until he had gained the very pinnacle of that ambition which he had determined to reach. About this time I was separated from him, having found it necessary, in order to accomplish my objects in life, to reside with a relation in another part of the country.

The period of my absence, I believe, was about fourteen years, during which space I heard no account of him whatsoever. At length, however, that inextinguishable attachment which turns the affections and memory to the friends of our early days—to those scenes which we traversed when the heart was light and the spirits buoyant—determined me to make a visit to my native place, that I might witness the progress of time and care upon those faces that were once so familiar to me; that I might once more look upon the meadows, and valleys, and groves, and mountains where I had so often played, and to which I still found

* Big Markets.

myself bound by a tie that a more enlightened view of life and nature only made stronger and more enduring. I accordingly set off, and arrived late in the evening of a December day, at a little town within a few miles of my native home. On alighting from the coach and dining, I determined to walk home, as it was a fine frosty night. The full moon hung in the blue unclouded firmament in all her lustre, and the stars shone out with that tremulous twinkling motion, so peculiarly remarkable in frost. I had been absent, I said, about fourteen years, and felt that the enjoyment of this night would form an era in the records of my memory and my feelings. I find myself indeed utterly incapable of expressing what I experienced; but those who have ever been in similar circumstances will understand what I mean. A strong spirit of practical poetry and romance was upon me; and I thought that a common-place approach in the open day would have rendered my return to the scenes of my early life a very stale and unedifying matter.

I left the inn at seven o'clock, and as I had only five miles to walk, I would just arrive about nine, allowing myself to saunter on at the rate of two miles and a half per hour. My sensations, indeed, as I went along, were singular; and as I took a solitary road that went across the mountains, the loneliness of the walk, the deep gloom of the valleys, the towering height of the dark hills, and the pale silvery light of a sleeping lake, shining dimly in the distance below, gave me such a distinct notion of the sublime and beautiful, as I have seldom since experienced. I recommend every man who has been fourteen years absent from his native fields to return by moonlight.

Well, there is a mystery yet undiscovered in our being, for no man can know his feelings or his capacities. Many a slumbering thought, and sentiment, and association, reposes within him, of which he is utterly ignorant, and which, except he come in contact with those objects whose influence over his mind can alone call them into being, may never be awakened, or give him one moment of either pleasure or pain. There is, therefore, a great deal in the position which we hold in society, and simply in situation. I felt this on *that* night: for the tenor of my reflections was new and original, and my feelings had a warmth and freshness in them, which nothing but the situation in which I then found myself could give them. The force of association, too, was powerful; for as I advanced nearer home, the names of hills, and lakes, and mountains, that I had utterly forgotten, as I thought, were distinctly revived in my memory; and a crowd of youthful thoughts and feelings, that I imagined my intercourse with the world and the finger of time had blotted out of my being, began to crowd afresh on my fancy. The name of a townland would instantly return with its appearance; and I could now remember the history of families and individuals that had long been effaced from my recollection.

But what is even more singular is, that the superstitious terrors of my boyhood began to come over me, as formerly, whenever a spot noted for supernatural appearances met my eye. It was in vain that I exerted myself to expel them, by throwing the barrier of philosophic reasoning in their way; they still clung to me, in spite of every effort to the contrary. But the fact is, that I was, for the moment, the slave of a morbid and feverish sentiment, that left me completely at the mercy of the dark and fleeting images that passed over my fancy. I now came to a turn where the road began to slope down into the depths of a valley that ran across it. When I looked forward into the bottom, all was darkness impenetrable, for the moon-beams were thrown off by the height of the mountains that rose on each side of it. I felt an indefinite sensation of fear, because at that moment I recollected that it had been, in my younger days, notorious as the scene of an apparition, where the spirit of a murdered pedlar had never been known to permit a solitary traveller to pass without appearing to him, and walking cheek-by-jowl along with him to the next house on the way, at which spot he usually vanished. The influence of my feelings, or, I should rather say, the physical excitement of my nerves, was by no means slight, as these old traditions recurred to me; although, at the same time, my moral courage was perfectly unimpaired, so that, notwithstanding this involuntary apprehension, I felt a degree of novelty and curiosity in descending the valley: "If it appear," said I, "I shall at least satisfy myself as to the truth of apparitions."

My dress consisted of a long, dark surtout, the collar of which, as the night was keen, I had turned up about my ears, and the corners of it met round my face. In addition to this I had a black silk handkerchief tied across my mouth, to keep out the night air, so that, as my dark fur travelling cap came down over my face, there was very little of my countenance visible. I now had advanced half way into the valley, and all about me was dark and still: the moon-light was not nearer than the top of the hill which I was descending; and I often turned round to look upon it, so silvery and beautiful it appeared at a distance. Sometimes I stood for a few moments, admiring its effect, and contemplating the dark mountains as they stood out against the firmament, then kindled into magnificent grandeur by the myriads of stars that glowed in its expanse. There was perfect silence and solitude around me; and, as I stood alone in the dark chamber of the mountains, I felt the impressiveness of the situation gradually supersede my terrors. A sublime sense of religious awe descended on me; my soul kindled into a glow of solemn and elevated devotion, which gave me a more intense perception of the presence of God than I had ever before experienced. "How sacred—how awful," thought I, "is this place!—how impressive is this hour!—surely, I feel myself at the footstool of God! The voice of worship is in this deep, soul-thrilling silence, and the tongue of praise speaks, as it were, from the very solitude of the mountains!" I then thought of Him who went up into a mountain-top to pray, and felt the majesty of those admirable descriptions of the Almighty, given in the Old Testament, blend in delightful harmony with the beauty and fitness of the Christian dispensation, that brought life and immortality to light. "Here," said I, "do I feel that I am indeed immortal, and destined for scenes of a more exalted and comprehensive existence!"

I then proceeded further into the valley, completely freed from the influence of old and superstitious associations. A few perches below me, a small river crossed the road, over which was thrown a little stone bridge of rude workmanship. This bridge was the spot on which the apparition was said to appear; and as I approached it, I felt the folly of those terrors which had only a few minutes before beset me so strongly. I found my moral energies recruited, and the dark phantasms of my imagination dispelled by the light of religion, which had refreshed me with a deep sense of the Almighty presence. I accordingly walked forward, scarcely bestowing a thought upon the history of the place, and had got within a few yards of the bridge, when on resting my eye accidentally upon the little elevation formed by its rude arch, I perceived a black coffin placed at the edge of the road, exactly upon the bridge!

It may be evident to the reader, that, however satisfactory the force of philosophical reasoning might have been upon the subject of the solitude, I was too much the creature of sensation for an hour before, to look on such a startling object with firm nerves. For the first two or three minutes, therefore, I exhibited as finished a specimen of the dastardly, as could be imagined. My hair absolutely raised my cap some inches off my head; my mouth opened to an extent which I did not conceive it could possibly reach; I thought my eyes shot out from their sockets; and my fingers spread out and became stiff, though powerless. The "*obstupui*" was perfectly realized in me, for, with the exception of a single groan, which I gave on first seeing the object, I found that if one word would save my life, or transport me to my own fire-side, I could not utter it. I was also rooted to the earth, as if by magic; and although instant tergiversation and flight had my most hearty concurrence, I could not move a limb, nor even raise my eye off the sepulchral-looking object which lay before me. I now felt the perspiration fall from my face in torrents, and the strokes of my heart fell audibly on my ear. I even attempted to say "God preserve me," but my tongue was dumb and powerless, and could not move. My eye was still upon the coffin, when I perceived that, from being motionless, it instantly began to swing, first in a lateral, then in a longitudinal direction, although it was perfectly evident that no human hand was nearer it than my own. At length I raised my eyes off it, for my vision was strained to an aching intensity, which I thought must have occasioned my eye-strings to crack. I looked instinctively about me for assistance—but all was dismal, silent, and solitary: even the moon had disappeared among a few clouds that I had not noticed in the sky.

As I stood in this state of indescribable horror, I saw the light gradually fade away from the tops of the mountains, giving the scene around me a dim and spectral ghastliness, which, to those who were never in such a situation, is altogether inconceivable.

At length I thought I heard a noise as it were of a rushing tempest, sweeping from the hills down into the valley; but, on looking up, I could perceive nothing but the dusky desolation that brooded over the place. Still the noise continued; again I saw the coffin move; I then felt the motion communicated to myself, and found my body borne and swung backwards and forwards, precisely according to the motion of the coffin. I again attempted to utter a cry for assistance, but could not: the motion of my body still continued, as did the approaching noise in the hills. I looked up a second time in the direction in which the valley wound off between them, but, judge of what I must have suffered, when I beheld one of the mountains moving, as it were, from its base, and tumbling down towards the spot on which I stood. In the twinkling of an eye the whole scene, hills and all, began to tremble, to vibrate and to fly round me, with a rapid, delirious motion; the stars shot back into the depths of heaven, and disappeared; the ground on which I stood began to pass from beneath my feet; a noise like the breaking of a thousand gigantic billows again burst from every direction, and I found myself instantly overwhelmed by some deadly weight, which protrasted me on the earth, and deprived me of sense and motion.

I know not how long I continued in this state; but I remember that, on opening my eyes, the first object that presented itself to me, was the sky glowing as before with ten thousand stars, and the moon walking in her unclouded brightness through the heavens. The whole circumstance then rushed back upon my mind, but with a sense of horror very much diminished; I arose, and, on looking towards the spot, perceived the coffin in the same place. I then stood, and endeavouring to collect myself, viewed it as calmly as possible; it was, however, as motionless and distinct as when I first saw it. I now began to reason upon the matter, and to consider that it was pusillanimous in me to give way to such boyish terrors. The confidence, also, which my heart, only a short time before this, had experienced in the presence and protection of the Almighty, again returned, and, along with it, a degree of religious fortitude, which invigorated my whole system. "Well," thought I, "in the name of God I shall ascertain what you are, let the consequence be what it may." I then advanced until I stood exactly over it, and raising my foot, gave it a slight kick. "Now," said I, "nothing remains but to ascertain whether it contains a dead body, or not;" but, on raising the end of it, I perceived, by its lightness, that it was empty. To investigate the cause of its being left in this solitary spot was, however, not within the compass of my philosophy, so I gave that up. On looking at it more closely, I noticed a plate, marked with the name and age of the person for whom it was intended, and on bringing my eye near the letters, I was able between fingering and reading, to make out the name of my old cudgel-fighting school-fellow, Denis Kelly.

This discovery threw a partial light upon the business; but I now remembered to have heard of individuals who had seen black, unearthly coffins, inscribed with the names of certain living persons; and that these were considered as ominous of the death of those persons. I accordingly determined to be certain that this was a real coffin; and as Denis's house was not more than a mile before me, I decided on carrying it that far: "If he be dead," thought I, "it will be all right, and if not, we will see more about it." My mind, in fact, was diseased by terror. I instantly raised the coffin, and as I found a rope lying on the ground under it, I strapped it about my shoulders and proceeded: nor could I help smiling when I reflected upon the singular transition which the man of sentiment and sensation so strangely underwent;—from the sublime contemplation of the silent mountain solitude and the spangled heavens to the task of carrying a coffin! It was an adventure, however, and I was resolved to see how it would terminate.

There was from the bridge an ascent in the road, not so gradual as that by which I descended on the other side; and as the coffin was rather heavy, I began to repent of having any thing to do with it; for I was by no means experienced in carrying coffins. The carriage of it was, indeed, altogether an irksome and unpleasant concern; for owing to my ignorance of using the rope that tied it skilfully, it was every moment sliding down my back, dragging along the stones, or bumping against my heels: besides, I saw no sufficient grounds I had for entering upon the ludicrous and odd employment of carrying another man's coffin, and was several times upon the point of washing my hands out of it altogether. But the novelty of the incident, and the mystery in which it was involved, decided me in bringing it as far as Kelly's house, which was exactly on my way home.

I had yet half a mile to go; but I thought it would be best to strap it more firmly about my body before I could start again: I therefore set it standing on its end, just at the turn of the road, until I should breathe a little, for I was rather exhausted by a trudge under it of half a mile and upwards. Whilst the coffin was in this position, I standing exactly behind it, (Kelly had been a tall man, consequently it was somewhat higher than I was) a crowd of people bearing lights, advanced round the corner; and the first object which presented itself to their vision, was the coffin in that position, whilst I was totally invisible behind it. As soon as they saw it, there was an involuntary cry of consternation from the whole crowd; at this time I had the coffin once more strapped firmly by a running knot to my shoulders, so that I could loose it whenever I pleased. On seeing the party, and hearing certain expressions which dropped from them, I knew at once that there had been some unlucky blunder in the business on their part; and I would have given a good deal to be out of the circumstances in which I then stood. I felt that I could not possibly have accounted for my situation, without bringing myself in for as respectable a portion of rank cowardice, as those who ran away from the coffin; for that it was left behind in a fit of terror, I now entertained no doubt whatever, particularly when I remembered the traditions connected with the spot in which I found it.

" *Manim a Yea agus a wurrah !**" exclaimed one of them, " if the black man hasn't brought it up from the bridge: *dher a lorna heena*,† he did; for it was above the bridge we first seen him: jist for all the world—the Lord be about us—as Antony and me war coming out on the road at the bridge, there he was standing—a headless man, all black, widout face or eyes upon him—and then we cut acrass the fields home."

" But where is he now, Eman?" said one of them, " are you sure you seen him?"

" Seen him!" both exclaimed, " do ye think we'd take to our scrapers like two hares, only we did; arrah, bad manners to you, do you think the coffin could walk up wid itself from the bridge to this, only he brought it?—isn't that enough?"

* My soul to God and the Virgin.

† By the *very* book.

"Thrue for yees," the rest exclaimed, "but what's to be done?"

"Why to bring the coffin home, now that we're all together," another observed; "they say he never appears to more than two at wanst, so he won't be apt to show himself now."

"Well, boys, let two of you go down to it," said one of them, "and we'll wait here till yees bring it up."

"Yes," said Eman Dhu, "do you go down, Owen, as you have the Scapular on you, and the jug of holy water in your hand, and let Billy M'Shane, here, repate the *confeethur* along wid you."

"Isn't it the same thing, Eman," replied Owen, "if I shake the holy water on you, and whoever goes wid you; sure you know that if only one dhrop of it touched you, the devil himself couldn't harm you!"

"And what needs yourself be afraid, then," retorted Eman; "and you has the Scapular on you to the back of that? Didn't you say, as you war coming out, that if it *was* the devil, you'd disparse him?"

"You had betther not be mintioning his name, you *omadhaun*," replied the other; "if I was your age, and hadn't a wife and childre on my hands, it's myself that would trust in God, and go down manfully; but the people are hen-hearted now, besides what they used to be in my time."

"During this conversation, I had resolved, if possible, to keep up the delusion, until I could get myself extricated with due secrecy out of this ridiculous situation; and I was glad to find that owing to their cowardice there was some likelihood of effecting my design.

"Ned," said one of them to a little man, "go down and speak to it, as it can't harm *you*."

"Why, sure," said Ned, with a tremor in his voice, "I can speak to it, where I am, widout going within rache of it. Boys, stay close to me: hem—In the name of—but don't you think I had betther spake to it in the Latin I sarve mass wid; it can't but answer that, for the *sowl* of it, seeing it's a blest language?"

"Very well," the rest replied; "try that, Ned; give it the best and ginteelest grammar you have, and maybe it may thrate us dacent."

Now it so happened that, in my school-boy days, I had joined, from mere frolic, a class of young fellows who were learning what is called the "*Sarvin' of Mass*," and had impressed it so accurately on a pretty retentive memory, that I never forgot it. At length, Ned pulled out his beads, and bedewed himself most copiously with the holy water. He then shouted out, with a voice which resembled that of a man in an ague fit—"*Dom-i-n-us vo-bis-cum ?*" "*Et cum spiritu tuo*," I replied, in a husky sepulchral tone, from behind the coffin. As soon as I uttered these words, the whole crowd ran back instinctively with affright; and Ned got so weak, that they were obliged to support him.

"Lord have marcy on us," said Ned; "boys, isn't it an awful thing to speak to a spirit: my hair is like I dunna what, it's sticking up so stiff upon my head."

"Spake to it in English, Ned," said they, "till we hear what it will say. Ax it does any thing trouble it; or whether its *sowl's* in Purgatory."

"Wouldn't it be betther," observed another, "to ax it who murdhered it—maybe it wants to discover that?"

"In the—na-me of—Go-o-d-ness," said Ned, down to me, "what are you?"

"I'm the soul," I replied, in the same voice, "of the pedlar that was murdered on the bridge below."

"And—who—was—it, Sur, wid—submission, that—murdhered—you?"

To this I made no reply.

"I say," continued Ned, "in—the—name—of —G-o-o-d-ness—who was it—that took the liberty of murdhering you, dacent man?"

"Ned Corrigan," I answered, giving his own name.

"Hem! God presarve us! Ned Corrigan!" he exclaimed. "What Ned, for there's two of them —Is it myself, or the *other* vagabone?"

"Yourself, you murderer!" I replied.

"Ho!" said Ned, getting quite stout—"Is that you, neighbour? Come, now, walk out wid yourself out of that coffin, you vagabone you, whoever you are."

"What do you mane, Ned, by spaking to it that-a-way?" the rest inquired.

"Hut," said Ned, "it's some fellow or other that's playing a thrick upon us. Sure I never knew neither act nor part of the murdher, nor of the murdherers; and you know, if it was any thing of that nature, it couldn't tell me a lie, and me a Scapularian, along wid axing it in God's name, wid Father Feasthalagh's Latin."

"Big tare-an'-ouns!" said the rest; "if we thought it was any man making fun of us, but we'd crop the ears off his head, to tache him to be joking!"

To tell the truth, when I heard this suggestion, I began to repent of my frolic; but I was determined to make another effort to finish the adventure creditably.

"Ned," said they, "throw some of the holy water on us all, and in the name of St. Pether and the Blessed Virgin, we'll go down and examine it in a body."

This they considered a good thought, and Ned was sprinkling the water about him in all directions, whilst he repeated some jargon which was completely unintelligible. They then began to approach the coffin at dead-march time, and I felt that this was the only moment in which my plan could succeed—for had I waited until they came down, all would have been discovered. As soon, therefore, as they began to move towards me, I also began, with equal solemnity, to retrograde towards *them;* so that, as the coffin was between us, it seemed to move without human means.

"Stop, for God's sake, stop," shouted Ned; "it's movin'! It has made the coffin alive; don't you see it stepping this way widout hand or foot, barring the boords!"

There was now a halt to ascertain the fact: but I still retrograded. This was sufficient—a cry of terror broke from the whole group, and, without waiting for further evidence, they set off in the direction they came from, at full speed, Ned fling-

THE FUNERAL

[illegible] by W.H.B. [illegible]

[illegible] cry of terror broke from [illegible] group!

Dublin, Published by Wm. F. Wakeman. Oct 18[illegible]

ing the jug of holy water at the coffin, lest the latter should follow, or the former encumber him in his flight. Never was there so complete a discomfiture; and so eager were they to escape, that several of them came down on the stones; and I could hear them shouting with desperation, and imploring the more advanced not to leave them behind. I instantly disentangled myself from the coffin, and left it standing exactly in the middle of the road, for the next passenger to give it a lift as far as Denis Kelly's, if he felt so disposed. I lost no time in making the best of my way home; and on passing poor Denis's house, I perceived, by the bustle and noise within, that he was dead.

I had given my friends no notice of this visit; my reception was, consequently the warmer, as I was not expected. That evening was a happy one, which I shall long remember. At supper I alluded to Kelly, and received from my brother a full account, as given in the following narrative, of the circumstances which caused his death.

"I need not remind you, Toby, of our schoolboy days, nor of the principles usually imbibed at such schools as that in which the two tiny factions of the Caseys and the Murphys qualified themselves—among the latter of whom you cut so distinguished a figure. You will not, therefore, be surprised to hear that those two factions are as bitter as ever; and that the boys who, at Pat Mulligan's school belaboured each other, in imitation of their brothers and fathers, continue to set the same iniquitous example to their children; so that this groundless and hereditary enmity is likely to descend to future generations—unless, indeed, the influence of a more enlightened system of education may check it. But, unhappily, there is a strong suspicion of the object proposed by such a system; so that the advantages likely to result from it to the lower orders of the people will be slow and distant."

"But, John," said I, "now that we are upon that subject, let me ask what really *is* the bone of contention between Irish factions?"

"I assure you," he replied, "I am almost as much at a loss, Toby, to give you a satisfactory answer, as if you asked me the elevation of the highest mountain on the moon; and I believe you would find equal difficulty in ascertaining the cause of their feuds from the factions themselves. I really am convinced they know not, nor, if I rightly understand them, do they much care. Their object is to fight, and the turning of a straw will at any time furnish them with sufficient grounds for that. I do not think, after all, that the enmity between them is purely personal: they do not hate each other individually; but having originally had one quarrel upon some trifling occasion, the beaten party could not bear the stigma of defeat without another trial of strength. Then, if they succeed, the *onus* of retrieving lost credit is thrown upon the party that was formerly victorious. If they fail a second time, the double triumph of their conquerors excites them to a greater determination to throw off the additional disgrace; and this species of alternation perpetuates the evil.

" These habits, however, familiarise our peasantry to acts of outrage and violence—the bad passions are cultivated and nourished, until crimes, which peaceable men look upon with fear and horror, lose their real magnitude and deformity in the eyes of Irishmen. I believe this kind of undefined hatred between either parties or nations, is the most dangerous and fatal spirit which could pervade any portion of society. If you hate a man for an obvious and palpable injury, it is likely that when he cancels that injury by an act of subsequent kindness, accompanied by an exhibition of sincere sorrow, you will cease to look upon him as your enemy; but where the hatred is such that, while feeling it, you cannot, on a sober examination of your heart, account for it, there is little hope that you will ever be able to stifle the enmity which you entertain against him. This, however, in politics and religion, is what is frequently designated as principle—a word on which men, possessing higher and greater advantages than the poor ignorant peasantry of Ireland, pride themselves. In sects and parties, we may mark its effects among all ranks and nations. I, therefore, seldom wish, Toby, to hear a man assert that he is of this party or that, from *principle;* for I am usually inclined to suspect that he is not, in this case, influenced by *conviction.*

"Kelly was a man who, but for these scandalous proceedings among us, might have been now alive and happy. Although his temperament was warm, yet that warmth communicated itself to his good as well as to his evil qualities. In the beginning his family were not attached to any faction—and when I use the word *faction,* it is in contradistinction to the word *party*—for faction, you know, is applied to a feud or grudge between Roman Catholics exclusively. But when he was young, he ardently attached himself to the Murphys; and, having continued among them until manhood, he could not abandon them, consistently with that sense of mistaken honour which forms so prominent a feature in the character of the Irish peasantry. But although the Kellys were not *faction-men,* they were bitter *party-men,* being the ringleaders of every quarrel which took place between the Catholics and Protestants, or, I should rather say, between the Orangemen and White-boys.

"From the moment when Denis attached himself to the Murphys, until the day he received the beating which subsequently occasioned his death, he never withdrew from them. He was in all their battles; and in course of time, induced his relations to follow his example; so that, by general consent, they were nicknamed 'the Errigle Slashers.' Soon after you left the country, and went to reside with my uncle, Denis married a daughter of little Dick Magrath's, from the Race-road, with whom he got a little money. She proved a kind, affectionate wife; and, to do him justice, I believe he was an excellent husband.—Shortly after his marriage his father died, and Denis succeeded him in his farm; for you know that, among the peasantry, the youngest usually gets the landed property—the elder children being obliged to provide for themselves according to their ability, as otherwise a population would multiply upon a portion of land inadequate to their support.

"It was supposed that Kelly's marriage would have been the means of producing a change in him for the better but it did not. He was, in fact, the slave of a low, vain ambition, which constantly occasioned him to have some quarrel or other on his hands; and, as he possessed great physical courage and strength, he became the champion of the parish. It was in vain that his wife used every argument to induce him to relinquish such practices; the only reply he was in the habit of making, was a good-humoured slap on the back and a laugh, saying,

" 'That's it, Honor; sure and isn't that the Magraths, all over, that would let the manest spalpeen that ever chewed cheese thramp upon them, widout raising a hand in their own defence; and I don't blame you for being a coward, seeing that you have their blood in your veins—not but that there ought to be something betther in you, afther all; for it's the M'Karrons, by your mother's side, that had the good dhrop of their own in them, any how—but you're a Magrath, out and out.'

" 'And, Denis,' Honor would reply, 'it would be a blessed day for the parish, if all in it were as peaceable as the same Magraths. There would be no sore heads, nor broken bones, nor fighting, nor slashing of one another in fairs and markets, when people ought to be minding their business. You're ever and always at the Magraths, bekase they don't join you agin the Caseys or the Orangemen, and more fools they'd be to make or meddle between you, having no spite agin either of them; and it would be wiser for you to be *sed* by the Magraths, and *red* your hands out of sich ways altogether. What did ever the Murphys do to sarve you or any of your family, that you'd go to make a great man of yourself fighting for them? Or what did the poor Caseys do to make you go agin the honest people? Arrah, bad manners to me, if you know what you're about, or, if *sonse*,* or grace can ever come of it; and mind my words, Denis, if God hasn't sed it, you'll live to rue your folly for the same work.'

"At this Denis would laugh heartily. 'Well said, Honor *Magrath*, but not *Kelly*. Well, it's one comfort that our childher aren't likely to follow your side of the house, any way.—Come here, Lanty—come over, acushla, to your father! Lanty, ma bouchal, what 'ill you do when you grow a man?'

"'I'll buy a horse of my own to ride on, daddy.'

"'A horse, Lanty!—and so you will, ma bouchal; but that's not it—sure that's not what I mane, Lanty. What'ill you do to the Caseys?'

* Good luck.

" 'Ho, ho! the Caseys!—I'll bate the blackguards wid your blackthorn, daddy!'

" 'Ha, ha, ha!—that's my stout man—my brave little sodger! *Wus dha lamh, avick!*—give me your hand, my son! Here, Nelly,' he would say to the child's eldest sister, 'give him a brave whang of bread, to make him able to bate the Caseys. Well, Lanty, who more will you leather, a-hagur?'

" 'All the Orangemen—I'll kill all the Orangemen!'

"This would produce another laugh from the father, who would again kiss and shake hands with his son, for these early manifestations of his own spirit.

" 'Lanty, ma bouchal,' he would say, 'thank God, you're not a *Magrath;* 'tis you that's a *Kelly*, every blessed inch of you!—and if you turn out as good a *buillagh batthah* as your father afore you, I'll be contint, avourneen!'

" 'God forgive you, Denis,' the wife would reply, 'it's long before you'd think of larning him his prayers, or his catechism, or any thing that's good! Lanty, agra, come over to myself, and never heed what that man says; for, except you have some poor body's blessing, he'll bring you to no good.'

"Sometimes, however, Kelly's own natural

good sense, joined with the remonstrances of his wife, prevailed for a short time, and he would withdraw himself from the connection altogether; but the force of habit and of circumstances was too strong in him, to hope that he could ever overcome it by his own firmness, for he was totally destitute of religion. The peaceable intervals of his life were, therefore, very short.

"One summer evening I was standing in my own garden, when I saw a man galloping up towards me at full speed. When he approached, I recognized him as one of the Murphy faction, and perceived that he was cut and bleeding.

"'Murphy,' said I, 'what's the matter?'

"'Hard fighting, Sir,' said he, 'is the matter. The Caseys gathered all their faction, bekase they heard that Denis Kelly has given us up, and they're sweeping the street wid us. I'm going hot foot for Kelly, Sir, for even the very name of him will turn the tide in our favour. Along wid that, I have sint in a score of the Duggans, and, if I get in Denis, plase God we'll clear the town of them!'

"He then set off, but pulled up abruptly, and said—

"'Arrah, Mr. Darcy, maybe you'd be civil enough to lind me the loan of a sword, or bagnet, or gun, or any thing that way, that would be sarviceable to a body on a pinch?'

"'Yes!' said I, 'and enable you to commit murder. No, no, Murphy: I'm sorry it's not in my power to put a final stop to such dangerous quarrels!'

"He then dashed off, and in the course of a short time, I saw him and Kelly, both on horseback, hurrying into the town in all possible haste, armed with their cudgels. The following day, I got my dog and gun, and sauntered about the hills, making a point to call upon Kelly. I found him with his head tied up, and his arm in a sling.

"'Well, Denis,' said I, 'I find you have kept your promise of giving up quarrels!'

"'And so I did, Sir,' said Denis; 'but, sure you wouldn't have me for to go desart them, when the Caseys war three to one over them. No: God be thanked, I'm not so mane as that, any how. Besides, they welted both my brothers within an inch of their lives.'

"'I think they didn't miss yourself,' said I.

"'You may well say they did not, Sir,' he replied; 'and, to tell God's thruth, they thrashed us right and left out of the town, although we rallied three times, and came in agin. At any rate, it's the first time, for the last five years, that they dare go up and down the street, calling out for the face of a Murphy, or a Kelly—for they're as bitter now agin us as agin the Murphys themselves.'

"'Well, I hope, Denis,' I observed, 'that what occurred yesterday will prevent you from entering into their quarrels in future. Indeed, I shall not give over, until I prevail on you to lead a quiet and peaceable life, as the father of a rising family ought to do.'

"'Denis,' said the wife, when I alluded to the children, looking at him with a reproachful and significant expression—'Denis, do you hear *that!* —the *father* of a family, Denis! Oh, then, God look down on that family, but it's——Musha, God bless you and yours, Sir,' said she to me, dropping that part of the subject abruptly—'it's kind of you to trouble yourself about him, at all at all; it's what them that has a betther right to do it, doesn't do.'

"'I hope,' said I, 'that Denis's own good sense will show him the folly and guilt of his conduct, and that he will not, under any circumstances, enter into their battles in future. Come, Denis, will you promise me this?"

"'If any man,' replied Denis, 'could make me do it, it's yourself, Sir, or any one of your family; but, if the priest of the parish was to go down on his two knees before me, I wouldn't give it up till we give them vagabone Caseys one glorious battherin', which, plase God, we'll do, and are well able to do, before a month of Sundays goes over us. Now, Sir, you needn't say another word,' said he, seeing me about to speak, 'for, by Him that made me, we'll do it. If any man, I say, could persuade me agin it, you could; but, if we don't pay them full interest for what we got, why, my name's not Denis Kelly—ay, sweep them like varmint out of the town, body and sleeves!'

"I saw argument would be lost on him, so I only observed that I feared it would, eventually, end badly.

"'Och, many and many's the time, Mr. Darcy,' said Honor, 'I prophesied the same thing; and if God hasn't said it, he'll be coming home a corpse to me some day or other, for he got as much bating, Sir, as would be enough to kill a horse; and to tell you God's truth, Sir, he's breeding up his childher——'

"'Honor,' said Kelly, irritated—'whatever I do, do I lave it in your power to say that I'm a bad husband; so don't *rise* me by your talk, for I don't like to be provoked. I *know* it's wrong, but what can I do? Would you have me for to show the *Garran bane** and lave them like a cow-

* The white Horse, i. e., be wanting in mettle.

ardly thraitor, now that the other faction is coming up to be their match?—no; let what will come of it, I'll never do the mane thing—death before dishonour!'

"In this manner, Kelly went on for years; sometimes, indeed, keeping quiet for a short period, but eventually drawn in, from the apprehension of being reproached with want of honour and truth to his connexion. This, truly, is an imputation which no peasant could endure; nor, were he thought capable of treachery, would his life be worth a single week's purchase. Many a time have I seen Kelly reeling home, his head and face sadly cut, the blood streaming from him, and his wife and some neighbour on each side of him—the poor woman weeping and deploring the senseless and sanguinary feuds in which her husband took so active a part.

"About three miles from this, down at the Long Ridge, where the Shannons live, dwelt a family of the M'Guigans, cousins to Denis. They were any thing but industrious, although they might have lived very independently, having held a farm on what they call an *old take*, which means a long lease taken out when the lands were cheap. It so happened, however, that, like too many of their countrymen, they paid little attention to the cultivation of their farm, the consequence of which neglect was, that they became embarrassed, and overburdened with arrears. Their landlord was old Sam Simmons, whose only fault to his tenants was an excess of indulgence, and a generous disposition wherever he could possibly get an opportunity, to scatter his money about him, upon the spur of a benevolence, which it would seem never ceased goading him to acts of the most Christian liberality and kindness. Along with these excellent qualities, he was remarkable for a most rooted aversion to law and lawyers; for he would lose one hundred pounds rather than recover that sum by legal proceedings, even when certain that five pounds would effect it; but he seldom or never was known to pardon a breach of the peace.

"I have always found that an *excess* of indulgence in a landlord never fails ultimately to injure and relax the industry of the tenant; at least, this was the effect which *his* forbearance produced on them. But the most extraordinary good-nature has its limits, and so had his; after repeated warning, and the most unparalleled patience on his part, he was at length compelled to determine on at once removing them from his estate, and letting his land to some more efficient and deserving tenant. He accordingly desired them to remove their property from the premises, as he did not wish, he said, to leave them without the means of entering upon another farm, if they felt so disposed. This they refused to do, adding, that they would at least put him to the expense of ejecting them. He then gave orders to his agent to seize; but they, in the mean time, had secreted their effects by night among their friends and relations, sending a cow to this one, and a horse to that; so that when the bailiff came to levy his execution, he found very little except the empty walls. They were, however, ejected without ceremony, and driven altogether off the farm, for which they had actually paid nothing for the three preceding years. In the mean time the farm was advertised to be let, and several persons had offered themselves as tenants; but what appeared very remarkable was, that the Roman Catholics seldom came a second time to make any further inquiry about it; or if they did, Simmons observed that they were sure to withdraw their proposals, and ultimately decline having any thing to do with it.

"This was a circumstance which he could not properly understand; but the fact was, that the peasantry were, to a man, members of a widely-extending system of Whiteboyism, the secret influence of which intimidated such of their own religion as intended to take it, and prevented them from exposing themselves to the penalty which they knew those who should dare to occupy it must pay. In a short time, however, the matter began to be whispered about, until it spread gradually, day after day, through the parish, that those who already had proposed, or intended to propose, were afraid to enter upon the land on any terms. Hitherto, it is true, these threats floated about only in the invisible form of rumour.

"The farm had been now unoccupied for about a year: party-spirit ran very high among the peasantry, and no proposals came in, or were at all likely to come. Simmons then got advertisements printed, and had them posted up in the most conspicuous parts of this and the neighbouring parishes. It was expected, however, that they would be torn down; but instead of that, there was a written notice posted up immediately under each, which ran in the following words:—

'TAKE NOTESS.

'*Any man that'll dare to take the farm belonging to yallow Sam Simmons, and sitivated at the long ridge, will be flayed alive.*

'MAT MIDNIGHT.

'B. N.—*It's it that was latterrally occupied by the M'Guigans.*'

"This occasioned Simmons and the other magistrates of the barony to hold a meeting, at which they subscribed to the amount of fifty pounds, as a reward for discovering the author or authors of the threatening notice; but the advertisement containing the reward, which was posted in the usual places through the parish, was torn down on the first night after it was put up. In the mean time, a man, nicknamed Vengeance—Vesey Vengeance, in consequence of his daring and fearless spirit, and his bitterness in retaliating injury—came to Simmons, and proposed for the farm. The latter candidly mentioned the circumstances of the notice, and fairly told him that he was running a personal risk in taking it.

"'Leave that to me, Sir,' said Vengeance; 'if you will set me the farm at the terms I offer, I am willing to become your tenant; and let them that posted up the notices go to old Nick, or if they annoy me, let them take care I don't send them there. I am a true-blue, Sir—a purple man—have lots of fire-arms, and plenty of stout fellows in the parish, ready and willing to back me; and, by the light-of-day! if they make or meddle with me or mine, we will hunt them in the face of the world, like so many mad dogs, out of the country: what are they but a pack of *ribles*,* that would cut our throats, if they dared ?'

" 'I have no objection," said Simmons, 'that you should express a firm determination to defend your life, and protect your property; but I utterly condemn the spirit with which you seem to be animated. Be temperate and sober, but be firm. I will afford you every assistance and protection in my power, both as a magistrate and a landlord; but if you speak so incautiously, the result may be serious, if not fatal, to yourself.'

" 'Instead of that,' said Vengeance, 'the more a man appears to be afeard, the more danger he is in, as I know by what I have seen; but, at any rate, if they injure me, I wouldn't ask better sport than taking down the ribles—the bloody-minded villains! Isn't it a purty thing, that a man darn't put one foot past the other, only as *they* wish? By the light-of-day, I'll pepper them!'

" Shortly, after this, Vengeance, braving all their threats, removed to the farm, and set about its cultivation with skill and vigour. He had not been long there, however, when a notice was posted one night on his door, giving him ten days to clear off from this interdicted spot, threatening, in case of non-compliance, to make a bon-

* Rebels.

fire of the house and offices, inmates included. The reply which Vengeance made to this was fearless and characteristic. He wrote another notice, which he posted on the chapel door, stating that he would not budge an inch—recommending, at the same time, such as intended paying him a nightly visit to be careful that they might not chance to go home with their heels foremost. This, indeed, was setting them completely at defiance, and would, no doubt, have been fatal to Vesey, were it not for a circumstance which I will now relate:—In a little dell below Vesey's house, lived a poor woman called Doran, a widow; she inhabited a small hut, and was principally supported by her two sons, who were servants—one to a neighbouring farmer, a Roman Catholic, and the other to Dr. Ableson, Rector of the parish. He who had been with the Rector lost his health shortly before Vengeance succeeded the M'Guigans as occupier of the land in question, and was obliged to come home to his mother. He was then confined to his bed, from which, indeed, he never rose.

"This boy had been his mother's principal support—for the other was unsettled, and paid her but little attention, being, like most of those in his situation, fond of drinking, dancing, and attending fairs. In short, he became a Ribbonman and consequently was obliged to attend their nightly meetings. Now it so happened that for a considerable time after the threatening notice had been posted on Vengeance's door, he received no annoyance, although the period allowèd for his departure had been long past, and the purport of the paper uncomplied with. Whether this proceeded from an apprehension on the part of the Ribbonmen of receiving a warmer welcome than they might wish, or whether they deferred the execution of their threat until Vengeance might be off his guard, I cannot determine; but the fact is, that some months had elapsed and Vengeance remained hitherto unmolested

"During this interval the distress of Widow Doran had become known to the inmates of his family, and his mother—for she lived with him—used to bring down each day some nourishing food to the sick boy. In these kind offices she was very punctual; and so great was the poverty of the poor widow, and so destitute the situation of her sick son, that, in fact, the burden of their support lay principally upon Vengeance's family.

"Vengeance was a small, thin man, with fair hair, and fiery eyes; his voice was loud and shrill, his utterance rapid, and the general expression of his countenance irritable. His motions were so quick, that he rather seemed to run than walk.

He was a civil, obliging neighbour, but performed his best actions with a bad grace; a firm, unflinching friend, but a bitter and implacable enemy. Upon the whole, he was generally esteemed and respected—though considered as an eccentric character, for such, indeed, he was. On hearing of Widow Doran's distress, he gave orders that a portion of each meal should be regularly sent down to her and her son; and from that period forward they were both supported principally from his table.

"In this way some months had passed, and still Vengeance was undisturbed in his farm. It often happened, however, that Doran's other son came to see his brother; and during these visits it was but natural that his mother and brother should allude to the kindness which they daily experienced from Vesey.

"One night, about twelve o'clock, a tap came to Widow Doran's door, who happened to be attending the invalid, as he was then nearly in the last stage of his illness. When she opened it, the other son entered, in an evident hurry, having the appearance of a man who felt deep and serious anxiety.

"'Mother,' said he, 'I was very uneasy entirely about Mick, and just started over to see him, although they don't know at home that I'm out, so

I can't stay a crack; but I wish you would go to the door for two or three minutes, as I have something to say to *him.*'

" 'Why, thin, Holy Mother!—Jack, a-hagur, is there any thing the matther, for you look as if you had seen something?'

" 'Nothing worse than myself, mother,' he replied; 'nor there's nothing the matther at all—only I have a few words to say to Mick here, that's all.'

" The mother accordingly removed herself out of hearing.

" 'Mick,' says the boy, 'this is a bad business—I wish to God I was clear and clane out of it.'

" 'What is it?' said Mick, alarmed.

" 'Murther, I'm afeard, if God doesn't turn it off of them, some how.'

" 'What do you mane, man, at all?' said the invalid, raising himself, in deep emotion, on his elbow, from his poor straw bed.

" 'Vengeance,' said he—'Vengeance, man—he's going to get it. I was out with the boys on Sunday evening, and *at last* it's agreed on to visit him to-morrow night. I'm sure and sartin he'll never escape, for there's more *in* for him than taking the farm, and daring them so often as he did—he shot two fingers off of a brother-in-law of Jem Reilly's one night that they war *on* for threshing him, and that's coming home to him along with the rest.'

" 'In the name of God, Jack,' inquired Mick, 'what do they intend to do to him?'

" 'Why,' replied Jack, 'it's agreed to put a coal in the thatch, in the first place; and although they were afeard to name what he's to get besides, I doubt they'll make a spatch-cock of *himself*. They won't meddle with any other of the family, though—but *he's down* for it.'

" 'Are *you* to be one of them?' asked Mick.

" 'I was the third man named,' replied the other, 'bekase, they said, I knew the place.'

" 'Jack,' said his emaciated brother, with much solemnity, raising himself up in the bed—'Jack, if you have act or part in that bloody business, God in his glory you'll never see. Fly the country—cut off a finger or toe—break your arm—or do something that may prevent you from being there. Oh, my God!' he exclaimed, whilst the tears fell fast down his pale cheeks—'to go to murder the man, and lave his little family widout a head or a father over them, and his wife a widow! To burn his place, widout rhime, or rason, or offince. Jack, if you go, I'll die cursing you. I'll appear to you—I'll let you rest neither night nor day, sleeping nor waking, in bed or out of bed. I'll haunt you, till you'll curse the very day you war born.'

"Whisht, Micky,' said Jack, 'you're frightening me: I'll not go—will that satisfy you?'

"'Well, dhrop down on your two knees, there,' said Micky, 'and swear before the God that has his eye upon you this minute, that you'll have no hand in injuring him or his, while you live. If you don't do this, I'll not rest in my grave, and maybe I'll be a corpse before mornin'.'

"'Well, Micky,' said Jack, who, though wild and unthinking, was a lad whose heart and affections were good, 'it would be hard for me to refuse you that much, and you not likely to be long wid me—I will;' and he accordingly knelt down and swore solemnly, in words which his brother dictated to him, that he would not be concerned in the intended murder.

"'Now, give me your hand, Jack,' said the invalid; 'God bless you—and so he will. Jack, if I depart before I see you again, I'll die happy. That man has supported me and my mother for near the last three months, bad as you all think him. Why, Jack, we would both be dead of hunger long ago, only for his family; and, my God! to think of such a murdhering intention makes my blood run cowld'——

"'You had better give him a hint, then,' said

Jack, 'some way, or he'll be done for, as sure as you're stretched on that bed; but don't mintion names, if you wish to keep me from being murdhered for what I did. I must be off now, for I stole out of the barn;* and only that Atty Laghy's gone along wid the master to the —— fair, to help him to sell the two coults, I couldn't get over at all.'

" 'Well, go home, Jack, and God bless you, and so he will, for what you did this night.'

" Jack accordingly departed, after bidding his mother and brother farewell.

" When the old woman came in, she asked her son if there was any thing wrong with his brother, but he replied that there was not.

" 'Nothing at all,' said he—'but will you go up airly in the morning, plase God, and tell Vesey Johnston that I want to see him; and—that—I have a great dale to say to him.'

" 'To be sure I will, Micky; but, Lord guard us, what ails you, avourneen, you look so frightened?'

" 'Nothing at all, at all, mother; but will you go where I say airly to-morrow, for me?'

" 'It's the first thing I'll do, God willin',' replied the mother. And the next morning Vesey

* Labouring servants in Ireland, usually sleep in barns.

was down with the invalid very early, for the old woman kept her word, and paid him a timely visit.

"'Well, Micky, my boy,' said Vengeance, as he entered the hut, 'I hope you're no worse this morning.'

"'Not worse, Sir,' replied Mick; 'nor, indeed, am I any thing better either, but much the same way. Sure it's I that knows very well that my time here is but short.'

"'Well, Mick, my boy,' said Vengeance, 'I hope you're prepared for death—and that you expect forgiveness, like a Christian. Look up, my boy, to God at once, and pitch the priests and their craft to ould Nick, where they'll all go at the long run.'

"'I blieve,' said Mick, with a faint smile, 'that you're not very fond of the priests, Mr. Johnston; but if you knew the power they possess as well as I do, you wouldn't spake of them so bad, any how.'

"'Me fond of them!' replied the other; 'why, man, they're a set of the most gluttonous, black-looking hypocrites, that ever walked on neat's leather; and ought to be hunted out of the country —hunted out of the country, by the light of day! every one of them; for they do nothing but egg up the people against the Protestants.'

" 'God help you, Mr. Johnston,' replied the invalid; 'I pity you from my heart for the opinion you hould about the blessed crathurs. I suppose if you were sthruck dead on the spot wid a blast from the fairies, that you think a priest couldn't cure you by one word's spaking?'

" 'Cure me!' said Vengeance, with a laugh of disdain; 'by the light of day, if I caught one of them curing me, I'd give him the purtiest chase you ever saw in your life, across the hills.'

" 'Don't you know,' said Mick, 'that priest Dannelly cured Bob Arthurs of the falling sickness—until he broke the vow that was laid upon him, of not going into a church, and the minute he crossed the church-door, didn't he dhrop down as bad as ever—and what could the minister do for him?'

" 'And don't *you* know,' rejoined Vengeance, 'that that's all a parcel of the most lying stuff possible; lies—lies—all lies—and vagabondism. Why, Mick, you Papishes worship the priests; you think they can bring you to heaven at a word. By the light of day, they must have good sport laughing at you, when they get among one another. Why don't they teach you, and give you the Bible to read, the ribelly rascals? but they're afraid you'd know too much then.'

" 'Well, Mr. Johnston,' said Mick, 'I blieve

you'll never have a good opinion of them, at any rate.'

" 'Ay, when the sky falls,' replied Vengeance; 'but you're now on your death-bed, and why don't you pitch them to ould Nick, and get a Bible? Get a Bible, man; there's a pair of them in my house, that's never used at all—except my mother's, and she's at it night and day. I'll send one of them down to you: turn yourself to God —to your Redeemer, that died on the mount of Jehoshaphat, or somewhere about Jerusalem, for your sins—and don't go out of the world from the hand of a rascally priest, with a band about your eyes, as if you were at blind-man's-buff; for, by the light of day, you're as blind as a bat in a religious way.'

" 'There's no use in sending me a Bible,' replied the invalid, 'for I can't read it: but, whatever you may think, I'm very willing to lave my salvation with my priest.'

" 'Why, man,' observed Vengeance, 'I thought you were going to have sense at last, and that you sent for me to give you some spiritual consolation.'

" 'No, Sir,' replied Mick; 'I have two or three words to spake to you.'

" 'Come, come, Mick, now that we're on a spiritual subject, I'll hear nothing from you till I try whether it's possible to give you a true insight into religion. Stop, now, and let us lay our heads together, that we may make out something of a dacenter creed for you to believe in, than the one you profess. Tell me truth, do you believe in the priests?'

"'How?' replied Mick; 'I believe that they're holy men—but I know they can't save me widout the Redeemer, and his blessed mother.'

"'By the light above us, you're shuffling, Mick—I say you *do* believe in them—now don't tell me to the contrary—I say you're shuffling as fast as possible.'

"'I tould you truth, Sir,' replied Mick, 'and if you don't blieve me, I can't help it.'

"'Don't trust in the priests, Mick; that's the main point to secure your salvation.'

"Mick, who knew his prejudices against the priests, smiled faintly, and replied—

"'Why, Sir, I trust in them as bein' able to make inthercession wid God for me, that's all.'

"'They make intercession! By the stool I'm sitting on, a single word from one of them would ruin you. They, a set of ribles, to make interest for you in heaven! Didn't they rise the rebellion in Ireland? answer me that.'

"'This is a subject, Sir, we would never agree on,' replied Mick.

" 'Have you the Ten Commandments?' enquired Vesey.

" 'I doubt my mimory's not clear enough to have them in my mind,' said the lad, feeling keenly the imputation of ignorance, which he apprehended from Vesey's blunt observations.'

" Vesey, however, had penetration enough to perceive his feelings, and with more delicacy than could be expected from him, immediately moved the question.

" 'No matter, Mick,' said he, 'if you would give up the priests, we would get over that point; as it is, I'll give you a lift in the Commandments; and as I said a while ago, if you take my advice I'll work up a creed for you, that you may depend upon. But now for the Commandments;—let me see.

" 'First:—Thou shalt have no other gods but me. Don't you see, man, how that peppers the priests?

" 'Second:—Remember that thou keep holy the Sabbath day.

" 'Third:—Thou shalt not make to thyself—no—hang it no—I'm out—that's the Second—very right—Third:—Honour thy Father and thy Mother—you understand that, Mick?—It means that you are bound to—to—just so—to honour your father and your mother, poor woman.'

" 'My father—God be good to him—is dead near fourteen years, Sir,' replied Mick.

" 'Well, in that case, Mick, you see all that's left for you is to honour your mother—although I'm not certain of that either; the Commandments make no allowance at all for death, and in that case, why, living, or dead, the surest way is to respect and obey them—that is—if the thing wern't impossible. I wish we had blind George M'Gin here, Mick, although he's as great a rogue as ever escaped hemp, yet he'd beat the devil himself at a knotty point.'

" 'His breath would be bad about a dying man,' observed Mick.

" 'Ay, or a living one,' said Vesey; 'however, let us get on—we were at the Third: Fourth :—Thou shalt do no murder.'

" At the word murder, Mick started, and gave a deep groan—whilst his eyes and features assumed a great and hollow expression, resembling that of a man struck with an immediate sense of horror and affright.

" 'Oh, for heaven's sake, Sir, stop there,' said Doran; 'that brings to my mind the business I had with you, Mr. Johnston.'

" 'What is it about?' enquired Vengeance, in his usual eager manner.

" 'Do you mind, said Mick, 'that a paper was

stuck one night upon your door, threatening you, if you wouldn't lave that farm you're in?

" 'I do; the blood-thirsty villians! but they knew a trick worth two of coming near me.'

" 'Well,' said Mick, 'a strange man that I never seen before, come into me last night, and tould me, if I'd see you, to say that you would get a visit from the boys this night, and to take care of yourself.'

" 'Give me the hand, Mick,' said Vengeance —'give me the hand: in spite of the priests, by the light of day, you're an honest fellow—This night, you say, they're to côme? And what are the bloody wretches to do, Mick? But I needn't ask that, for I suppose it's to murder myself, and to burn my place.'

" 'I'm afeard, Sir, you re not far from the truth,' replied Mick; 'but, Mr. Johnston, for God's sake, don't mintion my name; for, if you do, I'll get myself what they war laying out for you—be burned in my bed maybe.'

" 'Never fear, Mick,' replied Vengeance; 'your name will never cross my lips.'

" 'It's a great thing,' said Mick, 'that would make me turn informer; but sure, only for your kindness and the goodness of your family, the Lord spare you to one another, mightn't I be dead long ago? I couldn't have one minute's peace if you or yours came to any harm, when I could prevint it.'

"'Say no more, Mick,' said Vengeance, taking his hand again; 'I know that, leave the rest to me; but how do you find yourself, my poor fellow; you look weaker than you did, a good deal.'

"'Indeed I'm going very fast, Sir,' replied Mick; 'I know it'll soon be over with me.'

"'Hut, no, man,' said Vengeance, drawing his hand rapidly across his eyes, and clearing his voice—'not at all, don't say so: would a little broth serve you? or a bit of fresh meat?—or would you have a fancy for any thing that I could make out for you? I'll get you wine, if you think it would do you good.'

"'God reward you,' said Mick, feebly—'God reward you, and open your eyes to the truth. Is my mother likely to come in, do you think?'

"'She must be here in a few minutes,' the other replied; 'she was waiting till they'd churn, that she might bring you down a little fresh milk and butter.'

"'I wish she was wid me,' said the poor lad, 'for I'm lonely wantin' her—her voice, and the very touch of her hands goes to my heart. Mother, come to me—and let me lay my head upon your breast, agra machree, for I think it will be for the last time: we lived lonely, avourneen, wid none but ourselves—sometimes in happiness, when the nabours 'ud be kind to us—and sometimes in sorrow, when there 'ud be none to help us. It's over now, mother, and I'm lavin' you for ever?'

"Vengeance wiped his eyes—'Rouse yourself, Mick,' said he—'rouse yourself.'

"'Who is that sitting along with you on the stool?' said Mick.

"'No one,' replied his neighbour—'but what's the matter with you, Mick?——your face is changed.'

"Mick, however, made no reply; but after a few slight struggles, in which he attempted to call upon his mother's name, he breathed his last. When Vengeance saw that he was dead,—looked upon the cold, miserable hut in which this grateful and affectionate young man was stretched,—and then reflected on the important service he had just rendered him, he could not suppress his tears.

"After sending down some of the females to assist his poor mother in laying him out, Vengeance went among his friends and acquaintances, informing them of the intelligence he had received, without mentioning the source from which he had it. After dusk that evening, they all flocked, as privately as possible, to his house, to the number of thirty or forty, well provided with arms and ammunition. Some of them stationed themselves in the out-houses, some behind the garden hedge, and others in the dwelling-house."

When my brother had got thus far in his narrative, a tap came to the parlour-door, and immediately a stout-looking man, having the appearance of a labourer, entered the room.

"Well, Lachlin," said my brother, "what's the matter?"

"Why, Sir," said Lachlin, scratching his head, "I had a bit of a favour to ax, if it would be plasin' to you to grant it to me."

"What is that?" said my brother.

"Do you know, Sir," said he, "I haven't been at a wake—let us see—this two or three years, any how; and, if you'd have no objection, why, I'd slip up a while to Denis Kelly's; he's a distant relation of my own, Sir; and blood's thicker than wather, you know."

"I'm just glad you came in, Lachlin," said my brother; "I didn't think of you—take a chair here, and never heed the wake to-night, but sit down and tell us about the attack on Vesey Vengeance, long ago. I'll get you a tumbler of punch; and, instead of going to the wake, I will allow you to go to the funeral to-morrow."

"Ah, Sir," said Lachlin, "you know whenever

the punch is consarned, I'm aisily persuaded; but not making little of your tumbler, Sir," said the shrewd fellow, "I would get two or three of them if I went to the wake."

"Well, sit down," said my brother, handing him one, "and we won't permit you to get thirsty while you're talking, at all events."

"In throth, you haven't your heart in the likes of it," said Lachlin. "Gintlemen, your healths—*your* health, Sir, and we're happy to see you wanst more. Why, thin, I remember you, Sir, when you were a gorsoon, passing to school wid your satchell on your back; but, I'll be bound, you're by no means as soople now as you were thin. Why, Sir," turning to my brother, "he could fly, or kick football wid the rabbits.—Well, this is raal stuff!"

"Now, Lachlin," said my brother, "give us an account of the attack you made on Vesey Vengeance's house, at the Long Ridge, when all his party were chased out of the town."

"Why, thin, Sir, I ought to be ashamed to mintion it; but you see, gintlemen, there was no getting over being connected wid them—for a man's life wouldn't be his own if he refused;—but I hope your brother's *safe*, Sir!"

"Oh, perfectly safe, Lachlin; you may rest assured he'll never mention it."

"Well, Sir," said Lachlin, addressing himself to me, "Vesey Vengeance was——."

"Lachlin," said my brother, "he knows all about Vesey; just give an account of the attack."

"The attack, Sir!—no, but the chivey we got over the mountains. Why, Sir, we met in an ould empty house, you see, that belonged to the Farrells of Ballyboulteen, that went over to America that spring. There war none wid us, you may be sure, but them that war *up;* and in all we might be about sixty or seventy. The M'Guigans, one way or another, got it up first among them, bekase they expected that Mr. Simmons would take them back when he'd find that no one else dare venthur upon their land. There war at that time two fellows down from the county Longford in their neighbourhood, of the name of Collier—although that wasn't their right name—they were here upon their keeping, for the murder of a proctor in their own part of the country. One of them was a tall, powerful fellow, with sandy hair, and red brows; the other was a slender chap, that must have been drawn into it by his brother—for he was very mild and innocent, and always persuaded us agin evil. The M'Guigans brought lashings of whiskey, and made them that war to go foremost amost drunk—these war the two Colliers, some of the strangers from behind the mountains, and a son of Widdy Doran's, that knew every inch about the place, for he was bred and born jist below the house a bit. He wasn't wid us, however, in regard of his brother being *under boord* that night; but, instid of him, Tim M'Guigan went to show the way up the little glin to the house, though, for that matther, the most of us knew as well as he did—but we didn't like to be the first to put a hand to it, if we could help it.

"At any rate, we sot in Farrell's empty house, drinking whiskey, till they war all gathered, when about two dozen of them got the damp soot from the chimley, and rubbed it over their faces, making them so black, that their own relations couldn't know them. We then went across the country in little lots, of about six, or ten, or a score, and we war glad that the wake was in Widdy Doran's, seeing that, if any one would meet us, we war going to it you know, and the blackening of the faces would pass for a frolic; but there was no great danger of being met, for it was now long beyant midnight.

"Well, jintlemen, it puts me into a tremble, even at this time, to think of how little we cared about doing what we were bent upon. Them that had to manage the business war more than half drunk; and, hard fortune to me, but you would think it was to a wedding they went—some of them singing songs aginst the law—some of them quite merry, and laughing as if they had found a mare's nest. The big fellow, Collier, had a dark lanthern wid a half-burned turf in it to light the bonfire, as they said; others had guns and pistols—some of them charged, and some of them not; some had bagnets, and ould rusty swords, pitchforks, and so on. Myself had nothing in my hand but the flail I was thrashing wid that day; and to tell the thruth, the divil a step I would have gone with them, only for fraid cf my health: for, as I said awhile agone, if any discovery was made afterwards, them that promised to go, and turned tail, would be marked as the informers. Neither was I so blind, but I could see that there war plenty there that would stay away if they durst.

"Well, we went on till we came to a little dark corner below the house, where we met and held a council of war upon what we should do. Collier and the other strangers from behind the mountains war to go first, and the rest war to stand round the house at a distance—he carried the lantern, a bagnet, and a horse pistol; and half-a-dozen more war to bring over bottles of straw from Vengeance's own haggard, to hould up to the thatch. It's all past and gone now—but three of the Reillys were desperate against Vesey that night, particularly one of them that he had shot about a year and a-half before—that is peppered two of the right hand fingers off of him, one night in a scuffle, as Vesey came home from an Orange-lodge. Well, all went on purty fair; we had got as far as the out-houses, where we stopped, to see if we could hear any noise; but all was quiet as you plase.

" 'Now, Vengeance,' says Reilly, swearing a terrible oath out of him—'you murdering Orange villain, you're going to get your pay,' says he.

" 'Ay,' says M'Guigan, 'what he often threatened to others, he'll soon meet himself, plase God—come boys,' says he, 'bring the straw and light it, and just lay it up, my darlings, nicely to the thatch here, and ye'll see what a glorious bonfire we'll have of the black Orange villain's blankets, in less than no time.'

" 'Some of us could hardly stand this: 'Stop, boys,' cried one of Dan Slevin's sons—'stop, Vengeance is bad enough, but his wife and childher never offinded us—we'll not burn the plaee.'

" 'No,' said others, spaking out when they heard any body at all having courage to do so—'it's too bad, boys, to burn the place; for if we do,' says they, 'some of the innocent may be burned before they get out from the house, or even before they waken out of their sleep.'

" 'Knock at the door first,' says Slevin, 'and bring Vengeance out; let us cut the ears off of his head, and lave him.'

" 'Damn him!' says another, 'let us not take the vagabone's life; it's enough to take the ears from him, and to give him a *prod* or two of a bagnet on the ribs; but don't kill him.'

" 'Well, well,' says Reilly, 'let us knock at the door, and get himself and the family out,' says he; 'and then we'll see what can be done wid him.'

" 'Tattheration to me,' says the big Longford fellow, 'if he had sarved me, Reilly, as he did you, but I'd roast him in the flames of his own house,' says he.

" 'I'd have *you* to know, says Slevin, 'that you have no command here, Collier. I'm captain at the present time,' says he; 'and more nor what I wish shall not be done. Go over,' says he to the black faces, 'and rap him up.'

"Accordingly, they began to knock at the door, commanding Vengeance to get up and come out to them.

" 'Come, Vengeance,' says Collier, 'put on you, my good fellow, and come out till two or three of your neighbours, that wish you well, gets a sight of your purty face, you babe of grace!'

"'Who are you that wants me, at all?' says Vengeance, from within.

"'Come out first,' says Collier; 'a few friends that has a crow to pluck with you: walk out, avourneen; or if you'd rather be roasted alive, why you may stay where you are,' says he.

"'Gentlemen,' says Vengeance, 'I have never, to my knowledge, offinded any of you; and I hope you won't be so cruel as to take an industrious, hard-working man from his family, in the clouds of the night, to do him an injury. Go home, gentlemen, in the name of God, and let me and mine alone. You're all mighty dacent gentlemen, you know, and I'm determined never to make or meddle with any of you. Sure, I know right well it's purtecting me you would be, dacent gentlemen. But I don't think there's any of my neighbours there, or they wouldn't stand by and see me injured.'

"'Thrue for you, avick,' says they, giving, at the same time, a terrible pattherrara agin the door, with two or three big stones.

"'Stop, stop!' says Vengeance, 'don't break the door, and I'll open it. I know you're merciful, dacent gentlemen—I know you're merciful.'

" So the thief came and unbarred it quietly, and the next minute about a dozen of them that war within the house let slap at us. As God would have had it, the crowd didn't happen to be fornent the door, or numbers of them would have been shot, and the night was dark, too, which was in our favour. The first volley was scarcely over, when there was another slap from the out-houses; and after that, another from the gardens; and, after that, to be sure, we took to our scrapers. Several of them were badly wounded; but, as for Collier, he was shot dead, and M'Guigan was taken prisoner, with five more, on the spot. There never was such a chase as we got; and only that they thought there was more of us in it, they might have tuck most of us prisoners.

" 'Fly, boys!' says M'Guigan, as soon as they fired out of the house—'we've been sould,' says he, 'but I'll die game, any how,'—and so he did, poor fellow; for although he and the other four war transported, one of them never sould the pass or stagged. Not but that they might have done it, for all that, only that there was a whisper sent to them, that if they *did*, a single sowl belonging to one of them wouldn't be left living. The M'Guigans were cousins of Denis Kelly's, that's now laid out there above.

" From the time this tuck place till after the

sizes, there wasn't a stir among them, on any side; but when they war over, the boys began to prepare. Denis, heavens be his bed, was there in his glory. This was in the spring 'sizes, and the May fair soon followed. Ah! that was the bloody sight, I'm tould—for I wasn't at it—atween the Orangemen and them. The Ribbonmen war bate, though, but not till after there was a desperate fight on both sides. I was tould that Denis Kelly that day knocked down five-and-twenty men in about three quarters of an hour; and only that long John Grimes hot him a *polthoge* on the sconce with the butt-end of the gun, it was thought the Orangemen would be beat. That blow broke his skull, and was the manes of his death. He was carried home senseless."

"Well, Lachlin," said my brother, "if you didn't see it, I did. I happened to be looking out of John Carson's upper window—for it wasn't altogether safe to contemplate it within reach of the missiles. It was certainly a dreadful and a barbarous sight. You have often observed the calm, gloomy silence that precedes a thunder-storm; and had you been there that day, you might have seen it illustrated in a scene much more awful. The thick living mass of people extended from the corner-house, nearly a quarter of a mile, at this end of the town, up to the parsonage on the other side. During the early part of the day, every kind of business was carried on in a hurry and an impatience, which denoted the little chance they knew there would be for transacting it in the evening.

"Up to the hour of four o'clock, the fair was unusually quiet, and, on the whole, presented nothing in any way remarkable; but after that hour you might observe the busy stir and hum of the mass settling down into a deep, brooding, portentous silence, that was absolutely fearful. The females with dismay and terror pictured in their faces, hurried home; and in various instances you might see mothers, and wives, and sisters, clinging about the sons, husbands, and brothers, attempting to drag them by main force from the danger which they knew impended over them. In this they seldom succeeded; for the person so urged was usually compelled to tear himself from them by superior strength.

"The pedlars, and basket-women, and such as had tables and standings erected in the streets, commenced removing them with all possible haste. The shopkeepers, and other inhabitants of the town, put up their shutters, in order to secure their windows from being shattered. Strangers, who were compelled to stop in town that night, took shelter in the inns and other houses of entertainment where they lodged; so that about five o'clock the street was completely clear, and free for action.

"Hitherto there was not a stroke—the scene became even more silent and gloomy, although the moral darkness of their ill-suppressed passions was strongly contrasted with the splendour of the sun, that poured down a tide of golden light upon the multitude. This contrast between the natural brightness of the evening, and the internal gloom of their hearts, as the beams of the sun rested upon the ever-moving crowd, would, to any man who knew the impetuosity with which the spirit of religious hatred was soon to rage among them, produce novel and singular sensations. For, after all, Toby, there is a mysterious connection between natural and moral things, which often invests both nature and sentiment with a feeling that certainly would not come home to our hearts, if such a connection did not exist. A rose-tree beside a grave will lead us from sentiment to reflection; and any other association, where a painful or melancholy thought is clothed with a garb of joy or pleasure, will strike us more deeply in proportion as the contrast is strong. On seeing the sun or moon struggling through the darkness of surrounding clouds, I confess, although you may smile, that I feel for the moment a diminution of enjoyment—something taken, as it were, from the sum of my happiness.

"Ere the quarrel commenced, you might see a dark and hateful glare scowling from the countenances of the two parties, as they viewed and approached each other in the street—the eye was set in deadly animosity, and the face marked with an ireful paleness, occasioned at once by revenge and apprehension. Groups were silently hurrying with an eager and energetic step to their places of rendezvous, grasping their weapons more closely, or grinding their teeth in the impatience of their fury. The veterans on each side were surrounded by their respective followers, anxious to act under their direction; and the very boys seemed to be animated with a martial spirit, much more eager than that of those who had greater experience in party quarrels.

"Jem Finigan's public-house was the head quarters and rallying point of the Ribbonmen; the Orangemen assembled in that of Joe Sherlock, the master of an Orange lodge. About six o'clock, the crowd in the street began gradually to fall off to the opposite ends of the town—the Roman Catholics towards the north, and the Protestants towards the south. Carson's window, from which I was observing their motions, was exactly half way between them, so that I had a distinct view of both. At this moment I noticed Denis Kelly coming forward from the closely condensed mass formed by the Ribbonmen: he advanced with his cravat off, to the middle of the vacant space between the parties, holding a fine oak cudgel in his hand. He then stopped, and addressing the Orangemen, said,

" 'Where's Vengeance and his crew now? Is there any single Orange villain among you that dare come down and meet me here, like a man? Is John Grimes there? for if he is, before we begin to take you *out of a face*—to hunt you altogether out of the town, ye Orange villains—I would be glad that he'd step down to Denis Kelly here for two or three minutes—I'll not keep him longer.'

" There was now a stir and a murmur among the Orangemen, as if a rush was about to take place towards Denis; but Grimes, whom I saw endeavouring to curb them in, left the crowd, and advanced towards him.

" At this moment an instinctive movement among both masses took place; so that when Grimes had come within a few yards of Kelly, both parties were within two or three perches of them. Kelly was standing, apparently off his guard, with one hand thrust carelessly into the breast of his waistcoat, and the cudgel in the other; but his eye was fixed calmly upon Grimes as he approached. They were both powerful, fine men—brawney, vigorous, and active: Grimes had somewhat the advantage of the other in height; he also fought with his left hand, from which circumstance he was nicknamed *Kitthouge*. He was a man of a dark, stern-looking countenance; and the tones of his voice were deep, sullen, and of appalling strength.

"As they approached each other, the windows on each side of the street were crowded; but there was not a breath to be heard in any direction, nor from either party. As for myself, my heart palpitated with anxiety. What *they* might have felt I do not know: but they must have experienced considerable apprehension; for as they were both the champions of their respective parties, and had never before met in single encounter, their characters depended on the issue of the contest.

"'Well, Grimes,' said Denis, 'sure I've often wished for this same meetin', man, betune myself and you; I have what you're goin' to get, *in* for you this long time; but you'll get it now, avick, plase God——'

"'It was not to scould I came, you popish, ribly rascal,' replied Grimes, 'but to give you what you're long——'

"Ere the word had been out of his mouth, however, Kelly sprung over to him; and making a feint, as if he intended to lay the stick on his ribs, he swung it past without touching him, and, bringing it round his own head like lightning, made it tell with a powerful back-stroke, right on Grimes's temple, and in an instant his own face was sprinkled with the blood which sprung from the wound. Grimes staggered forward towards his antagonist, seeing which, Kelly sprung back, and was again meeting him with full force, when Grimes, turning a little, clutched Kelly's stick in his right hand, and being left-handed himself, ere the other could wrench the cudgel from him, he gave him a terrible blow upon the back part of the head, which laid Kelly in the dust.

"There was then a deafening shout from the Orange party; and Grimes stood until Kelly should be in the act of rising, ready then to give him another blow. The coolness and generalship of Kelly, however, were here very remarkable; for, when he was just getting to his feet, 'Look at your party coming down upon me!' he exclaimed to Grimes, who turned round to order them back, and, in the interim, Kelly was upon his legs.

"I was surprised at the coolness of both men; for Grimes was by no means inflated with the boisterous triumph of his party—nor did Denis get into a blind rage on being knocked down. They approached again, their eyes kindled into savage fury, tamed down into the wariness of experienced combatants; for a short time they stood eyeing each other, as if calculating upon the contingent advantages of attack or defence. This was a moment of great interest; for, as their huge and powerful frames stood out in opposition, strung and dilated by the impulse of passion and the energy of contest, no judgment, however experienced, could venture to anticipate the result of the battle, or name the person likely to be victorious. Indeed it was surprising how the natural sagacity of these men threw their attitudes and movements into scientific form and elegance. Kelly raised his cudgel, and placed it transversely in the air, between himself and his opponent; Grimes instantly placed his against it—both weapons thus forming a St. Andrew's cross—whilst the men themselves stood foot to foot, calm and collected. Nothing could be finer than their proportions, nor superior to their respective attitudes; their broad chests were in a line—their thick, well-set necks, laid a little back, as were their bodies—without, however, losing their balance—and their fierce, but calm features, grimly, but placidly scowling at each other, like men who were prepared for the onset.

"At length, Kelly made an attempt to repeat his former feint, with variations; for, whereas he had sent the first blow to Grimes's right temple, he took measures now to reach the left; his action was rapid, but equally quick was the eye of his antagonist, whose cudgel was up in ready guard to meet the blow. It met it; and with such surprising power was it sent and opposed, that both cudgels, on meeting, bent across each other into curves. An involuntary huzza followed this from their respective parties—not so much on account of the skill displayed by the combatants, as in admiration of their cudgels, and of the judgment with which they must have been selected. In fact, it was the staves, rather than the men, that were praised; and certainly the former did their duty. In a moment their shillelaghs were across each other once more, and the men resumed their former attitudes; their savage determination, their kindled eyes, the blood which disfigured the face of Grimes, and begrimmed also the countenance of his antagonist into a deeper expression of ferocity, occasioned many a cowardly heart to shrink from the sight. There they stood, gory and stern, ready for the next onset; it was first made by Grimes, who tried to practise on Kelly the feint which Kelly had before practised on him. Denis, after his usual manner, caught the blow in his open hand, and clutched the staff with an intention of holding it until he might visit Grimes—now apparently unguarded—with a levelling blow; but Grimes's effort to wrest the cudgel from his grasp, drew all Kelly's strength to that quarter, and prevented him from availing himself from the other's defenceless attitude. A trial of muscular power ensued, and their enormous bodily strength was exhibited in the stiff tug for victory. Kelly's address prevailed; for while Grimes pulled against him with all his collected vigour, the former suddenly let go his hold, and the latter, having lost his balance, staggered back: lightning could not be more quick than the action of Kelly, as, with tremendous force, his cudgel rung on the unprotected head of Grimes, who fell, or rather was shot to the ground, as if some superior power had dashed him against it; and there he lay for a short time, quivering under the blow he had received.

"A peal of triumph now arose from Kelly's party; but Kelly himself, placing his arms a-kimbo, stood calmly over his enemy, awaiting his return to the conflict. For nearly five minutes he stood in this attitude, during which time Grimes did not stir; at length, Kelly stooped a little, and peering closely into his face, exclaimed—

" 'Why, then, is it acting you are? any how, I wouldn't put it past you, you cunning vagabone; 'tis lying to take breath he is—get up, man, I'd scorn to touch you till you're on your legs; not all as one, for sure it's yourself would show *me* no such forbearance. Up with you, man alive, I've none of your own thrachery in me. I'll not *rise* my cudgel till you're on your guard.'

"There was an expression of disdain mingled with a glow of honest, manly generosity on his countenance, as he spoke, which made him at once the favourite with such spectators as were not connected with either of the parties. Grimes arose; and it was evident that Kelly's generosity deepened his resentment more than the blow which had sent him so rapidly to the ground; however, he was still cool, but his brows knit, his eye flashed with double fierceness, and his complexion settled into a dark blue shade, which gave to his whole visage an expression fearfully ferocious. Kelly hailed this as the first appearance of passion; *his* brow expanded as the other approached, and a dash of confidence, if not of triumph, softened, in some degree, the sternness of his features.

" With caution they encountered again, each collected for a spring, their eyes gleaming at each other like those of tigers. Grimes made a motion as if he would have struck Kelly with his fist; and, as the latter threw up his guard against the blow, he received a stroke from Grimes's cudgel in the under part of the right arm. This had been directed at his elbow, with an intention of rendering the arm powerless; it fell short, however, yet was sufficient to relax the grasp which Kelly held of his weapon. Had Kelly been a novice, this stratagem alone would have soon vanquished him; his address, however, was fully equal to that of his antagonist. The staff dropped instantly from his grasp, but a stout thong of black polished leather, with a shining tassel at the end of it had bound it securely to his massive wrist; the cudgel, therefore, only dangled from his arm, and did not, as the other expected, fall to the ground, or put Denis to the necessity of stooping for it—Grimes's object being to have struck him in that attitude.

" A flash of indignation now shot from Kelly's eye, and with the speed of lightning, he sprung within Grimes's weapon, determined to wrest it from him. The grapple that ensued was gigantic. In a moment Grimes's staff was parallel with the horizon between them, clutched in the powerful grasp of both. They stood exactly opposite, and rather close to each other; their arms sometimes stretched out stiff and at full length, again contracted, until their faces, glowing and distorted by the energy of the contest, were drawn almost together. Sometimes, the prevailing strength of one would raise the staff slowly, and with gradually developed power, up in a perpendicular position; again, the re-action of opposing strength would strain it back, and sway the weighty frame of the antagonist, crouched and set into desperate resistance, along with it; whilst the hard pebbles under their feet were crumbled into powder, and the very street itself furrowed into gravel by the shock of their opposing strength. Indeed, so well matched a pair never met in contest; their strength, their wind, their activity, and their natural science appeared to be perfectly equal.

"At length, by a tremendous effort, Kelly got the staff twisted nearly out of Grimes's hand, and a short shout, half encouraging, half indignant, came from Grimes's party. This added shame to his other passions, and threw an impulse of almost superhuman strength into him: he recovered his advantage, but nothing more; they twisted—they heaved their great frames against each other—they struggled—their action became rapid—they swayed each other this wav and that—their eyes like fire—their teeth locked, and their nostrils dilated. Sometimes they twined about each other like serpents, and twirled round with such rapidity, that it was impossible to distinguish them—sometimes, when a pull of more than ordinary power took place, they seemed to cling together almost without motion, bending down until their heads nearly touched the ground, their cracking joints seeming to stretch by the effort, and the muscles of their limbs standing out from the flesh, strung into amazing tension.

"In this attitude were they, when Denis, with the eye of a hawk, spied a disadvantage in Grimes's position; he wheeled round, placed his broad shoulder against the shaggy breast of the other, and giving him what is called an 'inside crook,' strained him, despite of every effort, until he fairly got him on his shoulder, and off the point of resistance. There was a cry of alarm from the windows, particularly from the females, as Grimes's huge body was swung over Kelly's shoulder, until it came down in a crash upon the hard gravel of the street, while Denis stood in triumph, with his enemy's staff in his hand. A loud huzza followed this from all present except the Orangemen, who stood bristling with fury and shame for the temporary defeat of their champion.

"Denis again had his enemy at his mercy; but he scorned to use his advantage ungenerously; he went over, and placing the staff in his hands—for the other had got to his legs—retrograded to his place, and desired Grimes to defend himself.

"After considerable manœuvering on both sides, Denis, who appeared to be the more active of the two, got an open on his antagonist, and by a powerful blow upon Grimes's ear, sent him to the ground with amazing force. I never saw such a blow given by mortal; the end of the cudgel came exactly upon the ear, and as Grimes went down, the blood spurted out of his mouth and nostrils; he then kicked convulsively several times as he lay upon the ground, and that moment I really thought he would never have breathed more.

"The shout was again raised by the Ribbonmen, who threw up their hats, and bounded from the ground with the most vehement exultation. Both parties then waited to give Grimes time to rise and renew the battle; but he appeared perfectly contented to remain where he was: for there appeared no signs of life or motion in him.

"'Have you got your *gruel*, boy?' said Kelly, going over to where he lay;—'Well, you met Denis Kelly, at last, didn't you? and there you lie; but, plase God, the most of your sort will soon lie in the same state. Come, boys,' said Kelly, addressing his own party, 'now for bloody Vengeance and his crew, that thransported the M'Guigans and the Caffries, and murdered Collier. Now, boys, have at the murderers, and let us have satisfaction for all!'

"A mutual rush instantly took place; but, ere the Orangemen came down to where Grimes lay, Kelly had taken his staff, and handed it to one of his own party. It is impossible to describe the scene that ensued. The noise of the blows, the shouting, the yelling, the groans, the scalped heads, and gory visages, gave both to the eye and the ear an impression that could not easily be forgotten. The battle was obstinately maintained on both sides for nearly an hour; and with a skill of manœuvering, attack, and retreat, that was astonishing.

"Both parties arranged themselves against each other, forming something like two lines of battle, and these extended along the town, nearly from one end to the other. It was curious to remark the difference in the persons and appearances of the combatants. In the Orange line, the men were taller and of more powerful frames; but the Ribbonmen were more hardy, active, and courageous. Man to man, notwithstanding their superior bodily strength, the Orangemen could never fight the others; the former depend too much upon their fire and side-arms, but they are by no means so well trained to the use of the cudgel as their enemies. In the district where the scene of this fight is laid, the Catholics generally inhabit the mountainous part of the country, to which, when the civil feuds of worse times prevailed, they had been driven at the point of the bayonet; the Protestants and Presbyterians, on the other hand, who came in upon their possessions, occupy the richer and more fertile tracts of the land, living, of course, more wealthy, with less labour, and on better food. The characteristic features produced by these causes are such as might be expected—the Catholic being, like his soil, hardy, thin, and capable of bearing all weathers; and the Protestants, larger, softer, and more inactive.

"Their advance to the first onset was far different from a faction fight. There existed a silence here, that powerfully evinced the inextinguishable animosity with which they encountered. For some time they fought in two compact bodies, that remained unbroken so long as the chances of victory were doubtful. Men went down, and were up, and went down in all directions with uncommon rapidity; and as the weighty phalanx of Orangemen stood out against the nimble line of their mountain adversaries, the intrepid spirit of the latter, and their surprising skill and activity soon gave symptoms of a gradual superiority in the conflict. In the course of about half an hour, the Orange party began to give way in the northern end of the town; and, as their opponents pressed them warmly and with unsparing hand, the heavy mass formed by their numbers began to break, and this decomposition ran up their line, until in a short time they were thrown into utter confusion. They now fought in detached parties; but these subordinate conflicts, though shorter in duration than the shock of the general battle, were much more inhuman and destructive; for whenever any particular gang succeeded in putting their adversaries to flight, they usually ran to the assistance of their friends in the nearest fight—by which means they often fought three to one. In these instances the persons inferior in number suffered such barbarities, as it would be painful to detail.

"There lived, a short distance out of the town, a man nicknamed Jemsy Boccagh, on account of his lameness—he was also sometimes called 'Hip-an'-go-constant'—who fell the first victim to party spirit. He had got arms on seeing his friends likely to be defeated, and had the hardihood to follow, with charged bayonet, a few Ribbonmen, whom he attempted to intercept, as they fled from a large number of their enemies, who had got them separated from their comrades. Boccagh ran across a field, in order to get before them on the road, and was in the act of climbing a ditch, when one of them, who carried a spade-shaft, struck him a blow on the head, which put an end to his existence.

"This circumstance imparted, of course, fiercer hatred to both parties—triumph inspiring the one, a thirst for vengeance nerving the other. Kelly inflicted tremendous punishment in every direction; for scarcely a blow fell from him which did not bring a man to the ground. It absolutely resembled a military engagement, for the number of combatants amounted at least to two thousand men. In many places the street was covered with small pools and clots of blood, which flowed from those who lay insensible—while others were borne away bleeding, groaning, or staggering, having been battered into a total unconsciousness of the scene about them.

"At length the Orangemen gave way, and their enemies, yelling with madness and revenge, began to beat them with unrestrained fury. The former, finding that they could not resist the impetuous tide which burst upon them, fled back past the church, and stopped not until they had reached an elevation, on which lay two or three heaps of stones, that had been collected for the purpose of paving the streets. Here they made a stand, and commenced a vigorous discharge of them against their pursuers. This checked the latter; and the others, seeing them hesitate, and likely to retreat from the missiles, pelted them with such effect, that the tables became turned, and the Ribbonmen made a speedy flight back into the town.

"In the mean time several Orangemen had gone into Sherlock's, where a considerable number of arms had been deposited, with an intention of resorting to them in case of a defeat at the cudgels. These now came out, and met the Ribbonmen on their flight from those who were pelting them with the stones. A dreadful scene ensued. The Ribbonmen, who had the advantage in numbers, finding themselves intercepted before by those who had arms, and pursued behind by those who had recourse to the stones, fought with un common bravery and desperation. Kelly, who was furious, but still collected and decisive, shouted out in Irish, lest the opposite party might understand him 'Let every *two* men seize upon *one* of those who have the arms.'

"This was attempted, and effected with partial success: and I have no doubt, but the Orangemen would have been ultimately beaten and deprived of their weapons, were it not that many of them, who had got their pistols out of Sherlock's, discharged them among their enemies, and wounded several. The Catholics could not stand this; but, wishing to retaliate as effectually as possible, lifted stones wherever they could find them, and kept up the fight at a distance, as they retreated. On both sides, wherever a solitary foe was caught straggling from the rest, he was instantly punished with a most cruel and blood-thirsty spirit.

"It was just about this time that I saw Kelly engaged with two men, whom he kept at bay with great ease—retrograding, however, as he fought, towards his own party. Grimes, who had for some time before this recovered and joined the fight once more, was returning, after having pursued several of the Ribbonmen past the market-house, where he spied Kelly thus engaged. With a Volunteer gun in his hand, and furious with the degradation of his former defeat, he ran over and struck him with the butt-end of it upon the temple—and Denis fell. When the stroke was given, an involuntary cry of 'Murder—foul, foul!' burst from those who looked on from the windows; and long John Steele, Grimes's father-in-law, in indignation, raised his cudgel to knock him down for this treacherous and malignant blow;—but a person out of Neal Cassidy's back-yard hurled a round stone, about six pounds in weight, at Grimes's head, that felled him to the earth, leaving him as insensible, and nearly in as dangerous a state, as Kelly—for his jaw was broken.

"By this time the Catholics had retreated out of the town, and Denis might probably have received more punishment, had those who were returning from the pursuit recognised him; but James Wilson, seeing the dangerous situation in which he lay, came out, and, with the assistance of his servant-man, brought him into his own house. When the Orangemen had driven their adversaries off the field, they commenced the most hideous yellings through the streets—got music, and played party tunes—offered any money for the face of a Papist; and any of that religion who were so unfortunate as to make their appearance, were beaten in the most relentless manner. It was precisely the same thing on the part of the Ribbonmen; if a Protestant, but above all an Orangeman, came in their way, he was sure to be treated with barbarity: for the retaliation on either side was dreadfully unjust—the innocent suffering as well as the guilty. Leaving the window, I found Kelly in a bad state below stairs.

"'What's to be done?' said I to Wilson.

" 'I know not,' replied he, 'except I put him between us on my jaunting car, and drive him home.'

"This appeared decidedly the best plan we could adopt; so, after putting to the horse, we placed him on the car, sitting one on each side of him, and, in this manner, left him at his own house."

"Did you run no risk," said I, "in going among Kelly's friends, whilst they were under the influence of party feeling and exasperated passion?"

"No," said he; "we had rendered many of them acts of kindness, and had never exhibited any spirit but a *friendly* one towards them; and such individuals, but only such, *might walk through a crowd of enraged Catholics or Protestants, quite unmolested.*"

"The next morning Kelly's landlord, Sir W. R——, and two magistrates, were at his house, but he lay like a log, without sense or motion. Whilst they were there, Surgeon S——e arrived, and, after examining his head, declared that the skull was fractured. During that and the following day, the house was surrounded by crowds, anxious to know his state; and nothing might be heard amongst most of them, but loud and undisguised expressions of the most ample revenge.

The wife was frantic; and, on seeing me, hid her face in her hands, exclaiming,

" 'Ah, Sir, I knew it would come to this; and you, too, tould him the same thing. *My* curse and *God's* curse on it for quarrelling! Will it never stop in the counthry, till they rise some time, and murdher one another out of the face!'

" As soon as the swelling in his head was reduced, Surgeon S——e performed the operation of trepanning, and thereby saved his life; but his strength and intellect were gone—and he just lingered for four months, a feeble, drivelling simpleton, until, in consequence of a cold, which produced inflammation in the brain, he died, as hundreds have died, the victim of party spirit."

Such was the account which I heard of my old school-fellow, Denis Kelly; and, indeed, when I reflected upon the nature of the education he received, I could not but admit, that the consequences were such as might naturally be expected to result from it.

The next morning a relation of Mrs. Kelly's came down to my brother, hoping that, as they wished to have as decent a funeral as possible, he would be so kind as to attend it.

" Musha, God knows, Sir," said the man, " it's poor Denis, heavens be his bed! that had the regard and reverence for every one, young and ould, of your father's family; and it's himself that would be the proud man, if he was living, to see you, Sir, riding after his coffin."

"Well," said my brother, "let Mrs. Kelly know, that I shall certainly attend, and so will my brother, here, who has come to pay me a visit.—Why, I believe, Tom, you forget him!"

"Your brother, Sir! Is it Master Toby, that used to cudgel the half of the counthry when he was at school? Gad's my life, *Masther* Toby, (I was now about thirty-six) but it's your four quarters, sure enough! Arrah, thin, Sir, who'd think it—you're grown so full and stout?—but, faix, you'd always the bone in you! Ah, Masther Toby!" said he, "he's lying cowld, this morning, that would be the happy man to lay his eyes wanst more upon you. Many an' many's the winther's evening did he spind, talking about the time when you and he were bouchals together, and of the pranks you played at school, but especially of the time you both leathered the four Grogans, and tuck the apples from them—my poor fellow!—and now to be stretched a corpse, lavin' his poor widdy and childher behind him!"

I accordingly expressed my sorrow for Denis's death, which, indeed, I sincerely regretted, for he possessed materials for an excellent character, had not all that was amiable and good in him been permitted to run wild.

As soon as my trunk and travelling-bag had been brought from the inn, where I had left them the preceding night, we got our horses, and, as we wished to show particular respect to Denis's remains, rode up, with some of our friends, to the house. When we approached, there were large crowds of the country-people before the door of his well-thatched and respectable-looking dwelling, which had three chimneys, and a set of sash-windows, clean and well glazed. On our arrival, I was soon recognised and surrounded by numbers of those to whom I had formerly been known, who received and welcomed me with a warmth of kindness and sincerity, which it would be in vain to look for among the peasantry of any other nation.

Indeed, I have uniformly observed, that when no religious or political feeling influences the heart and principles of an Irish peasant, he is singularly sincere and faithful in his attachments, and has always a bias to the generous and the disinterested. To my own knowledge, circumstances frequently occur, in which the ebullition of party spirit is altogether temporary, subsiding after the cause that produced it has passed away, and leaving the kind peasant to the natural, affectionate, and generous impulses of his character. But poor *Paddy*, unfortunately, is as combustible a material in politics or religion, as in fighting—thinking it his duty to take the weak* side, without any other consideration, than because it is the weak side.

When we entered the house I was almost suffocated with the strong fumes of tobacco-smoke, snuff, and whiskey; and, as I had been an old school-fellow of Denis's, my appearance was the signal for a general burst of grief among his relations, in which the more distant friends and neighbours of the deceased joined, to keep up the *keening*.

I have often, indeed always, felt that there is something extremely touching in the Irish cry; in fact, that it breathes the very spirit of wild and

* A gentleman once told me an anecdote, of which he was an eye-witness. Some peasants, belonging to opposite factions, had met under peculiar circumstances; there were, however, two on one side, and four on the other—in this case, there was likely to be no fight; but, in order to balance the number, one of the more numerous party joined the weak side—"bekase, boys, it would be a burnin' shame, so it would, for four to kick two; and, except I join them, by the powers, there's no chance of there being a bit of sport, or a row, at all at all!" Accordingly, he did join them, and the result of it was, that he and his party were victorious; so honestly did he fight!

natural sorrow. The Irish peasantry, whenever a death takes place, are exceedingly happy in seizing upon any contingent circumstances that may occur, and making them subservient to the excitement of grief for the departed, or the exultation and praise of his character and virtues. My entrance was a proof of this—I had scarcely advanced to the middle of the floor, when my intimacy with the deceased, our boyish sports, and even our quarrels, were adverted to with a natural eloquence and pathos, that, in spite of my firmness, occasioned me to feel the prevailing sorrow. They spoke, or chaunted mournfully, in Irish; but the substance of what they said was as follows:—

"Oh, Denis, Denis, avourneen! you're lying low, this morning of sorrow!—lying low are you, and does not know who it is (alluding to me) that is standing over you, weeping for the days you spent together in your youth! It's yourself, *acushla agus asthore machree*, (the pulse and beloved of my heart) that would stretch out the right hand warmly to welcome him to the place of his birth, where you had both been so often happy about the green hills and valleys with each other! He's here now, standing over you; and it's he, of all his family, kind and respectable as they are, that was your own favourite, Denis, *avourneen dheelish!* He alone was the companion that you loved!—with no other could you be happy!—For him did you fight, when he wanted a friend in your young quarrels! and if you had a dispute with him, were not you sorry for it? Are you not now stretched in death before him, and will he not forgive you?"

All this was uttered, of course, extemporaneously, and without the least preparation. They then passed on to an enumeration of his virtues as a father, a husband, son, and brother—specified his worth as he stood related to society in general, and his kindness as a neighbour and a friend.

An occurrence now took place, which may serve in some measure, to throw light upon many of the atrocities and outrages which take place in Ireland. Before I mention it, however, I think it necessary to make a few observations relative to it. I am convinced that those who are intimately acquainted with the Irish peasantry, will grant that there is not on the earth a class of people in whom the domestic affections of blood-relationship are so pure, strong, and sacred. The birth of a child will occasion a poor man to break in upon the money set apart for his landlord, in order to keep the christening among his friends and neighbours with due festivity. A marriage exhibits a spirit of joy, an exuberance of happiness and delight, to be found only in the Green Island; and the death of a member of a family is attended with a sincerity of grief, scarcely to be expected from men so much the creatures of the more mirthful feelings. In fact, their sorrow is a solecism in humanity—at once deep and loud—mingled up, even in its greatest paroxysms, with a laughter-loving spirit. It is impossible that an Irishman, sunk in the lowest depths of affliction, could permit his grief to flow in all the sad solemnity of affliction, even for a day, without some glimpse of his natural humour throwing a faint and rapid light over the gloom within him. No: there is an amalgamation of sentiments in his mind, which, as I said before, would puzzle any philosopher to account for. Yet it would be wrong to say, though his grief has something of an unsettled and ludicrous character about it, that he is incapable of the most subtle and delicate shades of sentiment, or the deepest and most desolating intensity of sorrow. But he laughs off those heavy vapours which hang about the moral constitution of the people of other nations, giving them a morbid habit, which leaves them neither strength nor firmness to resist calamity—which they feel less keenly than an Irishman, exactly as a healthy man will feel the pangs of death with more acuteness than one who is wasted away by debility and decay. Let any man witness an emigration, and he will satisfy himself that this is true. I am convinced that Goldsmith's inimitable description of one in his "Deserted Village," was a picture drawn from actual observation. Let him observe the emigrant, as he crosses the Atlantic, and he will find, although he joins the jest, and the laugh, and the song, that he will seek a silent corner or a silent hour to indulge the sorrow which he still feels for the friends, the companions, and the native fields that he has left behind him. This constitution of mind is beneficial: the Irishman seldom or never hangs himself, because he is capable of too much real feeling to permit himself to become the slave of that which is factitious. There is no void in his affections or sentiments, which a morbid and depraved sensibility could occupy; but his feelings, of what character soever they may be, are strong, because they are fresh and healthy. For this reason, I maintain, that when the domestic affections come under the influence of either grief or joy, the peasantry of no nation are capable of feeling so deeply. Even on the ordinary occasions of death, sorrow, though it alternates with mirth and cheerfulness, in a manner peculiar to themselves, lingers long in the unseen recesses of domestic life: *any hand there-*

fore, whether by law or violence, that plants a wound HERE, *will suffer to the death.*

When my brother and I entered the house, the body had just been put into the coffin; and it is usual after this takes place, and before it is nailed down, for the immediate relatives of the family to embrace the deceased, and take their last look and farewell to his remains. In the present instance, the children were brought over, one by one, to perform that trying and melancholy ceremony. The first was an infant on the breast, whose little innocent mouth was held down to that of its dead father; the babe smiled upon his still and solemn features, and would have played with his grave clothes, but that the murmur of unfeigned sorrow, which burst from all present, occasioned it to be removed. The next was a fine little girl, of three or four years, who inquired where they were going to bring her daddy, and asked if he would not soon come back to *her*.

"My daddy's sleepin' a long time," said the child, "but I'll waken him till he sings me 'Peggy Slevin.' I like my daddy best, bekase I sleep wid him—and he brings me good things from the fair, he bought me this ribbon," said she, pointing to a ribbon which he had purchased for her.

The rest of the children were sensible of their loss, and truly it was a distressing scene. His eldest son and daughter, the former about fourteen, the latter about two years older, lay on the coffin, kissing his lips, and were with difficulty torn away from it.

"Oh!" said the boy, "he is going from us, and night or day we will never see him or hear of him more! Oh! father—father—is that the last sight we are ever to see of your face? Why, father dear, did you die, and leave us for ever—for ever—wasn't your heart good to us, and your words kind to us—Oh! your last smile is smiled—your last kiss given—and your last kind word spoken to your childhre that you loved, and that loved you as we did. Father, core of my heart, are you gone for ever, and your voice departed? Oh! the murdherers, oh! the murdherers, the murdherers!" he exclaimed, "that killed my father; for only for them, he would be still wid us: but, by the God that's over me, if I live, night or day I will not rest, till I have blood for blood; nor do I care who hears it, nor if I was hanged the next minute."*

As these words escaped him, a deep and awful murmur of suppressed vengeance burst from his relations. At length their sorrow became too strong to be repressed; and as it was the time to

* Such were the words.

take their last embrace and look of him, they came up, and after fixing their eyes on his face in deep affliction, their lips began to quiver, and their countenance became convulsed. They then burst out simultaneously into a tide of violent grief, which, after having indulged in it for some time, they checked. But the resolution of revenge was stronger than their grief, for standing over his dead body—they repeated, almost word for word, the vow of vengeance which the son had just sworn. It was really a scene dreadfully and terribly solemn; and I could not avoid reflecting upon the mystery of nature, which can, from the deep power of domestic affection, cause to spring a determination to crime of so black a dye.—Would to God that our peasantry had a clearer sense of moral and religious duties, and were not left so much as they are to the headlong impulse of an ardent temperament, and an impetuous character; and would to God that the clergy who superintend their education and morals, had a better knowledge of human nature!

During all this time the heart-broken widow sat beyond the coffin, looking upon what passed with a stupid sense of bereavement; and when they had all performed this last ceremony, it was found necessary to tell her that the time was come for the procession of the funeral, and that they only waited for her to take, as the rest did, her last look and embrace of her husband. When she heard this, it pierced her like an arrow: she became instantly collected, and her complexion assumed a dark sallow shade of despairing anguish, which it was an affliction even to look upon. She then stooped over the coffin, and kissed him several times, after which she ceased sobbing, and lay silently with her mouth to his.

The character of a faithful wife sorrowing for a beloved husband, has that in it which compels both respect and sympathy. There was not at this moment a dry eye in the house. She still lay silent on the coffin; but, as I observed that her bosom seemed not to heave as it did a little before, I was convinced that she had become insensible. I accordingly beckoned to Kelly's brother, to whom I mentioned what I had suspected; and, on his going over to ascertain the truth, he found her as I had said. She was then brought to the air, and after some trouble recovered; but I recommended them to put her to bed, and not to subject her to any unnecessary anguish, by a custom which was really too soul-piercing to endure. This, however, was, in her opinion, the violation of an old rite, sacred to her heart and affections—she would not hear of it for an instant. Again she was helped out between her brother and brother-in-law; and, after stooping down, and doing as the other had done—

"Now," said she, "I will sit here, and keep him under my eye as long as I can—surely you won't blame me for it; you all know the kind husband he was to me, and the good right I have to be sorry for him! Oh!" she added, "is it thrue at all?—is he my own Denis, the young husband of my early—and my first love, in good arnest, dead, and going to leave me here—me, Denis, that you loved so tindherly, and our childher, that your brow was never clouded aginst? Can I believe myself, or is it a dhrame? Denis, *avick machree! avick machree!* your hand was dreaded, and a good right it had, for it was the manly hand, that was ever and always raised in defence of them that wanted a friend; abroad, in the faction-fight, against the oppressor, your name was ever feared, *acushla!*—but *at home*—AT HOME—*where was your fellow?* Denis achra, do you know the lips that's spaking to you?——your young bride—your heart's light—Oh! I remimber the day you war married to me like yesterday. Oh! avourneen, then and since wasn't the heart of your own Honor bound up in you—yet not a word even to me. Well, agrah machree, tisn't your fault, it's the first time you ever refused to spake to your own Honor. But you're dead, avourneen, or it wouldn't be so—you're dead before my eyes—husband of my heart, and all my hopes and happiness goes into the coffin and the grave along wid you, for ever!"

All this time she was rocking herself from side to side, her complexion pale and ghastly as could be conceived. When the coffin was about to be closed, she retired until it was nailed down, after which she returned with her bonnet and cloak on her, ready to accompany it to the grave. I was astonished—for I thought she could not have walked two steps without assistance; but it was the custom, and to neglect it, I found, would have thrown the imputation of insincerity upon her grief. While they were preparing to bring the coffin out, I could hear the chat and conversation of those who were standing in crowds before the door, and occasionally a loud, vacant laugh, and sometimes a volley of them, responsive to the jokes of some rustic wit, probably the same person who acted master of the revels at the wake.

Before the coffin was finally closed, Ned Corrigan, whom I had put to flight the preceding night, came up, and repeated the *De profundis* in very strange Latin, over the corpse. When this was finished, he got a jug of holy water, and after dipping his thumb in it, first made the sign of the cross upon his own forehead, and afterwards sprinkled it upon all present, giving my brother and myself an extra compliment, supposing, probably, that we stood most in need of it. When this was over, he sprinkled the corpse and the coffin in particular most profusely. He then placed two pebbles from Lough Derg, and a bit of holy candle, upon the breast of the corpse, and having said a *Pater* and *Ave*, in which he was joined by the people, he closed the lid, and nailed it down.

"Ned," said his brother, "are his feet and toes loose?"

"Musha, but that's more than myself knows," replied Ned—"Are they, Katty?" said he, inquiring from the sister of the deceased.

"Arrah, to be sure, avourneen!" answered Katty—"div you think we would lave him to be tied that-a-way, when he'd be risin' out of his last bed? Wouldn't it be too bad to have his toes tied thin, avourneen?"

The coffin was then brought out and placed upon four chairs before the door, to be keened; and, in the mean time, the friends and well-wishers of the deceased were brought into the room to get each a glass of whiskey, as a token of respect. I observed also, that such as had not seen any of Kelly's relations until then, came up, and shaking hands with them, said—"I'm sorry for your loss!" This expression of condolence was uniform, and the usual reply was—"Thank you, Mat, or Jim!" with a pluck of the skirts, accompanied by a significant nod, to follow. They then got a due share of whiskey; and it was curious, after they came out, their faces a little flushed, and their eyes watery with the strong, ardent spirits, to hear with what heartiness and alacrity they entered into Denis's praises.

When he had been keened in the street, there being no hearse, the coffin was placed upon two handspikes which were fixed across, but parallel to each other under it. These were borne by four men, one at the end of each, with the point of it crossing his body a little below his stomach; in other parts of Ireland, the coffin is borne on the shoulders, but this is more convenient and less distressing.

When we got out upon the road, the funeral was of great extent—for Kelly had been highly respected. On arriving at the *merin* which bounded the land he had owned, the coffin was laid down, and a loud and wailing *keena* took place over it. It was again raised, and the funeral proceeded in a direction which I was surprised to see it take, and it was not until an acquaintance of my brother's had explained the matter that I understood the cause of it. In Ireland when a murder is perpetrated, it is usual, as the funeral proceeds to the grave-yard, to bring the corpse to the house of him who committed the crime, and lay it down at his door, while the relations of the deceased kneel down, and, with an appalling solemnity, utter the deepest imprecations, and invoke the justice of heaven on the head of the murderer. This, however, is usually omitted if the residence of the criminal be completely out of the line of the funeral, but if it be possible, by any circuit, to approach it, this dark ceremony is never omitted. In cases where the crime is doubtful, or unjustly imputed, those who are thus visited come out, and laying their right hand upon the coffin, protest their innocence of the blood of the deceased, calling God to witness the truth of their asseverations; but, in cases where the crime is clearly proved against the murderer, the door is either closed, the ceremony repelled by violence, or the house abandoned by the inmates until the funeral passes.

The death of Kelly, however, could not be actually, or, at least, directly, considered a murder, for it was probable that Grimes did not inflict the stroke with an intention of taking away his life, and, besides, Kelly survived it four months.—Grimes's house was not more than fifteen perches from the road; and when the corpse was opposite the little bridle way that led up to it, they laid it down for a moment, and the relations of Kelly surrounded it, offering up a short prayer, with uncovered heads. It was then borne toward the house, whilst the keening commenced in a loud and wailing cry, accompanied with clapping of hands, and every other symptom of external sorrow. But, independent of their compliance with this ceremony, as an old usage, there is little doubt that the appearance of any thing connected with the man who certainly occasioned Kelly's death, awoke a keener and more intense sorrow for his loss. The wailing was thus continued until the coffin was laid opposite Grimes's door; nor did it cease then, but, on the contrary, was renewed with louder and more bitter lamentations.

As the multitude stood compassionating the affliction of the widow and orphans, it was the most impressive and solemn spectacle that could be witnessed. The very house seemed to have a condemned look; and, as a single wintry breeze waved a tuft of long grass that grew on a seat of turf at the side of the door, it brought the vanity of human enmity before my mind with melancholy force. When the keening ceased, Kelly's wife, with her children, knelt, their faces towards the house of their enemy, and invoked, in the strong language of excited passion, the justice of heaven upon the head of the man who had left her a widow, and her children fatherless. I was anxious to know if Grimes would appear to disclaim the intention of murder; but I understood that he was at market—for it happened to be market-day.

"Come out!" said the widow—"come out, and look at the sight that's here before you! Come and view *your own work!* Lay but your hand upon the coffin, and the blood of him you murdhered will spout, before God and these Christhen people, in your guilty face! But, oh! may the Almighty God bring *this home to you!**—May you never lave this life, John Grimes, till worse nor has overtaken me and mine falls upon you and yours! May our curse light upon you this day!—the curse, I say, of the widow and the orphans, that your bloody hand has made us, may it blast you! May you, and all belonging to you wither off of the 'arth! Night and day, sleeping and waking—like snow off the ditch may you melt, until your name and your place will be disremimbered, except to be cursed by them that

* Does not this usage illustrate the proverb of the guilt being brought home to a man, when there is no doubt of his criminality?

will hear of you and your hand of murdher! Amin, we pray God this day!—and the widow and orphan's prayer will not fall to the ground while your guilty head is above? Childhre, did you all say it?"

At this moment a deep, terrific murmur, or rather ejaculation, corroborative of assent to this dreadful imprecation, pervaded the crowd in a fearful manner; their countenances darkened, their eyes gleamed, and their scowling visages, stiffened into an expression of determined vengeance.

When these awful words were uttered, Grimes's wife and daughters approached the window in tears, sobbing, at the same time, loudly and bitterly.

"You're wrong," said the wife—"you're wrong, Widow Kelly, in saying that my husband *murdhered* him!—he did *not* murdher him; for, when you and yours were far from him, I heard John Grimes declare before the God who's to judge him, that he had no thought or intention of taking his life; he struck him in anger, and the blow did him an injury that was not intended. Don't curse him, Honor Kelly," said she—"don't curse him so fearfully; but, above all, don't curse me and my innocent childher, for *we* never harmed you, nor wished you ill! *But it was this party work did it!* Oh, my God!" she exclaimed, wringing her hands, in utter bitterness of spirit, "when will it be ended between friends and neighbours, that ought to live in love and kindness together, instead of fighting in this blood-thirsty manner!"

She then wept more violently, as did her daughters.

"May God give me mercy in the last day, Mrs. Kelly, as I pity from my heart and soul you and your orphans," she continued; "but don't curse us, for the love of God—for you know we should forgive our enemies, as we ourselves, that are the enemies of God, hope to be forgiven."

"May God forgive me, then, if I have wronged you or your husband," said the widow, softened by their distress; "but you know, that whether he intended his life or not, the stroke he gave him has left my childher without a father, and myself dissolate. Oh, heavens above me!" she exclaimed, in a scream of distraction and despair, "is it possible—is it thrue—that my manly husband—the best father that ever breathed the breath of life—my own Denis, is lying dead—murdhered before my eyes! Put your hands on my head, some of you—put your hands on my head, or it will go to pieces. Where are you, Denis—where are you, the strong of hand, and the tender of heart? Come to me, darling, I want you in my distress. I want comfort, Denis; and I'll take it from none but yourself, for kind was your word to me in all my afflictions!"

All present were affected; and, indeed, it was difficult to say, whether Kelly's wife or Grimes's was more to be pitied at the moment. The affliction of the latter and of her daughters was really pitiable; their sobs were loud, and the tears streamed down their cheeks like rain. When the widow's exclamations had ceased, or rather were lost in the loud cry of sorrow which were uttered by the keeners and friends of the deceased —they, too, standing somewhat apart from the rest, joined in it bitterly; and the solitary wail of Mrs. Grimes differing in character from that of those who had been trained to modulate the most profound grief into strains of a melancholy nature, was particularly wild and impressive. At all events, her Christian demeanour, joined to the sincerity of her grief, appeased the enmity of many; so true is it that a soft answer turneth away wrath. I could perceive, however, that the resentment of Kelly's male relations did not at all appear to be in any degree moderated.

The funeral again proceeded, and I remarked that whenever a strange passenger happened to meet it, he always turned back, and accompanied it for a short distance, after which he resumed his journey, it being considered unlucky to omit this usage on meeting a funeral. Denis's residence was not more than two miles from the churchyard, which was situated in the town where he had received the fatal blow. As soon as we had got on about the half of this way, the priest of the parish met us, and the funeral, after proceeding a few perches more, turned into a green field, in the corner of which stood a table with the apparatus for saying mass spread upon it.

The coffin was then laid down once more, immediately before this temporary altar; and the priest, after having robed himself, the wrong side of the vestments out, as is usual in the case of death, began to celebrate mass for the dead, the congregation all kneeling. When this was finished, the friends of the deceased approached the altar, and after some private conversation, the priest turned round, and inquired aloud—

"Who will give offerings?"

The people were acquainted with the manner in which this matter is conducted, and accordingly knew what to do. When the priest put the question, Denis's brother, who was a wealthy man, came forward, and laid down two guineas on the altar; the priest took this up, and putting it on a plate, set out among the multitude, accompanied by two or three of those who were best acquainted with the inhabitants of the parish. He thus continued putting the question, distinctly, after each man had paid; and according as the money was laid down, those who accompanied the priest pronounced the name of the person who gave it, so that all present might hear it. This is also done to enable the friends of the deceased to know not only those who show them this mark of respect, but those who neglect it, in order that they may treat them in the same manner on similar occasions. The amount of money so received is very great; for there is a kind of emulation among the people, as to who will act with most decency and spirit, that is exceedingly beneficial to the priest. In such instances the difference of religion is judiciously overlooked; for although the prayers of Protestants are declined on those occasions, yet it seems the same objection does not hold good against their money, and accordingly they pay as well as the rest. When the priest came round to where I stood, he shook hands with my brother, with whom he appeared to be on very friendly and familiar terms; he and I were then introduced to each other.

"Come," said he, with a very droll expression of countenance, shaking the plate at the same time up near my brother's nose—"Come, Mr. D'Arcy, down with your offerings, if you wish to have a friend with St. Peter when you go as far as the gates; down with your money, Sir, and you shall be remembered, depend upon it."

"Ah!" said my brother, pulling out a guinea, "I would with the greatest pleasure; but I fear this guinea is not orthodox. I'm afraid it has the heretical mark upon it."

"In that case," replied his reverence laughing heartily, "your only plan is to return it to the bosom of the church, by laying it on the plate here—it will then be *within the pale*, you know."

This reply produced a good deal of good-humour among that part of the crowd which immediately surrounded them—not excepting his nearest relations, who laughed heartily.

"Well," said my brother, as he laid it on the plate, "how many prayers will you offer up in my favour for this?"

"Leave *that* to myself," said his Reverence, looking at the *money*—"it will be before you when you go to St. Peter."

He then held the plate over to me in a droll manner; and I added another guinea to my brother's gift; for which I had the satisfaction of having my name called out so loud, that it might be heard a quarter of a mile off.

"God bless you, Sir," said the priest, "and I thank you."

"John," said I, when he left us, "I think that is a pleasant, and rather a sensible man?"

"He's as jovial a soul," replied my brother, "as ever gave birth to a jest, and he sings a right good song. Many a convivial hour have he and I spent together; but, as to being a Catholic in *their* sense—Lord help you! At all events, he is no bigot; but, on the contrary, a liberal—and, putting religion out of the question, a kind and benevolent man."

When the offerings were all collected, he returned to the altar, repeated a few additional prayers in prime style, as rapid as lightning; and after hastily shaking the holy water on the crowd, the funeral moved on. It was now two o'clock, the day clear and frosty, and the sun unusually bright for the season. During mass, many were added to those who formed the funeral train at the outset; so that, when we got out upon the road, the procession appeared very large. After this, few or none joined it; for it is esteemed by no means "*dacent*" to do so *after* mass—because, in that case, the matter is ascribed to an evasion of the offerings; but those whose delay has not really been occasioned by this motive, make it a point to pay them at the grave-yard, or after the interment, and sometimes even on the following day—so jealous are the peasantry of having any degrading suspicion attached to their generosity.

The order of the funeral now was as follows:—Foremost the women—next to them the corpse, surrounded by the relations—the eldest son, in deep affliction, "led the coffin," as chief mourner, holding in his hand the corner of a sheet or piece of linen, fastened to the *mort-cloth*. After the coffin came those who were on foot, and in the rear were the equestrians. When we were a quarter of a mile from the church-yard, the funeral was met by a dozen of singing boys, belonging to a chapel choir, which the priest, who was fond of music, had some time before formed. They fell in, two by two, immediately behind the corpse, and commenced singing the *Requiem*, or Latin hymn for the dead.

The scene through which we passed at this time, though not clothed with the verdure and luxuriant beauty of summer, was, nevertheless, marked by that solemn and decaying splendour which characterises a fine country, lit up by the melancholy light of a winter setting sun. It was, therefore, much more in character with the occasion. Indeed I felt it altogether beautiful; and, as the "dying day-hymn stole aloft," the dim sun-beams fell, through a vista of naked motionless trees, upon the coffin, which was borne with a slower and more funereal pace then before, in a manner that threw a solemn and visionary light upon the whole procession. This, however, was raised to something dreadfully impressive, when the long train, thus proceeding with a motion so mournful, was seen each covered with a profusion of crimson ribbons, to indicate that the corpse they bore owed his death to a deed of murder. The circumstance of the sun glancing his rays upon the coffin was not unobserved by the peasantry, who considered it as a good omen to the spirit of the departed.

As we went up the street which had been the scene of the quarrel that proved so fatal to Kelly, the coffin was again laid down on the spot where he received his death-blow; and, as was usual, the wild and melancholy *keena* was raised. My brother saw many of Grimes's friends among the spectators, but he himself was not visible. Whether Kelly's party saw them or not, we could not say; if they did, they seemed not to notice them, for no expression of revenge or indignation escaped them.

At length, we entered the last receptacle of the dead. The coffin was now placed upon the shoulders of the son and brothers of the deceased, and borne round the church-yard; whilst the priest, with his stole upon him, preceded it, reading prayers for the eternal repose of the soul. Being then laid beside the grave, a "*De profundis*" was repeated by the priest and the mass-server; after which, a portion of fresh clay, carried from the fields, was brought to his Reverence, who read a prayer over it, and consecrated it. This is a ceremony which is never omitted at the interment of a Roman Catholic. When it was over, the coffin was lowered into the grave, and the blessed clay shaken over it. The priest now took the shovel in his own hands, and threw in the three first shovelsful—one in the name of the Father, one in the name of the Son, and one in the name of the Holy Ghost. The sexton then took it, and in a short time Denis Kelly was fixed for ever in his narrow bed.

While these ceremonies were going forward, the church-yard presented a characteristic picture. Beside the usual groups who straggle through the place, to amuse themselves by reading the inscriptions on the tombs, you might see many individuals kneeling on particular graves, where some relation lay—for the benefit of whose soul they offered up their prayers, with an attachment and devotion which one cannot but admire. Sometimes all the surviving members of the family would assemble, and repeat a *Rosary* for the same purpose. Again, you might see an unhappy woman beside a newly-made grave, giving way to lamentation and sorrow for the loss of a husband, or of some beloved child. Here, you might observe the "last bed" ornamented with hoops, decked in white paper, emblematic of the virgin innocence of the individual who slept below;—there, a little board-cross informing you that "this monument was erected by a disconsolate husband to the memory of his beloved wife." But that which excited greatest curiosity was a sycamore tree, which grew in the middle of the burying ground.

It is necessary to inform the reader, that in Ireland many of the church-yards are exclusively appropriated to the interment of Roman Catholics, and, consequently, no Protestant corpse would be permitted to pollute or desecrate them. This was one of them: but it appears that, by some means or other, the body of a Protestant had been interred in it—and hear the consequence! The next morning heaven marked its disapprobation of this awful visitation by a miracle; for, ere the sun rose from the east, a full-grown sycamore had shot up out of the heretical grave, and stands there to this day, a monument at once of the profanation and its consequence. Crowds were looking at this tree, feeling a kind of awe, mingled with wonder, at the deed which drew down such a visible and lasting mark of God's displeasure. On the tomb-stones near Kelly's grave, men and women were seated, smoking tobacco to their very heart's content; for, with that profusion which characterises the Irish in every thing, they had brought out large quantities of tobacco, whiskey, and bunches of pipes. On such occasions it is the custom for those who attend the wake or the funeral to bring a full pipe home with them; and it is expected that as often as it is used, they will remember to say, "God be merciful to the soul of him that this pipe was over."

The crowd, however, now began to disperse; and the immediate friends of the deceased sent the priest, accompanied by Kelly's brother, to request that we would come in, as the last mark of respect to poor Denis's memory, and take a glass of wine and a cake.

"Come, Toby," said my brother, "we may as well go in, as it will gratify them; we need not make much delay, and we will still be at home in sufficient time for dinner."

"Certainly you will," said the priest; "for you shall both come and dine with me to-day."

"With all my heart," said my brother; "I have no objection, for I know you give it good."

When we went in, the punch was already reeking from immense white jugs, that couldn't hold less than a gallon each.

"Now," said his Reverence, very properly, "you have had a dacent and creditable funeral, and have managed every thing with great propriety; let me request, therefore, that you will not get drunk, nor permit yourselves to enter into any disputes or quarrels; but be moderate in what you take, and go home peaceably."

"Why, thin, your Reverence," replied the widow, "he's now in his grave, and, thank God, it's he that had the dacent funeral all out—ten good gallons did we put on you, astore, and it's yourself that liked the dacent thing, any how—but sure, Sir, it would shame him where he's lyin', if we disregarded him so far as to go home widout bringing in our friends, that didn't desart us in our throuble, an' thratin' them for their kindness."

While Kelly's brother was filling out all their glasses, the priest, my brother, and I, were taking a little refreshment. When the glasses were filled, the deceased's brother raised his in his hand, and said—

"Well, gintlemen," addressing us, "I hope you'll pardon me for not dhrinking your healths first; but people, you know, can't break through an ould custom, at any rate—so I give poor Denis's health, that's in his *warm* grave, and God be marciful to his sowl."*

The priest now winked at me to give them their own way; so we filled our glasses, and joined with the rest in drinking "Poor Denis's health, that's now in his warm grave, and God be merciful to his soul."

When this was finished, they then drank ours, and thanked us for our kindness in attending the funeral. It was now past five o'clock; and we left them just setting into a hard bout of drinking, and rode down to his Reverence's residence.

"I saw you smile," said he, on our way, "at the blundering toast of Mat Kelly; but it would be labour in vain to attempt setting them right. What do they know about the distinctions of more refined life? Besides, I maintain, that what they said was as well calculated to express their affection, as if they had drunk honest Denis's *memory*. It is, at least, unsophisticated. But did you hear," said he, "of the apparition that was seen last night, on the mountain road above Denis's?"

"I did not *hear* of it," I replied, equivocating a little.

* A fact.

"Why," said he, "it is currently reported that the spirit of a murdered pedlar, which haunts the hollow of the road at Drumfurrar, chased away the two servant men as they were bringing home the coffin, and that finding it a good bit, he then got into it, and walked half a mile along the road, with the wooden surtout upon him; and, finally, that to wind up the frolic, he left it on one end half-way between the bridge and Denis's house, after putting a crowd of the countrymen to flight. I suspect some droll knave has played them a trick. I assure you, that a deputation of them, who declared that they saw the coffin move along of itself, waited upon me this morning, to know whether they ought to have put him into the coffin, or gotten another."

"Well," said my brother, in reply to him, "after dinner we will probably throw some light upon that circumstance; for I believe my brother here knows something about it."

"So, Sir," said the priest, "I perceive you have been amusing yourself at their expense?"

I seldom spent a pleasanter evening than I did with Father Molloy, (so he was called,) who was, as my brother said, a shrewd, sensible man, possessed of convivial powers of the first order. He sang us several good songs; and, to do him justice, he had an excellent voice. He regretted very much the state of party and religious feeling, which he did every thing in his power to suppress.

"But," said he, "I have little co-operation in my efforts to communicate knowledge to my flock, and implant better feelings among them. You must know," he added, "that I am no great favourite among them. On being appointed to this parish by my bishop, I found that the young man who was curate to my predecessor, had formed a party against me, thinking, by that means, eventually to get the parish himself. Accordingly, on coming here, I found the chapel doors closed on me; so that a single individual among them would not recognise me as their proper pastor. By firmness and spirit, however, I at length succeeded, after a long struggle against the influence of the curate, in gaining admission to the altar; and, by a proper representation of his conduct to the bishop, I soon made my gentleman knock under. Although beginning to gain ground in the good opinion of the people, I am by no means yet a favourite. The curate and I scarcely speak; and a great number of my parishioners brand me with the epithet of the *Orange priest;* and this principally because I occasionally associate with Protestants—a habit, gentlemen, which they will find some difficulty in making me give up, as long as

I can have the pleasure," said he, bowing, "of seeing such guests at my table as those with whose company I am now honoured."

It was now near nine o'clock, and my brother was beginning to relate an anecdote concering the clergyman who had preceded Father Molloy in the parish, when a messenger from Mr. Wilson, already alluded to, came up in breathless haste, requesting the priest, for God's sake to go down into town instantly, as the Kellys and the Grimeses were engaged in a fresh quarrel.

"My God!" he exclaimed—"when will this work have an end? But, to tell you the truth, gentlemen, I apprehended it; and I fear that something still more fatal to the parties, will yet be the consequence. Mr. D'Arcy you must try what you can do with the Grimeses, and I will manage the Kellys."

We then proceeded to the town, which was but a very short distance from the priest's house; and, on arriving, found a large crowd before the door of the house in which the Kellys had been drinking, engaged in hard conflict. The priest was on foot, and had brought his whip with him, it being an argument, in the hands of a Roman Catholic pastor, which tells so home, that it is not to be gainsayed. Mr. Molloy and my brother now dashed in amongst them; and by remonstrance, abuse, blows, and entreaty, they with difficulty succeeded in terminating the fight. They were also assisted by Mr. Wilson and other persons, who dared not, until their appearance, run the risk of interfering between them. Wilson's servant, who had come for the priest, was still standing beside me, looking on; and, while my brother and Mr. Molloy were separating the parties, I asked him how the fray commenced.

"Why, Sir," said he, "it bein' market-day, the Grimeses chanced to be in town, and this came to the ears of the Kellys, who were drinking in Cassidy's here, till they got tipsy; some of them then broke out, and began to go up and down the street, shouting for the face of a murdhering Grimes. The Grimeses, Sir, happened at the time to be drinking with a parcel of their friends in Joe Sherlock's, and hearing the Kellys calling out for them, why, as the dhrop, Sir, was in on both sides, they were soon at it. Grimes has given one of the Kellys a great bating; but Tom M'Guigan, Kelly's cousin, a little before we came down, I'm tould, has knocked the seven senses out of him, with a pelt of a brick-bat in the stomach."

Soon after this, however, the quarrel was got under; and, in order to prevent any more bloodshed that night, my brother and I got the Kellys together, and brought them as far as our residence, on their way home. As we went along, they uttered awful vows, and determinations of the deepest revenge, swearing repeatedly, that they would shoot Grimes from behind a ditch, if they could not in any other manner have his blood. They seemed highly intoxicated; and several of them were cut and abused in a dreadful manner; even the women were in such a state of excitement and alarm, that grief for the deceased was, in many instances, forgotten. Several of both sexes were singing; some laughing with triumph at the punishment they had inflicted on the enemy; others of them, softened by what they had drunk, were weeping in tones of sorrow that might be heard a couple of miles off. Among the latter were many of the men, some of whom, as they staggered along, with their frieze big-coats hanging off one shoulder, clapped their hands, and roared like bulls, as if they intended, by the loudness of their grief then, to compensate for their silence when sober. It was also quite ludicrous to see the men kissing each other, sometimes in this maudling sorrow, and at others when exalted into the very madness of mirth. Such as had been cut in the scuffle, on finding the blood trickle down their faces, would wipe it off—then look at it, and break out into a parenthetical volley of curses against the Grimeses; after which, they would resume their grief, hug each other in mutual sorrow, and clap their hands as before. In short, such a group could be seen no where but in Ireland.

When my brother and I had separated from them, I asked him what had become of Vengeance, and if he were still in the country.

"No," said he; "with all his courage and watchfulness, he found that his life was not safe; he, accordingly, sold off his property, and collecting all his ready cash, emigrated to America, where, I hear, he is doing well."

"God knows," I replied, "I shouldn't be surprised if one half of the population were to follow his example, for the state of society here, among the lower orders, is truly deplorable"

THE HEDGE SCHOOL.

THE HEDGE SCHOOL.

There never was a more unfounded calumny, than that which would impute to the Irish peasantry an indifference to education. I may, on the contrary, fearlessly assert that the lower orders of no country ever manifested such a positive inclination for literary acquirements, and that, too, under circumstances strongly calculated to produce carelessness and apathy on this particular subject. Nay, I do maintain, that he who is intimately acquainted with the character of our countrymen, must acknowledge, that their zeal for book learning, not only is strong and ardent, when opportunities of scholastic education occur, but that it increases in proportion as these opportunities are rare and unattainable. The very name and nature of Hedge Schools are proof of this: for what stronger point could be made out, in illustration of my position, than the fact, that, despite of obstacles, whose very idea would crush ordinary enterprize—when not even a shed could be obtained in which to assemble the children of an Irish village, the worthy pedagogue selected the first green spot on the sunny side of a quick-set-thorn hedge, which he conceived adapted for his purpose, and there, under the scorching rays of a summer sun, and in defiance of spies and statutes, carried on the work of instruction. From this circumstance the name of Hedge School originated; and, however it may be associated with the ludicrous, I maintain, that it is highly creditable to the character of the people, and an encouragement to those who wish to see them receive pure and correct educational knowledge. A Hedge School, however, in its original sense, was but a temporary establishment, being only adopted until such a school-house could be erected, as was in those days deemed sufficient to hold such a number of children as were expected, at all hazards, to attend it.

The opinion, I know, which has been long entertained of Hedge Schoolmasters, was, and still is, unfavourable; but the character of these worthy and eccentric persons has been misunderstood, for the stigma attached to their want of knowledge should have rather been applied to their want of morals, because, on this latter point only were they indefensible. The fact is, that Hedge Schoolmasters were a class of men, from whom morality was not expected by the peasantry; for, strange to say, one of their strongest recommendations to the good opinion of the people, as far as their literary talents and qualifications were concerned, was an inordinate love of whiskey, and if to this could be added a slight touch of derangement, the character was complete.

On once asking an Irish peasant, why he sent his children to a schoolmaster who was notoriously addicted to spirituous liquors, rather than to a man of sober habits who taught in the same neighbourhood,

"Why do I sind them to Mat Meegan, is it?" he replied—"and do you think, Sir," said he, "that I'd sind them to that dry-headed dunce, Mr. Frazher, with his black coat upon him, and his caroline hat, and him wouldn't taste a glass of poteen wanst in seven years? Mat, Sir, likes it, and teaches the boys ten times betther whin he's dhrunk nor whin he's sober; and you'll never find a good tacher, Sir, but's fond of it. As for Mat, when he's *half gone*, I'd turn him agin the country for deepness in larning; for it's then he rhymes it out of him, that it would do one good to hear him."

"So," said I, "you think that a love of drinking poteen is a sign of talent in a schoolmaster."

"Ay, or in any man else, Sir," he replied. "Look at tradesmen, and 'tis always the cleverest that you'll find fond of the dhrink! If you had hard Mat and Frazher, the other evening, at it—what a hare Mat made of him; but he was just in proper tune for it, being, at the time, purty well I thank you, and did not lave him a leg to stand upon. He took him in Euclid's Ailments and Logicals, and proved in Frazher's teeth, that the candlestick before them was the church-steeple, and Frazher himself the parson; and so sign was on it, the other couldn't disprove it, but had to give in."

"Mat, then," I observed, "is the most learned man on this walk."

"Why, thin, I doubt that same, Sir," replied he, "for all he's so great in the books; for, you see, while they were ding dust at it, who comes in but mad Delany, and he attacked Mat, and, in less than no time, rubbed the consate out of *him*, as clane as *he* did out of Frazher."

"Who is Delany?" I inquired.

"He was the makings of a priest, Sir, and was in Maynooth a couple of years, but he took in the knowledge so fast, that, bedad, he got *cracked wid larnin'*—for a *dunce*, you see, never cracks wid it, in regard of the thickness of the skull: no doubt but he's too many for Mat, and can go far beyand him in the books; but then, like that, he's still brightest whin he has a sup in his head."

These are prejudices which the Irish peasantry have long entertained concerning the character of hedge schoolmasters; but, granting them to be unfounded, as they generally are, yet it is an indisputable fact, that hedge schoolmasters were as superior in literary knowledge and acquirements to the class of men who are now engaged in the general education of the people, as they were beneath them in moral and religious character.—The former part of this assertion will, I am aware, appear rather startling to many. But it is true; and one great cause why the character of Society Teachers is undervalued, in many instances, by the people, proceeds from a conviction on their parts, that they are, and must be, incapable, from the slender portion of learning they have received, of giving their children a sound and practical education.

But that we may put this subject in a clearer light, we will give a sketch of the course of instruction which was deemed necessary for a hedge schoolmaster, and, let it be contrasted with that which falls to the lot of those engaged in the conducting of schools patronized by the Education Societies of the present day.

When a poor man, about twenty or thirty years ago, understood from the schoolmaster who educated his sons, that any of them was particularly "cute at his larnin'," the ambition of the parent usually directed itself to one of three objects—he would either make him a priest, a clerk, or a schoolmaster. The determination once fixed, the boy was set apart from every kind of labour, that he might be at liberty to bestow his undivided time and talents to the objects set before him. His parents strained every nerve to furnish him with the necessary books, and always took care that his appearance and dress should be more decent than those of any other member of the family. If the church were in prospect, he was distinguished, after he had been two or three years at his Latin, by the appellation of "the young priest," an epithet to him of the greatest pride and honour; but if destined only to wield the ferula, his importance in the family, and the narrow circle of his friends, was by no means so great. If, however, the goal of his future ambition as a schoolmaster was humbler, that of his literary career was considerably extended. He usually remained at the next school in the vicinity until he supposed that he had completely drained the master of all his knowledge.

This circumstance was generally discovered in the following manner :—As soon as he judged himself a match for his teacher, and possessed sufficient confidence in his own powers, he penned him a formal challenge to meet him in literary contest, either in his own school, before competent witnesses, or at the chapel-green, on the Sabbath day, before the arrival of the priest, or probably after it—for the priest himself was generally the moderator and judge upon these occasions. This challenge was generally couched in rhyme, and either sent by the hands of a common friend, or posted upon the chapel door.

These contests, as the reader perceives, were always public, and were witnessed by the peasantry with intense interest. If the master sustained a defeat, it was not so much attributed to his want of learning, as to the overwhelming talent of his opponent; nor was the success of the pupil generally followed by the expulsion of the master—for this was but the first of a series of challenges which the former proposed to undertake, ere he eventually settled himself in the exercise of his profession.

I remember being present at one of them, and a ludicrous exhibition it was. The parish priest, a red-faced, jocular little man, was president, and his curate, a scholar of six feet two inches in height, and a schoolmaster from the next parish, were judges. I will only touch upon two circumstances in their conduct, which evinced a close, instinctive knowledge of human nature in the combatants. The master would not condescend to argue off his throne—a piece of policy to which, in my opinion, he owed his victory (for he won); whereas the pupil insisted that he should meet him on equal ground, face to face, in the lower end of the room. It was evident that the latter could not divest himself of his boyish terrors as long as the other sat, as it were, in the plenitude of his former authority, contracting his brows with habitual sternness, thundering out his arguments, with a most menacing and Stentorian voice, while he thumped his desk with his shut fist, or struck it with his great rule at the end of each argument, in a manner that made the youngster put his hands behind him several times, to be certain that that portion of his dress, which is *unmentionable*, was tight upon him.

If in these encounters the young candidate for the honours of the literary sceptre was not victorious, he again resumed his studies, under his old preceptor, with renewed vigour and becoming humility; but if he put the schoolmaster down, his next object was to seek out some other teacher, whose celebrity was unclouded within his own range. With him he had a fresh encounter, and its result was similar to what I have already related. If victorious, he sought out another and more learned opponent; and if defeated, he became the pupil of his conqueror—going night about, during his sojourn at the school, with the neighbouring farmers' sons, whom he assisted in their studies, as a compensation for his support. He was called, during these peregrinations, the *Poor Scholar*, a character which secured him the esteem and hospitable attention of the peasantry, who never fail in respect to any one characterised by a zeal for learning and knowledge.

In this manner he proceeded, a literary knight-errant, filled with a chivalrous love of letters, which would have done honour to the most learned peripatetic of them all; enlarging his own powers, and making fresh acquisitions of knowledge as he went along. His contests, his defeats, and his triumphs, of course, were frequent; and his habits of thinking and reasoning must have been considerably improved, his acquaintance with classical and mathematical authors rendered more intimate, and his powers of illustration and comparison more clear and happy. After three or four years spent in this manner, he usually returned to his native place, sent another challenge to the schoolmaster, in the capacity of a candidate for his situation, and, if successful, drove him out of the district, and established himself in his situation. The vanquished master sought a new district, sent a new challenge, in his turn, to some other teacher, and usually put him to flight in the same manner. The terms of defeat or victory, according to their application, were called *sacking* and *bogging*.

"There was a great argument entirely, Sir," said a peasant once, when speaking of these contests, "'twas at the chapel on Sunday week, betune young Tom Brady, that was a poor scholar in Munsther, and Mr. Hartigan, the schoolmaster."

"And who was victorious?" I inquired.

"Why, Sir, and maybe 'twas young Brady that didn't *sack* him clane, before the priest and all, and went nigh to *bog* the priest himself in Greek. His Reverence was only two words beyant him; but he sacked the masther, any how, and showed him in the Grammatical and Dixonary where he was wrong."

"And what is Brady's object in life?" I asked. "What does he intend to do?"

"Intend to do, is it? I'm tould nothing less nor going into Thrinity College in Dublin, and expects to bate them all there, out and out: he's first to make something they call a seizure;* and, afther making that good, he's to be a counsellor. So, Sir, you see what it is to resave good schoolin', and to have the larnin'; but, indeed, it's Brady that's the great head-piece entirely."

Unquestionably, many who received instruction in this manner have distinguished themselves in the Dublin University; and I have no hesitation in saying, that young men educated in Irish hedge-schools, as they were called, have proved themselves to be better classical scholars and mathematicians, generally speaking, than any proportionate number of those educated in our first-rate academies. The Munster masters have long been, and still are, particularly celebrated for making excellent classical and mathematical scholars.

That a great deal of ludicrous pedantry generally accompanied this knowledge is not at all surprising, when we consider the rank these worthy teachers held in life, and the stretch of inflation at which their pride was kept by the profound reverence excited by their learning among the people. It is equally true, that each of them had a stock of *crambos* ready for accidental encounter, which would have puzzled Euclid or Sir Isaac

* Sizar.

Newton himself; but even these trained their minds to habits of acuteness and investigation. When a schoolmaster of this class had established himself as a good mathematician, the predominant enjoyment of his heart and life was to write the epithet *Philomath* after his name; and this, whatever document he subscribed, was never omitted. If he witnessed a will, it was Timothy Fagan, Philomath; if he put his name to a promissory note, it was Tim. Fagan, Philomath; if he addressed a love-letter to his sweetheart, it was still Timothy Fagan—or whatever the name might be—Philomath; and this was always written in legible and distinct copyhand, sufficiently large to attract the observation of the reader.

It was also usual for a man who had been a pre-eminent and extraordiary scholar, to have the epithet GREAT prefixed to his name. I remember one of this description, who was called the *Great O'Brien, par excellence.* In the latter years of his life he gave up teaching, and led a circulating life, going round from school to school, and remaining a week or a month alternately among his brethren. His visits were considered an honour, and raised considerably the literary character of those with whom he resided; for he spoke of dunces with the most dignified contempt, and the general impression was, that he would scorn even to avail himself of their hospitality. Like most of his brethern, he could not live without the *po-teen;* and his custom was, to drink a pint of it in its native purity before he entered into any literary contest, or made any display of his learning at wakes or other Irish festivities; and most certainly, however blameable the practice, and injurious to health and morals, it threw out his talents and his powers in a most surprising manner.

It was highly amusing to observe the peculiarity which the consciousness of superior knowledge impressed upon the conversation and personal appearance of this decaying race. Whatever might have been the original conformation of their physical structure, it was sure, by the force of acquired habit, to transform itself into a stiff, erect, consequential, and unbending manner, ludicrously characteristic of an inflated sense of their extraordinary knowledge, and a proud and commiserating contempt of the dark ignorance by which, in despite of their own light, they were surrounded. Their conversation, like their own *crambos*, was dark and difficult to be understood; their words, truly sesquipedalian; their voice, loud and commanding in its tones; their deportment, grave and dictatorial, but completely indescribable, and certainly original to the last degree, in those instances where the ready, blundering, but genuine humour of their country maintained an unyielding rivalry in their disposition, against the natural solemnity which was considered necessary to keep up the due dignity of their character.

In many of these persons, where the original humour and gaiety of the disposition were known, all efforts at the grave and dignified were complete failures, and these were enjoyed by the peasantry and their own pupils, nearly with the sensations which the enactment of Hamlet by Liston would necessarily produce. At all events, their education, allowing for the usual exceptions, was by no means superficial; and the reader has already received a sketch of the trials which they had to undergo, before they considered themselves qualified to enter upon the duties of their calling. Their life was, in fact, a state of literary warfare; and they felt that a mere elementary knowledge of their business would have been insufficient to carry them, with suitable credit, through the attacks to which they were exposed from travelling teachers, whose mode of establishing themselves in schools, was, as I said, by driving away the less qualified, and usurping their places. This, according to the law of opinion, and the custom which prevailed, was very easily effected, for the peasantry uniformly encouraged those whom they supposed to be the most competent; as to moral or religious instruction, neither was expected from them, so that the indifference of the moral character was no bar to their success.

The village of Findramore was situated at the foot of a long green hill, the outline of which formed a low arch, as it rose to the eye against the horizon. This hill was studded with clumps of beeches, and sometimes enclosed as a meadow. In the month of July, when the grass on it was long, many an hour have I spent in solitary enjoyment, watching the wavy motion produced upon its pliant surface by the sunny winds, or the flight of the cloud-shadows, like gigantic phantoms, as they swept rapidly over it, whilst the murmur of the rocking trees, and the glancing of their bright leaves in the sun, produced a heartfelt pleasure, the very memory of which rises in my imagination, like some fading recollection of a brighter world.

At the foot of this hill ran a clear, deep-banked river, bounded on one side by a slip of rich, level meadow, and on the other by a kind of common for the village geese, whose white feathers, during the summer season, lay scattered over its green surface. It was also the play-ground for the boys of the village school; for there ran that part of the river, which, with very correct judgment, the urchins had selected as their bathing-place. A little slope, or watering-ground in the bank, brought them to the edge of the stream, where the bottom fell away into the fearful depths of the whirlpool, under the hanging oak on the other bank. Well do I remember the first time I ventured to swim across it, and even yet do I see, in imagination, the two bunches of water flaggons on which the inexperienced swimmers trusted themselves in the water.

About two hundred yards above this, the *boreen,** which led from the village to the main road, crossed the river, by one of those old narrow bridges, whose arches rise like round ditches across the road—an almost impassable barrier to horse and car. On passing the bridge, in a northern direction, you found a range of low thatched houses on each side of the road; and if one o'clock, the hour of dinner, drew near, you might observe columns of blue smoke curling up from a row of chimneys, some made of wicker creels plastered over with a rich coat of mud; some, of old, narrow, bottomless tubs; and others, with a greater appearance of taste, ornamented with thick, circu-

* A little road.

lar ropes of straw, sewed together like bees' skeps, with the peel of a brier; and many having nothing but the open vent above. But the smoke by no means escaped by its legitimate aperture, for you might observe little clouds of it bursting out of the doors and windows; the panes of the latter being mostly stopped at other times with old hats and rags, were now left entirely open for the purpose of giving it a free escape.

Before the doors, on right and left, was a series of dunghills, each with its concomitant sink of green, rotten water; and if it happened that a stout-looking woman, with watery eyes and a yellow cap, hung loosely upon her matted locks, came, with a chubby urchin on one arm, and a pot of dirty water in her hand, its unceremonious ejection in the aforesaid sink would be apt to send you up the village with your finger and thumb (for what purpose you would yourself perfectly understand) closely, but not knowingly, applied to your nostrils. But, independently of this, you would be apt to have other reasons for giving your horse, whose heels are by this time surrounded by a dozen of barking curs, and the same number of shouting urchins, a pretty sharp touch of the spurs, as well as for complaining bitterly of the odour of the atmosphere. It is no landscape without figures; and you might notice, if you are, as I suppose you to be, a man of observation, in every sink as you pass along, a "slip of a pig," stretched in the middle of the mud, the very *beau ideal* of luxury, giving occasionally a long, luxuriant grunt, highly expressive of his enjoyment; or, perhaps, an old farrower, lying in indolent repose, with half a dozen young ones justling each other for their draught, and punching her belly with their little snouts, reckless of the fumes they are creating; whilst the loud crow of the cock, as he confidently flaps his wings on his own dunghill, gives the warning note for the hour of dinner.

As you advance, you will also perceive several faces thrust out of the doors, and rather than miss a sight of you, a grotesque visage peeping by a short cut through the painless windows—or, a tattered female flying to snatch up her urchin that has been tumbling itself, heels up, in the dust of the road, lest "the gintleman's horse might ride over it;" and if you happen to look behind, you may observe a shaggy-headed youth in tattered frize, with one hand thrust indolently in his breast, standing at the door in conversation with the inmates, a broad grin of sarcastic ridicule on his face, in the act of breaking a joke or two upon yourself, or your horse; or, perhaps your jaw may be saluted with a lump of clay, just hard enough not to fall asunder as it flies, cast by some ragged gorsoon from behind a hedge, who squats himself in a ridge of corn to avoid detection.

Seated upon a hob at the door, you may observe a toil-worn man, without coat or waistcoat; his red, muscular, sun-burnt shoulder peering through the remnant of a shirt, mending his shoes with a piece of twisted flax, called a *lingel*—or, perhaps, sewing two footless stockings *(or martyeens)* to his coat, as a substitute for sleeves.

In the gardens, which are usually fringed with nettles, you will see a solitary labourer, working with that carelessness and apathy that characterise an Irishman when he labours *for himself*—leaning upon his spade to look after you, and glad of any excuse to be idle.

The houses, however, are not all such as I have described—far from it. You see, here and there, between the more humble cabins, a stout, comfortable-looking farm-house, with ornamental thatching, and well-glazed windows; adjoining to which is a hagyard, with five or six large stacks of corn, well trimmed and roped, and a fine, yellow, weather-beaten old hay-rick, half cut—not taking into account twelve or thirteen circular strata of stones, that mark out the foundations on which others had been raised. Neither is the rich smell of oaten or wheaten bread, which the good wife is baking on the griddle, unpleasant to your nostrils; nor would the bubbling of a large pot, in which you might see, should you chance to enter, a prodigious square of fat, yellow, and almost transparent bacon tumbling about, be an unpleasant object;—truly, as it hangs over a large fire, with well-swept hearth-stone, it is in good keeping with the white settle and chairs, and the dresser with noggins, wooden trenchers, and pewter dishes perfectly clean, and as well polished as a French courtier.

As you leave the village, you have, to the left, a view of the hill which I have already described, and, to the right, a level expanse of fertile country, bounded by a good view of respectable mountains, peering decently into the sky; and in a line that forms an acute angle from the point of the road where you ride, is a delightful valley, in the bottom of which shines a pretty lake; and a little beyond, on the slope of a green hill, rises a splendid house, surrounded by a park, well-wooded and stocked with deer. You have now topped the little hill above the village, and a straight line of level road, a mile long, goes forward to a country town which lies immediately behind that white church, with its spire cutting into the sky, before you. You descend on the other side, and, having advanced a few perches, look to the left, where you see a long, thatched chapel, only distinguished from a dwelling house by its want of chimneys, and a small stone cross that stands on the top of the eastern gable; behind it is a grave-yard, and beside it a snug public-house, well white-washed; then, to the right, you observe a door apparently in the side of a clay bank, which rises considerably above the pavement of the road. What! you ask yourself, can this be a human habitation?—but ere you have time to answer the question, a confused buzz of voices from within reaches your ear, and the appearance of a little "gorsoon," with a red, close-cropped head and Milesian face, having in his hand a short, white stick, or the thigh bone of a horse, which you at once recognise as "the pass" of a village school, gives you the full information. He has an ink-horn, covered with leather, dangling at the button-hole (for he has long since played away the buttons) of his frize jacket—his mouth is circumscribed with a streak of ink—his pen is stuck knowingly behind his ear—his shins are dotted over with blisters, black, red, and blue—on each heel a kibe—his "leather crackers," videlicet—breeches, shrunk up upon him, and only reaching as far down as the caps of his knees. Having spied you, he places his hand over his brows, to throw back the dazzling light of the sun, and peers at you from under it, till he breaks out into a laugh, exclaiming, half to himself, and half to you,

"You a gintleman!—no, nor one of your breed never was, you procthorin' thief you!"

You are now immediately opposite the door of the seminary, when half a dozen of those seated next it notice you.

"Oh, Sir, here's a gintleman on a horse!—masther, Sir, here's a gintleman on a horse, wid boots and spurs on him, that's looking in at us."

"Silence!" exclaims the masther; "back from the door, boys rehearse; every one of you rehearse, I say, you Bœotians, till the gintleman goes past!"

"I want to go out, if you plase, Sir."

"No, you don't, Phelim."

"I do, indeed, Sir."

"What! is it afther conthradictin' me you'd be?—don't you see the 'porter's' out, and you can't go."

"Well, 'tis Mat Meehan has it, Sir, and he's out this half hour, Sir. I can't stay in, Sir—iphfff—iphfff!"

"You want to be idling your time looking at the gintleman, Phelim."

"No indeed, Sir—iphfff!"

"Phelim, I know you of ould—go to your sate

—I tell you, Phelim, you were born for the encouragement of the hemp manufacture, and you'll die promoting it."

In the mean time, the master puts his head out of the door, his body stooped to a "half bend"—a phrase, and the exact curve which it forms, I leave for the present to your own sagacity—and surveys you until you pass. That is an Irish hedge school, and the personage who follows you with his eye, a hedge schoolmaster. His name is Matthew Kavanagh; and as you seem to consider his literary establishment rather a curiosity in its kind, I will, if you be disposed to hear it, give you the history of him and his establishment, beginning, in the first place, with—

THE
ABDUCTION OF MAT KAVANAGH,
THE HEDGE SCHOOLMASTER.

For about three years before the period of which I write, the village of Findramore, and the parish in which it lay, were without a teacher. Mat's predecessor was a James Garraghty, a lame young man, the son of a widow, whose husband lost his life in attempting to extinguish a fire that broke out in the dwelling-house of Squire Johnston, a neighbouring [illegible] boy at the time of this disaster, and the Squire, as some compensation for the loss of his father's life in his service, had him educated at his own expense; that is to say, he gave the master who taught in the village orders to educate him gratuitously, on the condition of being horse-whipped out of the parish, if he refused. As soon as he considered himself qualified to teach, he opened a school in the village on his own account, where he taught until his death, which happened in less than a year after the commencement of his little seminary. The children usually assembled in his mother's cabin; but as she did not long survive the son, this, which was at best a very miserable residence, soon tottered to the ground. The roof and thatch were burned for firing, the mud gables fell in, and were overgrown with grass, nettles, and docks; and nothing remained but a foot or two of the little clay side-walls, which presented, when associated with the calamitous fate of their inoffensive inmates, rather a touching image of ruin upon a small scale.

Garraghty had been attentive to his little pupils, and his instructions were sufficient to give them a relish for education—a circumstance which did not escape the observation of their parents, who duly appreciated it. His death, however, deprived them of this advantage; and as schoolmasters, under the old system, were always at a premium, it so happened, that for three years afterwards, none of that class presented himself to their acceptance. Many a trial had been made, and many a sly offer held out, as a lure to the neighbouring teachers, but they did not take; for although the country was densely inhabited, yet it was remarked that no schoolmaster ever "*thruv*" in the neighbourhood of Findramore. The place, in fact, had got a bad name. Garraghty died, it was thought, of poverty, a disease to which the Findramore schoolmasters had been always known to be subject. His predecessor, too, was hanged, along with two others, for burning the house of an "Aagint."

Then the Findramore boys were not easily dealt with, having an ugly habit of involving their unlucky teachers in those quarrels which they kept up with the Ballyscanlan boys, a fighting clan that lived at the foot of the mountains above them. These two factions, when they met, whether at fair or market, wake or wedding, could never part without carrying home on each side a dozen or two of bloody coxcombs. For these reasons, the parish of Aughindrum had for a few years been afflicted with an extraordinary dearth of knowledge; the only literary establishment which flourished in it being a parochial institution, which, however excellent in design, yet, like too many establishments of the same nature, it degenerated into a source of knowledge, morals, and education, exceedingly dry and unproductive to every person except the master, who was enabled by his honest industry to make a provision for his family absolutely surprising, when we consider the moderate nature of his ostensible income. It was, in fact, like a well dried up, to which scarcely any one ever thinks of going for water.

Such a state of things, however, could not last long. The youth of Findramore were parched for want of the dew of knowledge: and their parents and grown brethren met one Saturday evening in Barny Brady's shebeen-house, to take into consideration the best means for procuring a resident schoolmaster for the village and neighbourhood. It was a difficult point, and required great dexterity of management to enable them to devise any effectual remedy for the evil which they felt. There were present at this council, Tim Dolan, the senior of the village, and his three sons, Jem Coogan, Brian Murphy, Paddy Delany, Owen Roe O'Neil, Jack Traynor, and Andy Connell, with five or six others, whom it is not necessary to enumerate.

"Bring us in a quart, Barny," said Dolan to

Brady, whom on this occasion we must designate as the host; "and let it be rale hathen."

"What do you mane, Tim?" replied the host.

"I mane," continued Dolan, "stuff that was never christened, man alive."

"Thin I'll bring you the same that Father Maguire got last night on his way home, afther anointin' ould Katty Duffy," replied Brady. "I'm sure, whatever I might be afther givin' to strangers, Tim, I'd be long sorry to give *yees* any thing but the right sort."

"That's a gay man, Barny," said Traynor; "but off wid you like shot, an' let us get it under our tooth first, an' then we'll tell you more about it.—A big rogue is the same Barny," he added, after Brady had gone to bring in the poteen, "an' never sells a dhrop that's not one whiskey and five wathers."

"But he couldn't expose it on *you*, Jack," observed Connell; "you're too ould a hand about the *pot* for that. Warn't you in the mountains last week?"

"Ay: but the curse of Cromwell upon the thief of a gauger, Simpson—himself and a pack o' redcoats surrounded us when we war beginnin' to *double*, and the purtiest *runnin'* that even you seen was lost; for, you see, before you could cross yourself, we had the bottoms knocked clane out of the vessels; so that the villains didn't get a hole in our coats, as they thought they would."

"I tell you," observed O'Neil, "there's a *bad pill* somewhere about us."

"Ay is there, Owen," replied Traynor; "and what is more, I don't think he's a hundhred miles from the place where we're sittin' in."

"Faith, maybe so, Jack," returned the other.

"I'd never give in to that," said Murphy. "'Tis Barny Brady that would never turn informer—the same thing isn't in him, nor in any of his breed; there's not a man in the parish I'd thrust sooner."

"I'd jist thrust him," replied Traynor, "as far as I could throw a cow by the tail. Arrah, what's the rason that the gauger never looks next or near *his* place, an' it's well known that he sells poteen widout a licence, though he goes past his door wanst a week?"

"What the h—— is keepin' him at all?" inquired one of Dolan's sons.

"Look at him," said Traynor, "comin' in out of the garden; how much afeard he is! keepin' the whiskey in a phatie ridge—an' I'd kiss the book that he brought that bottle out in his pocket, instead of diggin' it up out o' the garden."

Whatever Brady's usual habits of *christening* his poteen might have been, that which he now placed before them was good. He laid the bottle on a little deal table with cross legs, and along with it a small drinking glass fixed in a bit of flat circular wood, as a substitute for the original bottom, which had been broken. They now entered upon the point in question, without further delay.

"Come, Tim," said Coogan, "you're the ouldest man, and must spake first."

"Throth, man," replied Dolan, "beggin' your pardon, I'll dhrink first—*shud-urth,* your sowl; success boys—glory to ourselves, and confusion to the Scanlan boys, any way."

"And maybe," observed Connell, "'tis we that didn't lick them well in the last fair—they're not able to meet the Findramore birds even on their own walk."

"Well, boys," said Delany, "about the masther? Our childhre will grow up like *bullockeens,* widout knowing a hap'orth; and larning, you see, is a burdyen that's asy carried."

"Ay," observed O'Neil, "as Solvester Maguire, the poet, used to say—

'Labour for larnin' before you grow ould,
For larnin' is better nor riches nor gould:
Riches an' gould they may vanquish away,
But larnin' alone it will never decay.'"

" Success, Owen! Why, you might put down the pot and warm an air to it," said Murphy.

" Well, boys, are we all safe?" asked Traynor.

" Safe!" said old Dolan. "Arrah, what are you talkin' about? Sure 'tisn't of that same spalpeen of a gauger that we'd be afraid?"

During this observation, young Dolan pressed Traynor's foot under the table, and they both went out for about five minutes.

" Father," said the son, when he and Traynor re-entered the room, " you're a wanting home."

" Who wants me, Larry, avick?" says the father.

The son immediately whispered him for a moment, when the old man instantly rose, got his hat, and after drinking another bumper of the poteen, departed.

" 'Twas hardly worth while," said Delany; " the ould fellow's mettle to the back-bone, an' would never show the *garran-bane* at any rate, even if he knew all about it."

" Bad end to the syllable I'd let the same ould cock hear," said the son; "the divil thrust any man that didn't *switch the primer** for it, though he *is* my father; but now, boys, that the coast's clear, and all safe—where will we get a school-

* Take an oath.

master? Mat Kavanagh won't budge from the Scanlan boys, even if we war to put our hands undher his feet: and small blame to him, when he heads them—sure, you would not expect him to be a thraitor to his own?"

"Faith, the gorsoons is in a bad state," said Murphy, "but, boys, where will we get a man that's *up?* Why, I know 'tis betther to have any body nor be without one; but we might kill two birds wid one stone—if we could get a masther that would carry 'Articles,'* an' swear in the boys, from time to time—an' between ourselves, if there's any danger of the hemp, we may as well lay it upon strange shoulders."

"Ay, but since Corrigan swung for the Aagint," replied Delany, "they're a little modest in havin' act or part wid us; but the best plan is to get an advartisment wrote out, an' have it posted on the chapel door."

This hint was debated with much earnestness; but as they were really anxious to have a master —in the first place, for the simple purpose of educating their children; and in the next, for filling the situation of director and regulator of their illegal Ribbon meetings—they determined on penning an advertisement, according to the sugges-

* A copy of the Whiteboy oath and regulations.

tion of Delany. After drinking another bottle, and amusing themselves with some further chat, one of the Dolans undertook to draw up the advertisement, which ran as follows:—

"ADVARTAAISMENT.

"*Notes to Schoolmasthers, and to all others whom it may consarn.*

"WANTED,

"For the nabourhood and vircinity of the Townland of Findramore, in the Parish of Aughindrum, in the Barony of Lisnamoghry, County of Sligo, Province of Connaught, Ireland.

"TO SCHOOLMASTERS.

"Take Notes—That any Schoolmaster who understands Spellin' gramatically — Readin' and Writin', in the raal way, according to the Dixonary—Arithmatick, that is to say, the five common rules, namely, simple addition, subtraction, multiplication, and division—and addition, subtraction, multiplication, and division, of Dives's denominations. Also reduction up and down—cross multiplication of coin—the Rule of Three direck—the Rule of Three in verse—the double Rule of Three—Frackshins taught according to the vulgar and decimatin' method; and must be well practised to tache the Findramore boys how to manage the *Scuffle*.

"N. B. He must be well grounded in *that.* Practis, Discount, and *Rebatin'*, N. B. Must be well grounded in *that* also.

"Tret and Tare—Fellowship—Allegation—Barther—Rates per Scent—Intherest—Exchange—Prophet in Loss—the Square Root—the Kibe Root—Hippothenuse—Arithmatical and Gommetrical Purgation—Compound Intherest—Loggerheadism—Questions for Exercise, and the Conendix to Algibbra. He must also know Jommithry accordin' to Grunther's scale—the Castigation of the Klipsticks—Surveying and the use of the Jacob-staff.

"N. B. Would get a good dale of Surveyin' to do in the vircinity of Findramore, particularly in *Con-acre time.* If he knew the use of the globe, it would be an accusation. He must also understand the Three Sets of Book-keeping, by single and double entry, particularly Loftus & Company of Paris, their Account of Cash and Company. And above all things, he must know how to tache the *Sarvin' of Mass in Latin*, and be able to read Doctor Gallaher's Irish Sarmints, and explain Kolumkill's and Pastorini's Prophecies.

"N. B. If he understands *Cudgel-fencin'*, it would be an accusation also—but mustn't tache us wid a staff that bends in the middle, bekase it breaks one's head across the guard. Any schoolmaster capacious and collified to instruct in the above-mintioned branches, would get a good school in the townland Findramore and its vircinity, be well fed, an' get the hoith o' good livin' among the farmers, an' would be ped—

"For Book-keepin', the three sets, *a ginny and half.*

"For Gommethry, &c. *half a ginny a quarther.*

"Arithmatic, *aight and three-hapuns.*

"Readin', Writin', &c. *six Hogs.*

"*Given under our hands, this 32d of June,* 18004.

"LARRY DOLAN,
"DICK DOLAN, his × mark.
"JEM COOGAN, his × mark.
"BRINE MURPHEY,
"PADDY DELANY, his × mark.
"JACK TRAYNOR,
"ANDY CONNELL,
"OWEN ROE O'NEIL, his × mark.

"N. B. *By making airly application to any of the undher-mintioned, he will hear of further particklers;* and if they find that he will shoot them, he may expect the best o' thratement, an' be well fed among the farmers.

"N. B. Would get also a good night-school among the vircinity."

Having penned the above advertisement, it was carefully posted early the next morning on the chapel doors, with an expectation on the part of the patrons that it would not be wholly fruitless. The next week, however, passed without an application—the second also—and the third produced the same result; nor was there the slightest prospect of a schoolmaster being blown by any wind to the lovers of learning at Findramore. In the mean time, the Ballyscanlan boys took care to keep up the ill-natured prejudice which had been circulated concerning the fatality that uniformly attended such schoolmasters as settled there; and when this came to the ears of the Findramore folk, it was once more resolved that the advertisement should be again put up, with a clause containing an explanation on that point. The clause ran as follows:—

"N. B. The two last masthers that was hanged out of Findramore, that is, Mickey Corrigan, who was hanged for killing the Aagent, and Jem Garraghty, that died of a declension—Jem died in quensequence of ill health, and Mickey was hanged contrary to his own wishes; so that it wasn't either of their faults—as witness our hands this 27th of July.

"DICK DOLAN, his ✕ mark."

This explanation, however, was as fruitless as the original advertisement; and week after week passed over without an offer from a single candidate. The "vircinity" of Findramore and its "nabourhood" seemed devoted to ignorance; and nothing remained except another effort at procuring a master by some more ingenious contrivance.

Debate after debate was, consequently, held in Barny Brady's; and, until a fresh suggestion was made by Delany, the prospect seemed as bad as ever. Delany, at length, fell upon a new plan; and it must be confessed, that it was marked in a peculiar manner by a spirit of originality and enterprise—it being nothing less than a proposal to carry off, by force or stratagem, Mat Kavanagh, who was at that time fixed in the throne of literature among the Ballyscanlan boys, quite unconscious of the honourable translation to the neighbourhood of Findramore which was intended for him. The project, when broached, was certainly a startling one, and drove most of them to a pause, before they were sufficiently collected to give an opinion on its merits.

"Nothin', boys, is asier," said Delany. "There's to be a patthern in Ballymagowan on next Sathurday—an' that's jist half way betune ourselves and the Scanlan boys. Let us musther an' go there, any how. We can keep an eye on Mat widout much trouble, an', when opportunity sarves, nick him at wanst, an' off wid him clane."

"But," said Traynor, "what would we do wid him when he'd be here? Wouldn't he *cut an' run* the first opportunity?"

"How can he, ye omadhawn, if we put a man-will in our pocket, an' sware him? But we'll butther him up when he's among us; or, be me sowks, if it goes to that, force him either to settle wid ourselves, or make himself scarce in the counthry entirely."

"Divil a much force it'll take to keep him, I'm thinkin'," observed Murphy. "He'll have three times a betther school here; and if he was wanst settled, I'll engage he would take to it kindly."

"See here, boys," says Dick Dolan, in a whisper, "if that bloody villain, Brady, isn't afther standin' this quarter of an hour, strivin' to hear what we're about; but it's well we didn't bring up any thing consarnin' the other business; didn't I tell yees the desate was in 'im? Look at his shadow on the wall forninst us."

"Hould yer tongues, boys," said Traynor; "jist keep never mindin', and, be my sowks, I'll make him sup sorrow for that thrick."

"You had betther neither make nor meddle wid him," observed Delany; "jist put him out o' that—but don't raise yer hand to him, or he'll sarve you as he did Jem Flanagan—put ye three or four months in the *Stone Jug*."

Traynor, however, had gone out while he was speaking, and in a few minutes dragged in Brady, whom he caught in the very act of eaves-dropping.

"Jist come in, Brady," said Traynor, as he dragged him along—"walk in, man alive; sure, and sich an honest man as you are needn't be afeard of lookin' his friend in the face!—ho!—an' be my sowl, is it a spy we've got? and, I suppose would be an informer, too, if he had heard any thing to tell!"

"What's the manin' of this, boys?" exclaimed the others, feigning ignorance—"let the honest man go, Traynor. What do ye hawl him that-a-way for, ye gallis pet?"

"Honest!" replied Traynor—"how very honest he is, the desavin' villain—to be standin' at the windy there, wantin' to overhear the little harmless talk we had."

"Come, Traynor," said Brady, seizing him in his turn by the neck, "take your hands off of me, or, bad fate to me, but I'll lave ye a mark."

Traynor, in his turn, had his hand twisted in Brady's cravat, which he drew tightly about his neck, until the other got nearly black in the face.

"Let me go, you villain!" exclaimed Brady, "or by this blessed night that's in it, it'll be worse for you."

"Villain! is id?" replied Traynor, making a blow at him, whilst Brady snatched at a pen-knife which one of the others had placed on the table, after picking the tobacco out of his pipe—intending either to stab Traynor, or to cut the knot of the cravat by which he was held. The others, however, interfered, and prevented further mischief.

"Brady," said Traynor, "you'll rue this night, if ever a man did, you tracherous informin' villain. What an honest spy we have among us!—and a short course to you!"

"Oh, hould yer tongue, Traynor!" replied Brady: "I blieve it's best known who is both the spy and the informer. The divil a pint of poteen ever you'll run in this parish, until you clear yourself of bringing the gauger on the Traceys, bekase they tuck Mick M'Kew in preference to yourself to run it for them."

Traynor made another attempt to strike him, but was prevented. The rest now interfered; and, in the course of an hour or so, an adjustment took place.

Brady took up the tongs, and swore "by that blessed iron," that he neither heard, nor intended to hear, any thing they said, and this exculpation was followed by a fresh bottle at his own expense.

"You omadhawn," said he to Traynor, "I was ony puttin' up a dozen o' bottles into the tatch of the house, when you thought I was listenin';" and, as a proof of the truth of this, he brought them out and showed them some bottles of poteen, neatly covered up under the thatch.

Before their separation they finally planned the abduction of Kavanagh from the Patron, on the Saturday following, and after drinking another round went home to their respective dwellings.

In this speculation, however, they experienced a fresh disappointment; for, ere Saturday arrived, whether in consequence of secret intimation of their intention from Brady or some friend, or in compliance with the offer of a better situation, the fact was, that Mat Kavanagh had removed to another school, distant about eighteen miles from Findramore. But they were not to be outdone; a new plan was laid, and in the course of the next week, a dozen of the most enterprising and intrepid of the "boys," mounted each upon a good horse, went to Mat's new residence for the express purpose of securing him.

Perhaps our readers may scarcely believe, that a love of learning was so strong among the inhabitants of Findramore, as to occasion their taking such remarkable steps for establishing a schoolmaster among them; but the country was densely inhabited, the rising population exceedingly numerous, and the outcry for a schoolmaster amongst the parents of the children loud and importunate. Besides this, the illegal principles of Whiteboyism were as deeply rooted in that neighbourhood as in others; and the young men stood in need of some person who might regulate their proceedings, keep their registries, preside at and appoint their meetings, and organize, with sufficient skill and precision, not only the vast numbers who had been already enrolled as members, but who were putting forward their claims, day after day, to be admitted as such.

God knows, it is no wonder that Ireland should be as she is, and as she long has been, when we consider the fact, that those who conducted the education of her peasantry were the most active instruments in disseminating among the rising generation, such pernicious principles as those which characterise this system, so deeply rooted among the people—men, whose moral characters were, with few exceptions, execrable—and nine-tenths of whom held situations of authority in these diabolical associations.

The fact, therefore, was, that a double motive

stimulated the inhabitants of Findramore in their efforts to procure a master. The old and middle-aged heads of families were actuated by a simple wish, inseparable from Irishmen, to have their children educated; and the young men, not only by a determination to have a properly qualified person to preside at their nightly orgies, but an inclination to improve themselves in reading, writing, and arithmetic. The circumstance I am now relating is one which actually took place; and any man acquainted with the remote parts of Ireland, may have often seen bloody and obstinate quarrels among the peasantry, in vindicating a priority of claim to the local residence of a schoolmaster among them. I could, within my own experience, relate two or three instances of this nature.

It was one Saturday night in the latter end of the month of May, that a dozen Findramore "boys," as they were called, set out upon this most singular of all literary speculations, resolved, at whatever risk, to secure the person and effect the permanent bodily presence among them of the redoubtable Mat Kavanagh. Each man was mounted on a horse, and one of them brought a spare steed for the accommodation of the schoolmaster. The caparison of this horse was somewhat remarkable: it consisted of a wooden straddle, such as is used by the peasantry for carrying wicker paniers or creels, which are hung upon two wooden pins, that stand up out of its sides. Under it was a straw mat, to prevent the horse's back from being stripped by the straddle. On one side of this hung a large creel, and on the other a strong sack, tied round a stone of sufficient weight to balance the empty creel. The night was warm and clear, the moon and stars all threw their mellow light from a serene, unclouded sky, and the repose of nature in the short nights of this delightful season, resembles that of a young virgin of sixteen—still, light, and glowing. Their way, for the most part of their journey, lay through a solitary mountain-road; and, as they did not undertake the enterprize without a good stock of poteen, their light-hearted songs and choruses awoke the echoes that slept in the mountain glens as they went along. The adventure, it is true, had as much of frolic as of seriousness in it; and merely as the means of a day's fun for the boys, it was the more eagerly entered into.

It was about midnight when they left home, and as they did not wish to arrive at the village to which they were bound, until the morning should be rather advanced, the journey was as slowly performed as possible. Every remarkable object on the way was noticed, and its history, if any particular association was connected with it, minutely detailed, whenever it happened to be known. When the sun rose, many beautiful green spots and hawthorn valleys excited, even from these unpolished and illiterate peasants, warm bursts of admiration at their fragrance and beauty. In some places, the dark flowery heath clothed the mountains to the tops, from which the grey mists, lit by a flood of light, and breaking into masses before the morning breeze, began to descend into the valleys beneath them; whilst the voice of the grouse, the bleating of sheep and lambs, the pee-weet of the wheeling lap-wing, and the song of the lark, threw life and animation over the previous stillness of the country. Sometimes a shallow river would cross the road, winding off into a valley that was overhung, on one side, by rugged precipices clothed with luxuriant heath and wild ash; whilst, on the other, it was skirted by a long sweep of greensward, skimmed by the twittering swallow, over which lay scattered numbers of sheep, cows, brood mares, and colts—many of them rising and stretching themselves ere they resumed their pasture, leaving the spots on which they lay of a deeper green. Occasionally, too, a sly-looking fox might be seen lurking about a solitary lamb, or brushing over the hills with a fat goose upon his back, retreating to his den among the inaccessible rocks, after having plundered some unsuspecting farmer.

As they advanced into the skirts of the cultivated country, they met many other beautiful spots of scenery among the upland, considerable portions of which, particularly in long sloping valleys, that faced the morning sun, were covered with hazel and brushwood, where the unceasing and simple notes of the cuckoo were incessantly plied, mingled with the more mellow and varied notes of the thrush and blackbird. Sometimes, the bright summer waterfall seemed, in the rays of the sun, like a column of light, and the springs that issued from the sides of the more distant and lofty mountains shone with a steady, dazzling brightness, on which the eye could scarcely rest. The morning, indeed, was beautiful, the fields in bloom, and every thing cheerful. As the sun rose in the heavens, nature began gradually to awaken into life and happiness; nor was the natural grandeur of a Sabbath summer morning among these piles of magnificent mountains—nor its heartfelt, but more artificial beauty in the cultivated country, lost, even upon the unphilosophical "boys" of Findramore, so true is it, that the appearance of nature will force enjoyment upon the most uncultivated heart.

When they had arrived within two miles of the little town in which Mat Kavanagh was fixed, they turned off into a deep glen, a little to the left; and, after having seated themselves under a white-thorn which grew on the banks of a rivulet, they began to devise the best immediate measures to be taken.

"Boys," said Tim Dolan, "how will we manage now with this thief of a schoolmaster, at all? Come, Jack Traynor, you that's up to still-house work—escapin' and carryin' away stills from gaugers, the bloody villains!—out wid yer *spake*, till we hear your opinion."

"Do ye think, boys," said Andy Connell, "that we could flatter him to come by fair mains?"

"Flatther him!" said Traynor; "and, by my sowl, if we flatther him at all, it must be by the hair of the head. No, no; let us bring him first whether he will or not, an' ax his consent afther-wards!"

"I'll tell you what it is, boys," continued Connell, "I'll hould a wager, if you lave him to me, I'll bring him wid his own consint."

"No, nor sorra that you'll do, nor could do," replied Traynor; "for, along wid every thing else, he thinks he's not jist doated on by the Findramore people, being one of the Ballyscanlan tribe.—No, no, let two of us go to his place, and purtind that we have other business in the fair of Clansallagh on Monday next, and ax him in to dhrink, for he'll not refuse that, any how; then, when he's half tipsy, ax him to convoy us this far; we'll then meet you here, an' tell him some palaver or other—sit down again where we are now, and, afther making him dead dhrunk, hoise a big stone in the creel, and Mat in the sack, on the other side, wid his head out, and off wid him; and he will know neither act nor part about it, till we're at Findramore."

Having approved of this project, they pulled out each a substantial complement of stout oaten bread, which served, along with the whiskey, for breakfast. The two persons pitched on for decoying Mat were Dolan and Traynor, who accordingly set out, full of glee at the singularity and drollness of their undertaking. It is unnecessary to detail the ingenuity with which they went about it—because, in consequence of Kavanagh's love of drink, very little ingenuity was necessary. One circumstance, however, came to light, which gave them much encouragement, and that was a discovery that Mat by no means relished his situation.

In the mean time, those who staid behind in the glen felt their patience begin to flag a little, because of the delay made by the others, who had promised, if possible, to have the schoolmaster in the glen before two o'clock. But the fact was, that Mat, who was far less deficient in hospitality than in learning, brought them into his house, and not only treated them to plenty of whiskey, but made the wife prepare a dinner, for which he detained them, swearing, that except they stopped to partake of it, he would not convoy them to the place appointed. Evening was, therefore, tolerably far advanced, when they made their appearance at the glen, in a very equivocal state of sobriety—Mat being by far the steadiest of the three, but still considerably the worse for what he had taken. He was now welcomed by a general huzza; and on his expressing his surprise at the appearances, they pointed to their horses, telling him that they were bound for the fair of Clansallagh, for the purpose of selling them. This was the more probable, as, when a fair occurs in Ireland, it is usual for cattle-dealers, particularly horse-jockeys, to effect sales, and "show" their horses on the evening before.

Mat now sat down, and was vigorously plied with strong poteen—songs were sung, stories told, and every device resorted to that was calculated to draw out and heighten his sense of enjoyment; nor were their efforts without success; for, in the course of a short time, Mat was free from all earthly care, being incapable of either speaking or standing.

"Now, boys," said Dolan, "let us do the thing clane an' dacent. Let you, Jem Coogan, Brian Murphy, Paddy Delany, and Andy Connell, go back, and tell the wife and two childher a cock-and-a-bull story about Mat—say that he is coming to Findramore for good and all, and that'll be thruth, you know; and that he ordhered yees to bring her and them afther him; and we can come back for the furniture to-morrow."

A word was enough—they immediately set off; and the others, not wishing that Mat's wife should witness the mode of his conveyance, proceeded home, for it was now dusk. The plan succeeded admirably; and in a short time the wife and children, mounted behind the "boys" on the horses, were on the way after them to Findramore.

The reader is already aware of the plan they had adopted for translating Mat; but, as it was extremely original, I will explain it somewhat more fully. The moment the schoolmaster was intoxicated to the necessary point—that is to say, totally helpless and insensible—they opened the sack and put him in, heels foremost, tying it in such a way about his neck as might prevent his head from getting into it, thus avoiding the danger of suffocation. The sack, with Mat at full length in it, was then fixed to the pin of the straddle, so that he was in an erect posture during the whole journey. A creel was then hung at the other side, in which was placed a large stone, of sufficient weight to preserve an equilibrium; and, to prevent any accident, a droll fellow sat astride behind the straddle, amusing himself and the rest by breaking jokes upon the novelty of Mat's situation.

"Well, Mat, *ma bouchal,* how duv ye like your sitivation? I believe, for all your larnin', the Findramore boys have *sacked* you at last?"

"Ay," exclaimed another, "he *is* sacked at last, in spite of his Matthew-maticks."

"An', be my sowks," observed Traynor, "he'd be a long time goin' up a Maypowl in the state he's in—his own snail would bate him."*

"Yes," said another, "but he desarves credit for travellin' from Clansallagh to Findramore, widout layin' a foot to the ground—

Wan day wid Captain Whiskey I wrastled a fall,
But faith I was no match for the captain at all—
But faith I was no match for the captain at all,
Though the landlady's measures they were damnable small.
Tooral, looral, looral, looral, lido.

* This alludes to a question in Gough's Arithmetic, which is considered difficult by hedge schoolmasters.

Whoo—hurroo! my darlings—success to the Findramore boys! Hurroo—hurroo—the Findramore boys for ever!"

"Boys, did ever yees hear the song Mat made on Ned Mullen's fight wid Jemmy Connor's gander? Well, here it is to the tune of 'Brian O'Lynn'—

As Ned and the gander wor basting each other,
I hard a loud cry from the grey goose his mother;
I ran to assist him, wid my great speed,
Bud before I arrived the poor gander did bleed.
'Alas!' says the gander, 'I'm very ill-trated,
For tracherous Mullen has me fairly defated;
Bud had you been here for to show me fair play,
I could leather his *puckan** around the lee bray.

"Bravo! Mat," addressing the insensible schoolmaster—"success, poet. Hurroo for the Findramore boys! the Bridge boys for ever!"

They then commenced, in a tone of mock gravity, to lecture him upon his future duties—detailing the advantages of his situation, and the comforts he would enjoy among them—although they might as well have addressed themselves to the stone on the other side. In this manner they got along, amusing themselves at Mat's expense, and highly elated at the success of their under-

* Paunch.

taking. About two o'clock in the morning they reached the top of the little hill above the village, when, on looking back along the level stretch of road which I have already described, they noticed their companions, with Mat's wife and children, moving briskly after them. A general huzza now took place, which, in a few minutes, was answered by two or three dozen of the young folks, who were assembled in Barny Brady's waiting for their arrival. The scene now became quite animated—cheer after cheer succeeded—jokes, laughter, and rustic wit, pointed by the spirit of Brady's poteen, flew briskly about. When Mat was unsacked, several of them came up, and, shaking him cordially by the hand, welcomed him among them. To the kindness of this reception, however, Mat was wholly insensible, having been for the greater part of the journey in a profound sleep. The boys next slipped the loop of the sack off the straddle-pin; and, carrying Mat into a farmer's house, they deposited him in a settle-bed, where he slept, unconscious of the journey he had performed, until breakfast-time on the next morning. In the mean time, the wife and children were taken care of by Mrs. Connell, who provided them with a bed, and every other comfort which they could require. The next morning, when Mat awoke, his first call was for a drink. I should have here observed, that Mrs. Kavanagh had been sent for by the good woman in whose house Mat had slept, that they might all breakfast and have a drop together, for they had already succeeded in reconciling *her* to the change.

"Wather!" said Mat—"a drink of wather, if it's to be had for love or money, or I'll split wid druth—I'm all in a state of conflagration; and my head—by the sowl of Newton, the inventor of fluxions, but my head is a complete illucidation of the centrifugle motion, so it is. Tundher-an'-turf! is there no wather to be had? Nancy, I say, for God's sake, quicken yourself wid the hydraulics, or the best mathematician in Ireland's gone to the abode of Euclid and Pythagoras, that first invented the multiplication table."

On cooling his burning blood with the "hydraulics," he again lay down, with the intention of composing himself for another sleep; but his eye having noticed the novelty of his situation, he once more called Nancy.

"Nancy, avourneen," he inquired, "will you be afther resolving me one single proposition—Where am I at the present spaking? Is it in the *Siminary* at home, Nancy?"

Nancy, in the mean time, had been desired to answer in the affirmative, hoping that if his mind was made easy on that point, he might refresh himself easy by another hour or two's sleep, as he appeared to be not at all free from the effects of his previous intoxication.

"Why, Mat, jewel, where else would you be, a lannah, but at home? Sure, isn't here Jack, an' Biddy, an' myself, Mat, agra, along wid me. Your head isn't well, but all you want is a good rousin' sleep."

"Very well, Nancy; very well, that's enough —quite satisfacthory—*quod erat demonstrandum.* May all kinds of bad luck rest upon the Findramore boys, any way! The unlucky vagabonds— I'm the *third* they've done up. Nancy, off wid ye, like quicksilver, for the priest."

"The priest! Why, Mat, jewel, what puts that in your head? Sure, there's nothing wrong wid ye, only the sup o' drink you tuck yestherday."

"Go, woman," said Mat, "did you ever know me to make a wrong *calculation?* I tell you, I'm *non compos mentis* from head to heel. Head! by my sowl, Nancy, it'll soon be a *caput mortuum* wid me—I'm far gone in a disease they call an ophtical delusion—the devil a thing less it is— me bein' in my own place, an' to think I'm lyin' in a settle-bed; that there is a large dresser, covered wid pewter dishes and plates; and, to crown all, the door on the wrong side of the house. Off wid ye, an' tell his Reverence that I want to be anointed, and to die in pace and charity wid all men. May the most especial kind of bad luck light down upon you, Findramore, and all that's in you, both man and baste —you have given *me* my gruel along wid the rest; but, thank God, you won't hang me, any how! Off, Nancy, for the priest, till I die like a Christhan, in pace and forgiveness wid the world; —all kinds of hard fortune to them! Make haste, woman, if you expect me to die like a Christhan. If they had let me alone till I'd publish to the world my Treatise upon Conic Sections—but to be cut off on my march to fame! Another draught of the hydraulics, Nancy, an' then for the priest: but see, bring Father Connell, the curate, for he understands something about Matthew-maticks; an' never heed Father Roger, for little he knows about them, not even the difference between a right line and a curve—in the page of histhory, to his everlasting disgrace, be it recorded!"

"Mat," replied Nancy, scarcely preserving her gravity, "keep yourself from talkin', an' fall asleep, then you'll be well enough."

"Is there e'er a sup at all in the house?" said Mat; "if there is, let me get it; for there's an ould proverb, though it's a most unmathematical axiom as ever was invinted—'try a hair of the same dog that bit you;' give me a glass, Nancy, any how, an' you can go for Father Connell after. Oh, by the sowl of Isaac, that invented fluxions, what's this for?"

A general burst of laughter followed this demand and ejaculation; and Mat sat up once more in the settle, and examined the place with keener scrutiny. Nancy herself laughed heartily; and, as she handed him the full glass, entered into an explanation of the circumstances attending his translation.

Mat, at all times rather of a pliant disposition, felt rejoiced on finding that he was still *compos mentis;* and on hearing what took place, he could not help entering into the humour of the enterprise, at which he laughed as heartily as any of them.

"Mat," said the farmer, and half a dozen of the neighbours, "you're a happy man; there's a hundred of the boys have a school-house half built for you this same blessed sunshiny mornin', while you're lying at ase in your bed."

"By the sowl of Newton, that invinted fluxions!" replied Mat, "but I'll take revenge for the disgrace you put upon my profession, by stringing up a schoolmaster among you, and I'll hang you all! It's death to stale a four-footed animal; but what do you desarve for stalin' a Christian baste, a two-legged schoolmaster without feathers, eighteen miles, and he not to know it?"

In the course of a short time Mat was dressed, and having found benefit from the "hair of the dog that bit him," he tried another glass, which strung his nerves, or, as he himself expressed it —"they've got the raal mathematical tinsion agin." What the farmer said, however, about the school-house, had been true. Early that morning all the growing and grown young men of Findramore and its "vircinity" had assembled, selected a suitable spot, and, with merry hearts, were then busily engaged in erecting a school-house for their general accommodation.

The manner of building hedge school-houses being rather curious, I will describe it. The usual spot selected for their erection is a ditch on the road-side, in some situation where there will be as little damp as possible. From such a spot an excavation is made equal to the size of the building, so that, when this is scooped out, the back side-wall and the two gables are already formed, the banks being dug perpendicularly. The front side-wall, with a window in each side of the door, is then built of clay or green sods laid along in rows; the gables are also topped with sods, and, perhaps, a row or two laid upon the back side-wall, if it should be considered too low. Having got the erection of Mat's house thus far, they procured a scraw-spade, and repaired with a couple of dozen of cars to the next bog, from which they cut the light heathy surface in stripes the length of the roof. A scraw-spade is an instrument resembling the letter T, with an iron plate at the lower end, considerably bent, and well adapted to the purpose for which it is intended. Whilst one party cut the scraws, another bound the *couples* and *bauks*, and a third cut as many green branches as were sufficient to wattle it. The couples, being bound, were raised—the ribs laid on—then the wattles, and afterwards the scraws.

Whilst these successive processes went forward, many others had been engaged all the morning cutting rushes; and the scraws were no sooner laid on, than half a dozen thatchers mounted the roof, and long before the evening was closed, a school-house, capable of holding near a hundred children, was finished. But among the peasantry no new house is ever put up without a hearth-warming, and a dance. Accordingly the clay floor was paired—a fiddler procured—Barny Brady and his stock of poteen sent for; the young women of the village and surrounding neighbourhood attended in their best finery; dancing commenced—and it was four o'clock the next morning when the merry-makers departed, leaving Mat a new home and a hard floor, ready for the reception of his scholars.

Business now commenced. At nine o'clock the next day Mat's furniture was settled in a small cabin, given to him at a cheap rate by one of the neighbouring farmers; for, whilst the school-house was being built, two men, with horses and cars, had gone to Clansallagh, accompanied by Nancy, and removed the furniture, such as it was, to their new residence. Nor was Mat, upon the whole, displeased at what had happened; he was now fixed in a flourishing country—fertile and well cultivated; nay, the bright landscape which his school-house commanded was sufficient in itself to reconcile him to his situation. The inhabitants were in comparatively good circumstances; many of them wealthy, respectable farmers, and capable of remunerating him very decently for his literary labours; and what was equally flattering, there was a certainty of his having a numerous and well attended school, in a neighbourhood with whose inhabitants he was acquainted.

Honest, kind-hearted Paddy!—pity that you should ever feel distress or hunger!—pity that you should be compelled to seek, in another land, the hard-earned pittance by which you keep the humble cabin over the head of your chaste wife and naked children! Alas! what noble materials for composing a national character, of which humanity might be justly proud, do the lower orders of the Irish possess, if raised and cultivated by a Christian education! Pardon me, gentle readers, for this momentary ebullition; I grant I am a little dark now. I assure you, however, the tear of enthusiastic admiration, is warm on my eye-lids, when I remember the flitches of bacon, the sacks of potatoes, the bags of meal, the *miscawns* of butter, and the dishes of eggs—not omitting crate after crate of turf, which came in such rapid succession to Mat Kavanagh, during the first week on which he opened his school. Ay, and many a bottle of stout poteen, when

"The eye of the gauger saw it not,"

was, with a sly, good-humoured wink, handed over to Mat, or Nancy, no matter which, from under the comfortable crab jock, with velvet-covered collar, erect about the honest, ruddy face of a warm, smiling farmer; or even the tattered frize of a poor labourer—anxious to secure the attention of the "masther" to his little "*Shoneen*," whom, in the extravagance of his ambition, he destined to "wear the robes as a clargy."

Let no man say, I repeat, that the Irish are not fond of education.

In the course of a month Mat's school was full to the door-posts, for, in fact, he had the parish to himself—many attending from a distance of three, four, and five miles. His merits, however, were believed to be great, and his character for learning stood high, though unjustly so: for a more superficial, and at the same time, a more presuming dunce never existed; but his character alone could secure him a good attendance; he, therefore, belied the unfavourable prejudices against the Findramore folk, which had gone abroad, and was a proof, in his own person, that the reason of the former schoolmasters' miscarriage, lay in the belief of their incapacity, which existed among the people. But Mat was one of those showy, shallow fellows, who did not lack for assurance.

The first step a hedge schoolmaster took, on establishing himself in a school, was to write out, in his best copperplate hand, a flaming advertisement, detailing, at full length, the several branches he professed himself capable of teaching. I have seen many of these—as who that is acquainted with Ireland has not?—and, beyond all doubt, if the persons that issued them were acquainted with the various heads recapitulated, they must have been buried in the most profound obscurity, as no man but a walking Encyclopædia—an Admirable Crichton—could claim an intimacy with them, embracing, as they often did, the whole circle of human knowledge. 'Tis true, the vanity of the pedagogue had full scope in these advertisements, as there was none to bring him to an account, except some rival, who could only attack him on those practical subjects which were known to both. Independently of this, there was a good-natured collusion between them on these points which were beyond their knowledge, inasmuch as they were not practical but speculative, and by no means involved their character or personal interests. On the next Sunday, therefore, after Mat's establishment at Findramore, you might see a circle of the peasantry assembled at the chapel door, perusing, with suitable reverence and admiration on their faces, the following advertisement; or, perhaps, Mat himself, with a learned, consequential air, in the act of explaining it to them.

"EDUCATION.

"*Mr. Matthew Kavanagh, Philomath and Professor of the Learned Languages, begs leave to inform the Inhabitants of Findramore and its vircinity, that he Lectures on the following Branches of*

Education, in his Seminary at the above recited place :—

" Spelling, Reading, Writing, and Arithmetic, upon altogether *new* principles, hitherto undiscovered by any excepting himself, and for which he expects a *Patent* from Trinity College, Dublin; or at any rate, from Squire Johnston, Esq., who paternizes many of the pupils: Book-keeping, by single and double entry—Geometry, Trigonometry, Stereometry, Mensuration, Navigation, Gauging, Surveying, Dialling, Astronomy, Astrology, Austerity, Fluxions, Geography, ancient and modern—Maps, the Projection of the *Spear*—Algebra, the Use of the Globes, Natural and Moral Philosophy, Pneumatics, Optics, Dioptics, Catroptics, Hydraulics, Ærostatics, Geology, Glorification, Divinity, Mythology, Midicinality, Physic, by theory only, Metaphysics practically, Chemistry, Electricity, Galvanism, Mechanics, Antiquities, Agriculture, Ventilation, Explosion, &c.

" In Classics—Grammar, Cordery, Æsop's Fables, Erasmus' Colloquies, Cornelius Nepos, Phœdrus, Valerius Maximus, Justin, Ovid, Sallust, Virgil, Horace, Juvenal, Persius, Terence, Tully's Offices, Cicero, Manouverius Turgidus, Esculapius, Regerius, Satanus Nigrus, Quinctilian,

Livy, Thomas Aquinas, Cornelius Agrippa, and Cholera Morbus.

"Greek Grammar, Greek Testament, Lucian, Homer, Sophocles, Eschylus, Thucydides, Aristophanes, Xenophon, Plato, Aristotle, Socrates, and the Works of Alexander the Great; the manners, habits, customs, usages, and meditations of the Grecians; the Greek digamma resolved, Prosody, Composition, both in prose-verse, and oratory, in English, Latin, and Greek; together with various other branches of learning and scholastic profundity—*quos enumerare longum est*—along with Irish Radically, and a small taste of Hebrew upon the Masoretic text.

"MATTHEW KAVANAGH, *Philomath.*"

Having posted this document upon the chapel-door, and in all the public places and cross roads of the parish, Mat considered himself as having done his duty. He now began to teach, and his school continued to increase to his heart's content, every day bringing him fresh scholars. In this manner he flourished till the beginning of winter, when those boys, who, by the poverty of their parents, had been compelled to go to service to the neighbouring farmers, flocked to him in numbers, quite voracious for knowledge. An addition was consequently built to the school-house, which was considerably too small; so that, as Christmas approached, it would be difficult to find a more numerous or merry establishment under the roof of a hedge school. But it is time to give an account of its interior.

The reader will then be pleased to picture to himself such a house as I have already described —in a line with the hedge; the eave of the back roof within a foot of the ground behind it; a large hole exactly in the middle of the "*riggin*," as a chimney; immediately under which is an excavation in the floor, burned away by a large fire of turf, loosely heaped together. This is surrounded by a circle of urchins, sitting on the bare earth, and exhibiting a series of speckled shins, all radiating towards the fire, like sausages on a *Poloni* dish. There they are—wedged as close as they can sit; one with half a thigh off his breeches—another with half an arm off his tattered coat—a third without breeches at all, wearing, as a substitute, a piece of his mother's old petticoat, pinned about his loins—a fourth, no coat—a fifth, with a cap on him, because he has got a scald, from having sat under the juice of fresh hung bacon—a sixth with a black eye—a seventh with two rags about his heels to keep his kibes clean—an eighth crying to get home, because he has got a head-ache, though it may be as well to hint, that there is a drag-hunt to start from beside his father's in the course of the day. In this ring, with his legs stretched in a most lordly manner, sits, upon a deal chair, Mat himself, with his hat on, basking in the enjoyment of unlimited authority. His dress consists of a black coat, considerably in want of repair, transferred to his shoulders through the means of a clothes-broker in the county town; a white cravat, round a large stuffing, having that part which comes in contact with the chin somewhat streaked with brown—a black waistcoat with one or two "tooth-an'-egg" metal buttons sewed on where the original had fallen off—black corduroy inexpressibles, twice dyed, and sheep's-grey stockings. In his hand is a large, broad ruler, the emblem of his power, the woful instrument of executive justice, and the signal of terror to all within his jurisdiction. In a corner below is a pile of turf, where, on entering, every boy throws his two sods, with a pitch from under his left arm. He then comes up to the master, catches his forelock with finger and thumb, and bobs down his head, by way of making him a bow and goes to his seat. Along the walls on the ground is a series of round stones, some of them capped with a straw collar or hassock, on which the boys sit; others have bosses, and many of them hobs—a light but compact kind of boggy substance found in the mountains. On these several of them sit; the greater number of them, however, have no seats whatever, but squat themselves down, without compunction, on the hard floor. Hung about, on wooden pegs driven into the walls, are the shapeless yellow "*caubeens*" of such as can boast the luxury of a hat, or caps made of goat or hare skin, the latter having the ears of the animal rising ludicrously over the temples, or cocked out at the sides, and the scut either before or behind, according to the taste or the humour of the wearer. The floor, which is only swept every Saturday, is strewed over with tops of quills, pens, pieces of broken slate, and tattered leaves of "Reading made Easy," or fragments of old copies. In one corner is a knot engaged at "Fox-and-geese," or the "Walls of Troy," on their slates; in another, a pair of them are "fighting bottles," which consists in striking the bottoms together, and he whose bottle breaks first, of course, loses. Behind the master is a third set, playing "heads and points"—a game of pins. Some are more industriously employed in writing their copies, which they perform seated on the ground, with their paper on a copy-board—a piece of planed deal the size of the copy, an appendage now nearly exploded—their cheek-bones laid within half an inch of the left side of the copy, and the eye set to guide the motion of the hand across, and to regulate the straightness of the lines and the forms of the letters. Others, again, of the more grown boys, are working their sums with becoming industry. In a dark corner are a pair of urchins thumping each other, their eyes steadily fixed on the master, lest he might happen to glance in that direction. Near the master himself are the larger boys, from twenty-two to fifteen—shaggy-headed slips, with loose-breasted shirts lying open about their bare chests; ragged colts, with white, dry, bristling beards upon them, that never knew a razor; strong stockings on their legs; heavy brogues, with broad, nail-paved soles; and breeches open at the knees. Nor is the establishment altogether without females; but these, in hedge schools, were too few in number to form a distinct class. They were, for the most part, the daughters of wealthy farmers, who considered it necessary to their respectability, that they should not be altogether illiterate; such a circumstance being a considerable draw back, in the opinion of an admirer, from the character of a young woman for whom he was about to propose—a draw back, too, which was always weighty in proportion to her wealth or respectability.

Having given our readers an imperfect sketch

of the interior of Mat's establishment, we will now proceed, however feebly, to represent him at work—with all the machinery of the system in full operation.

"Come, boys, rehearse—(buz, buz, buz)—I'll soon be after calling up the first spelling lesson—(buz, buz, buz)—then the mathematician—bookkeepers—Latinists, and Grecians, successfully. (Buz, buz, buz)—Silence there below!—your pens. Tim Casey, isn't this a purty hour o' the day for you to come into school at; arrah, and what kept you, Tim? Walk up wid yourself here, till we have a confabulation together; you see I love to be talking to you."

"Sir, Larry Branagan, here; he's throwing spits at me out of his pen."—(Buz, buz, buz.)

"By my sowl, Larry, there's a rod in steep for you."

"Fly away, Jack—fly away, Jill; come again, Jack—"

"I had to go to Paddy Nowlan's for tobaccy, Sir, for my father." (Weeping, with his hand knowingly across his face—one eye laughing at his comrades.)

"You lie, it wasn't."

"If you call me a liar agin, I'll give you a dig in the mug."

"It's not in your jacket."

" Isn't it?"

" Behave yourself; ha! there's the masther looking at you—ye'll get it now."

" None at all, Tim? And she's not after sinding an excuse wid you? What's that undher your arm?"

" My Gough, Sir."—(Buz, buz, buz.)

" Silence, boys. And, you blackguard Lilliputian, you, what kept you away till this?"

" One bird pickin', two men thrashing; one bird pickin', two men thrashin'; one bird pickin'—

" Sir, they're stickin' pins in me, here.'

" Who is, Briney?"

" I don't know, Sir, they're all at it."

" Boys, I'll go down to yous."

" I can't carry him, Sir, he'd be too heavy for me: let Larry Toole do it, he's stronger nor me; any way, there he's putting a corker pin in his mouth."—(Buz, buz, buz.)

" Whoo-hoo-hoo-hoo—I'll never stay away agin, Sir; indeed I won't, Sir. Oh, Sir, dear, pardon me this wan time; and if ever you cotch me doing the like agin, I'll give you lave to welt the sowl out of me."—(Buz, buz, buz.)

" Behave yourself, Barny Byrne."

" I'm not touching you."

"Yes, you are; didn't you make me blot my copy."

"Ho, by the livin', I'll pay you goin' home for this."

"Hand me the taws."

"Whoo-hoo-hoo-hoo-hoo-hoo—what'll I do, at all at all! Oh, Sir dear, Sir dear, Sir dear—hoo-hoo-hoo."

"Did she send no message good or bad, before I lay on?"

"Oh, not a word, Sir, only that my father killed a pig yestherday, and he wants you to go up to-day at dinner time."—(Buz, buz, buz.)

"It's time to get lave, it isn't, it is—it isn't, it is," &c.

"You lie, I say, your faction never was able to fight ours; didn't we lick all your dirty breed in Buillagh-battha fair?"

"Silence there."—(Buz, buz, buz.)

"Will you meet us on Sathurday, and we'll fight it out clane?"

"Ha-ha-ha! Tim, but you got a big fright, any how: whist, ma bouchal, sure I was only jokin' you; and sorry I'd be to bate your father's son, Tim. Come over, and sit beside myself at the fire here. Get up, Micky Donoghue, you big burnt-shinn'd spalpeen you, and let the dacent boy sit at the fire."

"Hullabaloo hoo-hoo-hoo—to go to give me such a welt, only for sitting at the fire, and me brought turf wid me."

"To-day, Tim?"

"Yes, Sir."

"At dinner time, is id?"

"Yes, Sir."

"Faith, the dacent strain was always in the same family."—(Buz, buz, buz.)

"Horns, horns, cock horns: oh, you up'd wid them, you lifted your fingers—that's a mark, now—hould your face, till I blacken you."

"Do you call thim two sods, Jack Lanigan? why, 'tis only one long one broke in the middle; but you must make it up to-morrow, Jack; how is your mother's tooth?—did she get it pulled out yet?"

"No, Sir."

"Well, tell her to come to me, an' I'll write a charm for it, that'll cure her—What kept you till now, Paddy Magouran?"

"Couldn't come any sooner, Sir."

"You couldn't, Sir—and why, Sir, couldn't you come any sooner, Sir?"

"See, Sir, what Andy Nowlan done to my copy."—(Buz, buz, buz.)

"Silence, I'll massacree yees, if yees don't make less noise."—(Buz, buz, buz.)

"I was down with Mrs. Kavanagh, Sir."

"You were, Paddy—an' Paddy, *ma bouchal*, what war you doing there, Paddy?"

"Masther, Sir, spake to Jem Kenny here; he made my nose bleed."

"Eh, Paddy?"

"I was bringin' her a layin' hen, Sir, that my mother promised her at mass on Sunday last."

"Ah, Paddy, you're a game bird, yourself, wid your layin' hens; you're as full o' mischief as an egg's full o' mate—(*omnes*—ha, ha, ha, ha!)—Silence, boys—what are you laughin' at?—ha, ha, ha!—Paddy, can you spell Nebachodnazure for me?"

"No, Sir."

"No, nor a better scholar, Paddy, could not do that, *ma bouchal;* but *I'll* spell it for you. Silence, boys—whist, all of yees, till I spell Nebachodnazure for Paddy Magouran. Listen; and you yourself, Paddy, are one of the letthers:

A turf and a *clod* spells Nebachod—
A knife and a razure, spells Nebachodnazure—
Three pair of boots and five pair of shoes—
Spells Nebachodnazure, the king of the Jews.

Now, Paddy, that's spelling Nebachodnazure by the science of Ventilation; but you'll never go that deep, Paddy."

"I want to go out, if you plase, Sir."

"Is that the way you ax me, you vagabone?"

"I want to go out, Sir"—(pulling down the fore lock.)

"Yes, that's something dacenter; by the sowl of Newton, that invinted fluxions, if ever you forget to make a bow again, I'll flog the enthrils out of you—wait till the pass comes in."

Then comes the spelling lesson.

"Come, boys, stand up to the spelling lesson."

"Micky, show me your book, till I look at *my* word. I'm fifteenth."

"Wait till I see my own."

"Why do you crush for."

"That's my place."

"No, it's not."

"Sir spake to——I'll tell the masther."

"What's the matther there?"

"Sir he won't let me into my place."

"I'm before you."

"No, you're not."

"I say, I am."

"You lie, pug-face: ha! I called you pug-face, tell now if you dare."

"Well, boys, down with your pins in the book; who's king?"

"I am, Sir."

"Who's queen?"

"Me, Sir."

"Who's prince?"

"I am prince, Sir."

"Tag rag and bob-tail, fall into your places."

"I've no pin, Sir."

"Well, down with you to the tail——now, boys."

Having gone through the spelling task, it was Mat's custom to give out six *hard words* selected according to his judgment—as a final test; but he did not always confine himself to that. Sometimes he would put a number of syllables arbitrarily together, forming a most heterogeneous combination of articulate sounds.

"Now, boys, here's a deep word, that'll thry yees: come, Larry, spell *me-mo-man-dran-san-ti-fi-can-du-ban-dan-ti-al-i-ty*, or *mis-an-thro-po-mor-phi-ta-ni-a-nus-mi-ca-li-a-tion*;—that's too hard for you, is it? Well, then, spell phthisic. Oh, that's physic you're spellin'. Now, Larry, do you know the difference between physic and phthisic?"

"No, Sir."

"Well, I'll expound it: phthisic, you see, manes—whisht, boys; will yees hould yer tongues there—phthisic, Larry, signifies—that is, phthisic—mind, it's not physic I'm expounding, but phthisic—boys, will yees stop yer noise there—signifies——but, Larry, it's so deep a word in larnin' that I should draw it out on a slate for you: and now I remimber, man alive, you're not far enough on yet to undherstand it: but what's physic, Larry?"

"Isn't that, Sir, what my father tuck, the day he got sick, Sir?"

"That's the very thing, Larry; it has what larned men call a medical property, and resembles little ricketty Dan Reilly there—it retrogrades. Och! och! I'm the boy that knows things——you see now how I expounded them two hard words for yees, boys—don't yees?"

"Yes, Sir," &c. &c.

"So, Larry, you haven't the larnin' for that either: but here's an 'asier one—spell me Ephabridotas (Epaphroditas)—you can't! hut! man—you're a big dunce entirely, that little shoneen Sharkey there below would *sack*. God be wid the day when I was the likes of you—it's I that was the bright gorsoon entirely—and so sign was on it, when a great larned traveller—silence, boys, till I tell yees this, [a dead silence]—from Thrinity College, all the way in Dublin, happened to meet me one day—seeing the slate and Gough, you see, undher my arm, he axes me—'Arrah, Mat,' says he, 'what are you *in*?' says he. 'Faix, I'm in my waistcoat, for one thing,' says I, off hand—silence, childhre, and don't laugh so loud—(ha, ha, ha!) So he looks closer at me: 'I see that,' says he, 'but what are you reading?' 'Nothing, at all at all,' says I; 'bad manners to the taste, as you may see, if you've your eye-sight.' 'I think,' says he, 'you'll be apt to *die* in your waistcoat;' and set spurs to a fine saddle mare he rid—faith he did so—thought me so *cute*—(*omnes*—ha, ha, ha!) Whisht, boys, whisht; isn't it a terrible thing that I can't tell yees a joke, but you split your sides laughing at it—(ha, ha, ha!)—don't laugh so loud, Barney Casey."—(ha, ha, ha!)

Barney—"I want to go out, if you plase, Sir"

"Go, avick; you'll be a good scholar yet, Barney. Faith, Barney knows whin to laugh, any how."

"Well, Larry, you can't spell Ephabridotas?—thin, here's a short weeshy one, and whoever spells it will get the pins;—spell a red rogue wid three letters. You, Micky? Dan? Jack? Natty? Alick? Andy? Pether? Jim? Tim? Pat? Rody? you? you? you? Now, boys, I'll hould ye my little Andy here, that's only beginning the *Rational Spelling Book*, bates you all; come here, Andy, alanna: now, boys, if he bates you, you must all bring him a little *miscaun* of butter between two kale blades, in the mornin', for himself; here, Andy avourneen, spell red rogue wid three letthers."

Andy—"M, a, t—Mat."

"No, no, avick, that's myself, Andy; it's red rogue, Andy—hem!—*F*—."

"F, o, x—fox."

"That's a man, Andy. Now, boys, mind what you owe Andy in the mornin', plase God, won't yees?"

"Yes, Sir." "Yes, Sir." "Yes, Sir." "I will, Sir." "And I will, Sir." "And so will I, Sir." &c. &c. &c.

I know not whether the Commissioners of Education found the monitorial system of instruction in such of the old hedge schools as maintained an obstinate resistance to the innovations of modern plans. That Bell and Lancaster deserve much credit for applying and extending the principle (I speak without any reference to its merits) I do not hesitate to grant; but it is unquestionably true, that the principle was reduced to practice in Irish hedge schools long before either of these worthy gentlemen were in existence. I do not, indeed, at present remember, whether or not they claim it as a discovery, or simply as an adaptation of a practice which experience, in accidental cases, had found useful, and which they considered capable of more extensive benefit. I remember many instances, however, in which it was applied—and applied, in my opinion, though not as a permanent system, yet more judiciously than it is at present. I think it a mistake to suppose that silence, among a number of children in school, is conducive to the improvement either of health or intellect. That the chest and the lungs are benefited by giving full play to the voice, I think will not be disputed; and that a child is capable of more intense study and abstraction in the din of a school-room, than in partial silence, (if I may be permitted the word,) is a fact, which I think any rational observation would establish. There is something cheering and cheerful in the noise of friendly voices about us—it is a restraint taken off the mind, and it will run the lighter for it—it produces more excitement, and puts the intellect in a better frame for study. The obligation to silence, though it may give the master more ease, imposes a new moral duty upon the child, the sense of which must necessarily weaken his application. Let the boy speak aloud, if he pleases—that is, to a certain pitch; let his blood circulate; let the natural secretions take place, and the physical effluvia be thrown off by a free exercise of voice and limbs: but do not keep him dumb and motionless as a statue—his blood and his intellect both in a state of stagnation, and his spirit below zero. Do not send him in quest of knowledge alone, but let him have cheerful companionship on his way; for, depend upon it, that the man who expects too much either in discipline or morals from a boy, is not, in my opinion, acquainted with human nature. If an urchin titter at his own joke, or that of another—if he give him a jagg of a pin under the desk, imagine not that it will do him an injury, whatever phrenologists may say concerning the organ of destructiveness. It is an exercise to the mind, and he will return to his business with greater vigour and effect. Children are not men, nor influenced by the same motives—they do not reflect, because their capacity for reflection is imperfect; so is their reason: whereas, on the contrary, their faculties for education (excepting judgment, which strengthens my argument) are in greater vigour in youth than in manhood. The general neglect of this distinction is, I am convinced, a stumbling block in the way of youthful instruction, though it characterises all our modern systems. We should never forget that they are children; nor should we bind them by a system, whose standard is taken from the maturity of human intellect. We may bend our reason to theirs, but we cannot elevate their capacity to our own. We may produce an external appearance, sufficiently satisfactory to ourselves; but, in the mean time, it is propable that the child may be growing in hypocrisy, and settling down into the habitual practice of a fictitious character.

But another and more serious objection may be urged against the present strictness of scholastic discipline—which is, that it deprives the boy of a sense of free and independent agency. I speak this with limitations, for a master should be a monarch in his school, but by no means a tyrant; and decidedly the very worst species of tyranny is that which stretches the young mind upon the bed of too rigorous a discipline—like the despot who exacted from his subjects so many barrels of perspiration, whenever there came a long and severe frost. Do not familiarize the mind when young to the toleration of slavery, lest it prove afterwards incapable of recognising and relishing the principle of an honest and manly independence. I have known many children, on whom a rigour of discipline, affecting the mind only, (for corporal punishment is now almost exploded,) impressed a degree of timidity almost bordering on pusillanimity. Away, then, with the specious and long-winded arguments of a false and mistaken philosophy. A child will be a child, and a boy a boy, to the conclusion of the chapter. Bell or Lancaster would not relish the pap or caudle-cup three times a day: neither would an infant on the breast feel comfortable after a gorge of ox beef. Let them, therefore, put a little of the mother's milk of human kindness and consideration into their strait-laced systems.

A hedge schoolmaster was the general scribe of the parish, to whom all who wanted letters or petitions written, uniformly applied—and these were glorious opportunities for the pompous display of pedantry: the remuneration usually consisted of a bottle of whiskey.

A poor woman, for instance, informs Mat that she wishes to have a letter written to her son, who is a soldier abroad.

"An', how long is he gone, ma'am?"

"Och, thin, masther, he's from me goin' an fifteen years; an' a comrade of his was spakin' to Jim Dwyer, an' says his ridgment's lyin' in the Island of Budanages, somewhere in the back parts of Africa."

"An' is it a letther or petition you'd be afther havin' me to indite for you, ma'am?"

"Och, a letther, Sir—a letther, masther; an' may the Lord grant you all kinds of luck, good, bad, an' indifferent, both to you an' yours: an well it's known, by the same token, that it's yourself has the nice hand at the pen entirely, an' can indite a letther or pertition, that the priest o' the parish mightn't be ashamed to own to it."

"Why, thin, 'tis I that 'ud scorn to deteriorate upon the superiminence of my own execution at inditin' wid a pen in my hand: but would you feel a delectability in my superscriptionizin' the epistolary correspondency, ma'am, that I'm about to adopt?"

"Eagh? och, what am I sayin'!—*Sir*—masther—*Sir?*—the noise of the crathurs, you see, is got into my ears; and, besides, I'm a bit bothered on both sides of my head, ever since I had that weary *weed*."

"Silence, boys; bad manners to yees will ye be asy, you Lilliputian Bœotians—by my s—— hem—upon my credit, if I go down to that corner, I'll castigate yees in dozens: I can't spake to this dacent woman, with your insuperable turbulentiality."

"Ah, avourneen, masther, but the larnin's a fine thing, any how; an' maybe 'tis yourself that hasn't the tongue in your head, an' can spake the tall, high-flown English; a wurrah, but your tongue hangs well, any how—the Lord increase it!"

"Lanty Cassidy, are you gettin' on wid yer Stereometry? *festina, mi discipuli; vocabo Homerum, mox atque mox.* You see, ma'am I must tache thim to spake an' effectuate a translation of the larned languages sometimes."

"Arrah, masther, dear, how did you get it all into your head, at all at all?"

"Silence, boys—*tace*—'*conticuere omnes intentique ora tenebant.*' Silence, I say agin'

"You could slip over, maybe, to Doran's, masther, do you see? You'd do it betther there, I'll engage: sure an' you'd want a dhrop to steady your hand, any how."

"Now, boys, I am goin' to indite a small taste of literal correspondency over at the public-house here; you *literati* will hear the lessons for me, boys, till afther I'm back agin; but mind, boys, *absente domino, strepuunt servi*—meditate on the philosophy of that; and, Mick Mahon, take your slate and put down all the names; and, upon my sou—hem—credit, I'll castigate any boy guilty of *misty manners* on my retrogadation thither;—*ergo momentote, cave ne titubes mandataque frangas.*"

"In throth, Sir, I'd be long sarry to throuble you; but he's away fifteen years, and I wouldn't thrust it to another; and the corplar that commands the ridgment would regard your hand-write and your inditin'.

"Don't, ma'am, plade the smallest taste of apology"

"Eagh?"

"I'm happy that I can sarve you, ma'am."

"Musha, long life to you, masther, for that same, any how—but it's yourself that's deep in the larnin' and the langridges; the Lord incrase yer knowledge—sure, an' we all want his blessin', you know."

THE RETURN.

"Well, boys, ye've been at it—here's swelled faces and bloody noses. What blackened your eye, Callaghan? You're a purty prime ministher, ye boxing blackguard you: I left you to keep pace among these factions, and you've kicked up a purty dust. What blackened your eye—egh?"

"I'll tell you, Sir, whin I come in, if you plase."

"Ho, you vagabones, this is the ould work of the faction between the Bradys and the Callaghans—bastin' one another; but, by my sowl, I'll baste you all through other. You don't want to go out, Callaghan. You had fine work here since; there's a dead silence now; but I'll pay you presently. Here, Duggan, go out wid Callaghan, an' see that you bring him back in less than no time. It's not enough for your fathers and brothers to be at it, who have *a right* to fight, but you must battle betune you—have your field days itself!"

(*Duggan returns*)—"Hoo—hoo—Sir, my nose. Oh, *murdher sheery*, my nose is broked!"

"Blow your nose, you spalpeen you—where's Callaghan?"

"Oh, Sir, bad luck to him every day he rises out of his bed; he got a stone in his fist, too, that he *hot* me a pelt on the nose wid, and then made off home."

"Home, is id? Start, boys, off—chase him, lie into him—asy, curse yees, take time gettin' out: that's it—keep to him—don't wait for me: take care, you little spalpeens, or you'll brake your bones, so you will: blow the dust of this road, I can't see my way in it!"

"Oh! murdher, Jem, agra, my knee's out o' joint."

"My elbow's smashed, Paddy. Bad luck to him—the divil fly away wid him—oh! ha! ha! --oh! ha! ha! murdher—hard fortune to me, but little Mickey Geery fell, an thripped the masther, an' himself's disabled now—his black breeches split too—look at him feelin' them—oh! oh! ha! ha!—by tare-an'-outy, Callaghan will be murdhered, if they cotch him."

This was a specimen of civilization which Ireland only could furnish: nothing, indeed, could be more perfectly ludicrous than such a chase; and such scenes were by no means uncommon in hedge schools; for, wherever severe punishment was dreaded—and, in truth, most of the hedge-masters were unfeeling tyrants—the boy, if sufficiently grown to make a good race, usually broke away, and fled home at the top of his speed. The pack then were usually led on by the master, who mostly headed them himself, all in full cry, exhibiting such a scene as should be witnessed, in order to be enjoyed. The neighbours, men, women, and children, ran out to be spectators; the labourers suspended their work to enjoy it, assembling on such eminences as commanded a full view of the pursuit.

"Bravo, boys—success, masther; lie into him—where's your huntin'-horn, Mr. Kavanagh—he'll bate yees, if ye don't take the wind of him. Well done, Callaghan, keep up your heart, your sowl, and you'll do it asy—yer gaining on them, *ma bouchal*—the masther's down, you gallows clip, an' there's none but the scholars afther ye—he's safe."

"Not he; I'll hould a naggin, the poor scholar has him; don't you see he's close at his heels."

"*Done*, by my song—they'll never come up wid him; listen to their leather crackers and cord-a-roys, as their knees bang agin one another. Hark forrit, boys! hark forrit! huzzaw, you thieves, huzzaw!"

"Yer beagles is well winded, Mr. Kavanagh, an' gives good tongue."

"Well, masther, you had your chase for nothin', I see."

"Mr. Kavanagh," another would observe, "I didn't think you war so stiff in the hams, as to let the gorsoon bate you that-a-way—your wind's failin', Sir."

"The schoolmaster was abroad" then, and never was the "march of intellect" at once so rapid and unsuccessful.

During the summer season, it was the usual practice for the scholars to transfer their paper, slates, and books, to the green which lay immediately behind the school house, where they stretched themselves on the grass, and resumed their business. Mat would bring out his chair, and, placing it on the shady side of the hedge, sit with his pipe in his mouth, the contented lord of his little realm, whilst nearly a hundred and fifty scholars of all sorts and sizes, lay scattered over the grass, basking under the scorching sun in all the luxury of novelty, nakedness, and freedom. The sight was original and characteristic, and such as Mr. Brougham would have been delighted with—"The schoolmaster was abroad again."

As soon as one o'clock drew near, Mat would

pull out his *Ring-dial*, holding it against the sun, and declare the hour.

"Now, boys, to yer dinners, and the rest to play."

"Hurroo, darlins, to play—the masther says its dinner-time!—whip-spur-an'-away-grey—hurroo—whack—hurroo!"

"Masther, Sir, my father bid me ax you home to yer dinner."

"No, he'll come to huz—come wid me if you plase, Sir."

"Sir, never heed them; my mother, Sir, has some of what you know—of the flitch I brought to Shoneen on last Aisther, Sir."

This was a subject on which the boys gave themselves great liberty, an invitation, even when not accepted, being an indemnity for the day; it was usually followed by a battle between the claimants, and bloody noses were the issue. The master himself, after deciding to go where he was certain of getting the best dinner, generally put an end to the quarrels by a reprimand, and then gave notice to the disappointed claimants of the successive days on which he would attend at their respective houses.

"Boys, you all know my maxim; to go, for fear of any jealousies, boys, wherever I get the *worst* dinner; so tell me now, boys, what yer dacent mothers have all got at home for me?"

"My mother killed a fat hen yesterday, Sir, an' you'll have a lump of bacon and 'flat dutch' along wid it."

"We'll have hang beef and greens, Sir."

"We tried the praties this mornin', Sir, an' we'll have new praties, and bread and butther, Sir."

"Well, it's all good, boys; but rather than show favour or affection, do you see, I'll go wid Andy, here, and take share of the hen an' bacon; but, boys, for all that, I'm fonder of the other things, you persave; and as I can't go wid you, Mat, tell your respectable mother that I'll be with her to-morrow; and with you, Larry, ma bouchal, the day afther."

If a master were a single man, he usually "went round" with the scholars each night; but there were generally a few comfortable farmers, leading men in the parish, at whose house he chiefly resided; and the children of these men were treated with the grossest and most barefaced partiality. They were altogether privileged persons, and had liberty to beat and abuse the other children of the school, who were certain of being most unmercifully flogged, if they even dared to prefer a complaint against the favourites. Indeed the instances of atrocious cruelty in hedge schools, were almost incredible, and such as, in the present enlightened time, would not be permitted. As to the state of the "poor scholar," it exceeded belief; for he was friendless and unprotected. But though legal prosecutions in those days were never resorted to, yet, according to the characteristic notions of the Irish retributive justice, certain cases occurred, in which a signal, and, at times; a fatal vengeance was executed on the person of the brutal master. Sometimes the brothers and other relatives of the mutilated child would come in a body to the school, and flog the pedagogue with his own taws, until his back was lapped in blood. Sometimes they would beat him until few symptoms of life remained.

Occasionally he would get a nocturnal notice to quit the parish in a given time, under a penalty which seldom proved a dead letter in case of non-compliance. Not unfrequently did those whom he had, when boys, treated with such barbarity, go back to him, when young men, not so much for education's sake, as for the especial purpose of retaliating upon him for his former cruelty. When cases of this nature occurred, he found himself a mere cipher in his school, never daring to practice excessive severity in their presence. Instances have come to our own knowledge, of masters, who, for their mere amusement, would go out to the next hedge, cut a large branch of furze or thorn, and having first carefully arranged the children in a row round the walls of the school, their naked legs stretched out before them, would sweep round the branch, bristling with spikes and prickles, with all his force against their limbs, until, in a few minutes, a circle of blood was visible on the ground where they sat, their legs appearing as if they had been scarified. This the master did, whenever he happened to be drunk, or in a remarkably good humour. The poor children, however, were obliged to laugh loud, and enjoy it, though the tears were falling down their cheeks, in consequence of the pain he inflicted. To knock down a child with the fist, was considered nothing harsh; nor, if a boy were cut, or prostrated by a blow of a cudgel on the head, did he ever think of representing the master's cruelty to his parents. Kicking on the shins with the point of a brogue or shoe, bound round the edge of the sole with iron nails, until the bone was laid open, was a common punishment; and as for the usual slapping, horsing, and flogging, they were inflicted with a brutality that in every case richly deserved for the tyrant, not only a peculiar whipping by the hand of the common executioner, but a separation from civilized society by transportation for life. It is a fact, however, that in consequence of the general severity practised in hedge schools, excesses of punishment did not often produce retaliation against the master; these were only exceptions, isolated cases that did not affect the general character of the discipline in such schools.

Now, when we consider the total absence of all moral and religious principles in these establishments, and the positive presence of all that was wicked, cruel, and immoral, need we be surprised at the character of Ireland at this enlightened day. But her education and herself were neglected, and now behold the consequence!

I am sorry to perceive the writings of many respectable persons on Irish topics, imbued with a tinge of spurious liberality, that frequently occasions them to depart from truth. To draw the Irish character as it *is*, as the model of all that is generous, hospitable, and magnanimous, is in some degree fashionable; but although I am as warm an admirer of all that is really excellent and amiable in my countrymen as any man, yet I cannot, nor will I, extenuate their weak and indefensible points. That they possess the *elements* of a noble and exalted national character, I grant; nay, that they actually do possess such a character, under limitations, I am ready to maintain. Irishmen, setting aside their religious and political prejudices, are grateful, affectionate, honourable, faithful, generous, and even magnanimous; but, under the stimulus of religious and political feeling, they are treacherous, cruel, and inhuman—will murder, burn, and exterminate, not only without compunction, but with a satanic delight, worthy of a savage. Their education, indeed, was truly barbarous; they were trained and habituated to cruelty, revenge, and personal hatred, in their schools. Their knowledge was directed to evil purposes—disloyal principles were industriously insinuated into their minds by their teachers, every one of whom was a leader of some illegal association. The matter placed in their hands was of a most inflammatory and pernicious nature, as regarded politics: and as far as religion and morality were concerned, nothing could be more gross and superstitious than the books which circulated among them. Eulogiums on murder, robbery, and theft, were read with delight in the histories of Freney the Robber, and the Irish Rogues and Rapparees; ridicule of the Word of God, and hatred to the Protestant religion, in a book called Ward's Cantos, written in Hudibrastic verse; the downfal of the Protestant Establishment, and the exaltation of the Romish Church, in Columbkill's Prophecy, and latterly in that of Pastorini; a belief in every species of religious imposture, in the Lives of the Saints, of St. Patrick, of St. Columbkill, of St. Teresa, St. Francis Xavier, the Holy Scapular, and several other works, disgraceful to human reason. Political and religious ballads of the vilest doggrel, miraculous legends of holy friars persecuted by Protestants, and of signal vengeance inflicted by their divine power on their persecutors, were in the mouths of the young and old, and of course, firmly fixed in their credulity.

Their weapons of controversy were drawn from the Fifty Reasons, the Doleful Fall of Andrew Sall, the Catholic Christian, the grounds of the Catholic Doctrine, a Net for the Fishers of Men, and several other publications, of the same class. The books of amusement read in these schools, including the first mentioned in this list, were, the Seven Champions of Christendom, the Seven Wise Masters and Mistresses of Rome, Don Belianis of Greece, the Royal Fairy Tales, the Arabian Nights Entertainments, Valentine and Orson, Gesta Romanorum, Dorastus and Faunia, the History of Reynard the Fox, the Chevalier Faublax; to those I may add, the Battle of Aughrim, Siege of Londonderry, History of the Young Ascanius, a name by which the Pretender was designated, and the Renowned History of the Siege of Troy; the Forty Thieves, Robin Hood's Garland, the Garden of Love and Royal Flower of Fidelity, Parimus and Parismenus; along with others, the names of which shall not appear on these pages. With this specimen of education before our eyes, is it at all extraordinary that Ireland should be as she is?

"Thady Bradly, will you come up wid your slate, till I examine you in your figures? Go out, Sir, and blow your nose first, and don't be after making a looking-glass out of the sleeve of your jacket. Now that Thady's out, I'll hould you, boys, that none of yees know how to expound his name—eh? do yees? But I needn't ax—well, 'tis Thadeus; and, maybe, that's as much as the priest that christened him knew. Boys, you see what it is to have the larnin'—to lade the life of a gintleman, and to be able to talk deeply wid the clargy! Now, I could run down any man in arguin', except a priest; and if the bishop was afther consecratin' me, I'd have more larnin' than the most of them; but you see I'm not consecrated—and—well, 'tis no matther—I only say that the more's the pity.

"Well, Thady, when did you go into subtraction?"

"The day beyond yesterday, Sir; yarra musha, sure 'twas yourself, Sir, that shet me the first sum."

"Masther, Sir, Thady Bradly stole my cutter—that's *my* cutter, Thady Bradly.'

"No it's not," (in a low voice).

"Sir, that's my cutter—an' there's three nicks in id."

"Thady, is that his cutter?"

"There's your cutter for you. Sir, I found it on the flure and didn't know who own'd it."

"You know'd very well who own'd it; didn't Dick Martin see you liftin' it off o' my slate, when I was out?"

"Well, if Dick Martin saw him, it's enough: an' 'tis Dick that's the tindher-hearted boy, an' would knock you down wid a lump of a stone, if he saw you murtherin' but a fly!

"Well, Thady—throth Thady, I fear you'll undherstand subtraction better nor your tacher: I doubt you'll apply it to 'Practice' all your life, ma bouchal, and that you'll be apt to find it 'the Rule of False' at last. Well, Thady, from one thousand pounds, no shillings and no pince, how will you subtract one pound? Put it down on your slate—this way,

1000 00 00
1 00 00

"I don't know how to shet about it, masther."

"You don't? an' how dare you tell me so, you *shingawn* you—you Cornelius Agrippa you—go to your sate and study it, or I'll—ha! be off, you"—

"Pierce Mahon, come up wid your multiplication. Pierce, multiply four hundred by two—put it down—that's it,

400
By 2

"Twice nought is one." (Whack, whack.) "Take that as an illustration—is that one?"

"Faith, masther, that's two, any how; but, Sir, is not wanst nought nothin'; now, masther, sure there can't be less than nothin'."

"Very good, Sir."

"If wanst nought be nothin', then twice nought must be somethin,' for it's double what wanst nought is—see how *I'm* sthruck for *nothin'*, an' me knows it—hoo! hoo! hoo!"

"Get out, you Esculapian; bud I'll give you *somethin'*, by-and-by, just to make you remimber that you know *nothin'*—off wid you to your sate, you spalpeen you—to tell me that there can't be less than nothin', when it's well known that sporting Squire O'Canter is worth a thousand pounds less than nothin'."

"Paddy Doran, come up to your 'Intherest,' Well, Paddy, what's the intherest of a hundred pound, at five per cent? Boys, have manners, you thieves you."

"Do you mane, masther, *per cent. per annum?*"

"To be sure I do—how do you state it?"

"I'll say, as a hundher pound is to one year, so is five per cent. per annum."

"Hum—why—what's the number of the sum, Paddy?"

"'Tis No. 84, Sir." (The master steals a glance at the Key to Gough.)

"I only want to look at it in the Gough, you see, Paddy—an' how dare you give me such an answer, you big-headed dunce, you—go off an' study it, you rascally Lilliputian—off wid you, and don't let me see your ugly mug till you know it."

"Now, *gintlemen*, for the Classics; and first for the Latinaarians—Larry Cassidy, come up wid your Asop. Larry, you're a year at Latin, an' I don't think you know Latin for *frize*, what your own coat is made of, Larry. But, in the first place, Larry, do you know what a man that taches Classics is called?"

"A schoolmasther, Sir." (Whack, whack, whack.)

"Take that for your ignorance—and that to the back of it—ha! that'll tache you—to call a man that taches Classics a schoolmasther, indeed! 'Tis a Profissor of Humanity itself, he is—(whack,

whack, whack,)—ha! you ringleader, you; you're as bad as Dick O'Connell, that no masther in the county could get any good of, in regard that he put the whole school together by the ears, wherever he'll be, though the spalpeen wouldn't stand fight himself. Hard fortune to you! to go to put such an affront upon me, an' me a Profissor of Humanity. What's Latin for pantaloons?"

"Fem—fem—femi."

"No, it's not, Sir."

"Femora—"

"Can you do it?"

"Don't strike me, Sir; don't strike me, Sir, an' I will."

"I say, can you do it?"

"Femorali,"—(whack, whack, whack,)—"*Ah*, Sir! *ah*, Sir! 'tis femorali—*ah*, Sir! 'tis femorali—*ah*, Sir!"

"This thratement to a Profissor of Humanity—(drives him head over heels to his seat.)—Now, Sir, maybe you'll have Latin for throwsers agin, or, by my sowl, if you don't, you must peel, and I'll tache you what a Profissor of Humanity is!

"Dan Shiel, you little starved-looking spalpeen, will you come up to your Illocution?—and a purty figure you cut at it, wid a voice like a penny thrumpet, Dan! Well, what speech have you got now, Dan, ma bouchal. Is it, 'Romans, counthrymin, and lovers?' "

"No, Shir; yarrah, didn't I *spake* that speech before? 'tis wan, masther, that I'm afther *pennen'* myself!"

"No, you didn't, you fairy; ah, Dan, little as you are, you take credit for more than ever you spoke, Dan, agrah; but, faith, the same thrick will come agin you some time or other, avick! Go and get that speech betther; I see by your face, you haven't it: off wid you, and get a patch upon your breeches, your little knees are through them, though 'tisn't by prayin' you've wore them, any how, you little hop-o'-my-thumb you, wid a voice like a rat in a thrap; and yet you'll be practisin' Illocution: off wid you, man alive! You little spitfire you, if you and your school-fellow, Dick O'Connell, had been wid the Jews whin they wanted to burn down the standin' corn of the Philistins, the divil a fox they might bother their heads about, for yees both would have carried fire-brands by the hundher for them. Spake the next speech bitther—between you and Dick, you keep the school in perpetual agitation."

Sometimes the neighbouring gentry used to call into Mat's establishment, moved probably by a curiosity excited by his character, and the general conduct of the school. On one occasion Squire Johnston and an English gentleman paid him rather an unexpected visit. Mat had that morning got a new scholar, the son of a dancing tailor in the neighbourhood; and as it was reported that the son was nearly equal to the father in that accomplishment, Mat insisted on having a specimen of his skill. He was the more anxious on this point, as it would contribute to the amusement of a travelling schoolmaster, who had paid him rather a hostile visit, which Mat, who dreaded a literary challenge, feared might occasion him some trouble.

"Come up here, you little *sartor*, till we get a dacent view of you. You're a son of Ned Malone's—aren't you?"

"Yes, and of Mary Malone, my mother, too, Sir."

"Why thin, that's not bad, any how—what's your name?"

"Dick, Sir."

"Now, Dick, ma bouchal, isn't it true that you can dance a hornpipe?"

"Yes, Sir."

"Here, Larry Brady, take the door off the hinges, an' lay it down on the flure, till Dick Malone dances the Humours of Glynn: silence, boys, not a word; but just keep lookin' an."

"Who'll sing, Sir? for I can't be afther dancin' a step widout the music."

"Boys, which of yees 'ill sing for Dick? I say, boys, will none of yees give Dick the Harmony? Well, come, Dick, I'll sing for you myself:—

> "Torral lol, lorral lol, lorral lol, lorral, lol—
> Toldherol, lorral lol, lorral lol, lol," &c. &c.

"I say, Misther Kavanagh," said the strange master, "what angle does Dick's heel form in the second step of the treble, from the kibe on the left foot to the corner of the door forninst him?"

To this mathematical poser Mat made no reply, only sang the tune with redoubled loudness and strength, whilst little Dicky pounded the old crazy door with all his skill and alacrity. The "boys" were delighted.

"Bravo, Dick, that's a man—welt the flure—cut the buckle—murdher the clocks—rise upon suggaun, and sink upon gad—down the flure flat, foot about—keep one foot on the ground, and t'other never off it," saluted him from all parts of the house.

Sometimes he would receive a sly hint, in a feigned voice, to call for "Devil stick the Fiddler," alluding to the master. Now a squeaking voice would chime in; by and by another, and so on, until the master's bass had a hundred and forty trebles, all in chorus to the same tune.

Just at this moment the two gentlemen entered; and, reader, you may conceive, but I cannot describe the face which Mat (who sat with his back to the door, and did not see them until they were some time in the house,) exhibited on the occasion. There he sung *ore rotundo*, throwing forth an astounding tide of voice; whilst little Dick, a thin, pale-faced urchin, with his head, from which the hair stood erect, sunk between his hollow shoulders, was performing prodigious feats of agility.

"What's the matter? what's the matter?" said the gentlemen. "Good morning, Mr. Kavanagh?"

"——Tooral lol, lol——

Oh, good——oh, good morning——gintlemen, with extrame kindness," replied Mat, rising suddenly up, but not removing his hat, although the gentlemen instantly uncovered.

"Why, thin, gintlemen," he continued, "you have caught us in our little relaxations to-day; but—hem!—I mane to give the boys a holiday for the sake of this honest and respectable gintleman in the frize jock, who is not entirely ignorant, you persave, of litherature; and we had a small taste, gintlemen, among ourselves, of Sathurnalian licentiousness, *ut ita dicam*, in regard of—hem!—in regard of this lad here, who was dancing a hornpipe upon the door, and we, in absence of betther music, had to supply him with the harmony; but, as your honours know, gintlemen, the greatest men have bent themselves on espacial occasions."

"Make no apology, Mr. Kavanagh; it's very commendable in you to *bend* yourself by condescending to amuse your pupils."

"I beg your pardon, Squire, I can take freedoms with you; but perhaps the concomitant gintleman, your friend here, would be pleased to take my stool. Indeed, I always use a chair, but the back of it, if I may be permitted the use of a small portion of jocularity, was as frail as the fair sect: it went home yisterday to be minded. Do, Sir, condescind to be *sated*. Upon my reputation, Squire, I'm sorry that I have not accommodation for you, too, Sir; except one of these hassocks, which, in joint considheration with the length of your honour's legs, would be, I anticipate, rather low; but *you*, Sir, will honour me by taking the stool."

By considerable importunity he forced the gentleman to comply with his courtesy; but no sooner had he fixed himself upon the seat, than it overturned, and stretched him, black coat and all, across a wide concavity in the floor, nearly filled up with white ashes produced from mountain turf. In a moment he was completely white on one side, and exhibited a most laughable appearance; his hat, too, was scorched, and nearly burned on the turf coals. Squire Johnston laughed heartily, as did the other schoolmaster, whilst the Englishman completely lost his temper—swearing that so uncivilized an establishment was not between the poles.

"I solemnly supplicate upwards of fifty pardons," said Mat; "bad manners to it for a stool! but, your honour, it was my own defect of speculation, bekase, you see, it's *minus* a leg—a circumstance of which you warn't in a proper capacity to take cognation, as not being personally acquainted with it. I humbly supplicate upwards of fifty pardons."

The Englishman was now nettled, and determined to wreak his ill temper on Mat, by turning him and his establishment into ridicule.

"Isn't this, Mister —— I forget your name, Sir."

"Mat Kavanagh, at your sarvice."

"Very well, my learned friend, Mr. Mat Kavanagh, isn't this precisely what is called *a hedge school?*"

"A hedge-school!" replied Mat, highly offended; "My siminary a hedge-school! No, Sir; I scorn the *cognomen, in toto.* This, Sir, is a Classical and Mathematical Siminary, under the personal superintendance of your humble servant."

"Sir," replied the other master, who till then was silent, wishing, perhaps, to *sack* Mat in presence of the gentleman, "it *is* a hedge-school; and he is no scholar, but an ignoramus, whom I'd sack in three minutes, that would be ashamed of a hedge-school."

"Ay," says Mat, changing his tone, and taking the cue from his friend, whose learning he dreaded, "it's just, for argument's sake, a hedge-school; and, what is more, I scorn to be ashamed of it."

"And do you not teach occasionally under the hedge behind the house here?"

"Granted," replied Mat; "and now, where's your *vis consequentiæ?*"

"Yes," subjoined the other, "produce your *vis consequentiæ.*"

The Englishman himself was rather at a loss for the *vis consequentiæ,* and replied, "Why don't you live, and learn, and teach like civilized beings, and not assemble like wild asses——pardon me, my friend, for the simile——at least like wild colts, in such clusters behind the ditches?"

"A clusther of wild coults!" said Mat; "that

shows what you are; no man of classical larnin' would use such a word."

"Permit me, Sir," replied the strange master, "to ax your honour one question—did you receive a *classical* education? Are you college-bred?"

"Yes," replied the Englishman; "I can reply to both in the affirmative. I'm a Cantabrigian."

"You're a *what*?" asked Mat.

"I am a Cantabrigian."

"Come, Sir, you must explain yourself, if you plase. I'll take my oath that's neither a classical nor a mathematical tarm."

The gentleman smiled. "I was educated in the English College of Cambridge."

"Well," says Mat, "and may be you would be as well off, if you had picked up your larnin' in our own Thrinity; there's good picking in Thrinity, for gintlemen like you, that are sober and harmless about the brains, in regard of not being overly bright."

"You talk with contempt of a hedge school," replied the other master. "Did you never hear, for all so long as you war in Cambridge, of a nate little spot in Greece, called the Groves of Academus?

Inter lucos Academi quærere verum.

What was Plato himself but a hedge schoolmaster? and, with humble submission, it casts no slur on an Irish tacher to be compared to him, I think. You forget, also, Sir, that the Dhruids taught under their oaks."

"Ay," added Mat, "and the Tree of Knowledge, too. Faith, an' if that same tree was now in being, if there wouldn't be hedge schoolmasters, there would be plinty of hedge scholars, any how—particularly if the fruit was well tasted."

"I believe, Millbank, you must give in," said Squire Johnston. "I think you have got the worst of it."

"Why," said Mat, "if the gintleman's not afther bein' sacked clane, I'm not here."

"Are you a mathematician," enquired Mat's friend, determined to follow up his victory; "do you know Mensuration?"

"Come, I do know Mensuration," said the Englishman, with confidence.

"And how would you find the solid contents of *a load of thorns?*" said the other.

"Ay, or how will you consther and parse me this sintince?" said Mat——

"Regibus et clotibus solemus stopere windous,
Nos numerus sumus fruges consumere nati,
Stercora flat stiro rara terra-tantaro bungo."

"Aisy, Mister Kavanagh," replied the other,

"let the Cantabrigian resolve the one I propounded him first."

"And let the Cantabrigian then take up mine," said Mat: "and if he can expound it, I'll give him a dozen more to bring home in his pocket, for the Cambridge folk to crack after their dinner, along wid their nuts."

"Can you do the 'Snail?'" inquired the stranger.

"Or 'A and B on opposite sides of a wood,' without the Key?" said Mat.

"Maybe," said the stranger, who threw off the frize jock, and exhibited a muscular frame of great power, cased in an old black coat—"maybe the gintleman would like to get a small taste of the '*Scuffle.*'"

"Not at all," replied the Englishman; "divel the least curiosity I have for it—I assure you I have not. What the deuce do they mean, Johnston? I hope you have influence over them."

"Hand me down that cudgel, Jack Brady, till I show the gintleman the 'Snail' and the 'Maypole,'" said Mat.

"Never mind, my lad; never mind, Mr. —— a——Mr. Kavanagh. I give up the contest, I resign you the palm, gentlemen. The hedge school has beaten Cambridge hollow."

"One poser more, before you go, Sir," said Mat—"Can you give Latin for a *game-egg* in two words?"

"Eh, a game egg? No, by my honor, I cannot—gentlemen, I yield."

"Ay, I thought so," replied Mat; "bring it home to Cam-bridge, anyhow, and let them chew their cuds upon it, you persave; and, by the sowl of Newton, it will puzzle the whole establishment, or my name's not Kavanagh."

"It will, I am convinced," replied the gentleman, eyeing the herculean frame of the strange teacher, and the substantial cudgel in Mat's hand; "it will, undoubtedly. But who is this most miserable, naked lad here, Mr. Kavanagh?"

"Why, Sir," replied Mat, with his broad Milesian face, expanding with a forthcoming joke, "he is, Sir, in a sartin and especial particularity, a namesake of your own."

"How is that, Mr. Kevanagh?"

"My name's not K*e*vanagh," replied Mat, "but K*a*vanagh; the Irish A for ever!"

"Well, but how is the lad a namesake of mine?" said the Englishman.

"Bekase, you see, he's a *poor scholar*, Sir," replied Mat; "an' hope your honour will pardon me for the facetiousness——

Quid vetat ridentem dicere verum?

as Horace says to Mæcenas, on the first of the Sathirs?"

"There, Mr. Kavanagh, is the price of a suit of clothes for him."

"Michael, will you rise up, Sir, and make the gintleman a bow? he has given you the price of a shoot of clothes, ma bouchal."

Michael came up with a thousand rags dangling about him; and, catching his fore-lock, bobbed down his head after the usual manner, saying—"Musha yarrah, long life to your honour every day you rise, an' the Lord grant your sowl a short stay in purgatory, wishin' ye, at the same time, a happy death aftherwards!"

The gentlemen could not stand this, but laughed so heartily that the argument was fairly knocked up.

It appeared, however, that Squire Johnston did not visit Mat's school from mere curiosity.

"Mr. Kavanagh," said he, "I would be glad to have a little private conversation with you, and will thank you to walk down the road a little with this gentleman and me."

When the gentlemen and Mat had gone ten or fifteen yards from the school door, the Englishman heard himself congratulated in the following phrases:

"How do you feel afther bein' *sacked*, gintleman? The masther sacked you! You're a purty scholar! It's not you, Mr. Johnston, it's the other. You'll come to argue agin, will you? Where's your head, now? Bah! Come back till we put the *soogaun** about your neck. Bah! You must go to school to Cam-bridge agin, before you can argue an Irisher! Look at the figure he cuts! Why duv ye put the one foot past the other, when ye walk, for? Bah! Dunce!!"

"Well, boys, never heed yees for that," shouted Mat; "never fear but I'll castigate yees, ye spalpeen villains, as soon as I go back. Sir," said Mat, "I supplicate upwards of fifty pardons. I assure you, Sir, I'll give them a most inordinate castigation, for their want of respectability."

"What's the Greek for tobaccy?" they continued—"or for Larry O'Toole? or for bletherum skite? How many beans make five? What's Latin for poteen, and flummery? You a mathemathitician! could you measure a snail's horn? How does your hat stay up and nothing undher it? Will you fight Barny Farrell wid one hand tied? I'd lick you myself! What's Greek for gosther?" with many other expressions of a similar stamp.

"Sir," said Mat, "lave the justice of this in my hands. By the sowl of Newton, your own

* The *soogaun* was a collar of straw which was put round the necks of the dunces, who were then placed at the door, that their disgrace might be as public as possible.

counthryman, ould Isaac, I'll flog the marrow out of them."

"You have heard, Mr. Kavanagh," continued Mr. Johnston, as they went along, "of the burning of Moore's stable and horses, the night before last. The fact is, that the magistrates of the county are endeavouring to get the incendiaries, and would render a service to any person capable, either directly or indirectly, of facilitating that object, or stumbling on a clew to the transaction."

"And how could I do you a sarvice in it, Sir?" inquired Mat.

"Why," replied Mr. Johnston, "from the children. If you could sift them in an indirect way, so as, without suspicion, to ascertain the absence of a brother, or so, on that particular night, I might have it in my power to serve you, Mr. Kavanagh. There will be a large reward offered to-morrow, besides."

"Oh, damn the penny of the reward ever I'd finger, even if I knew the whole conflagration," said Mat: "but lave the siftin' of the children wid myself, and if I can get any thing out of them, you'll hear from me; but your honour must keep a close mouth, or you might have occasion to lend me the money for my own funeral some o' these days. Good morning, gintlemen."

The gentlemen departed.

"May the most ornamental kind of hard fortune pursue you every day you rise, you desavin' villian, that would have me turn *informer*, bekase your brother-in-law, rack-rintin' Moore's stable and horses were burnt; but I'd see you and all your breed in the flames o' hell first." Such was Mat's soliloquy as he entered the school on his return.

"Now, boys, I'm afther givin' yees to-day and to-morrow for a holy-day: to-morrow we will have our Gregory; a fine faste, plinty of poteen, and a fiddle; and you will tell your brothers and sisters to come in the evening to the dance. You must bring plinty of bacon, hung beef, and fowls, bread and cabbage—not forgetting the phaties, and sixpence a-head for the *crathur*, boys, won't yees?"

The next day, of course, was one of festivity: every boy brought, in fact, as much provender as would serve six; but the surplus gave Mat some good dinners for three months to come. This feast was always held upon St. Gregory's day, from which circumstance it had its name. The pupils were at liberty for that day to conduct themselves as they pleased: and the consequence was, that they became generally intoxicated, and were brought home in that state to their parents.

If the children of two opposite parties chanced to be at the same school, they usually had a fight, of which the master was compelled to feign ignorance; for if he identified himself with either faction, his residence in the neighbourhood would be short. In other districts, where Protestant schools were in existence, a battle-royal commonly took place between the opposite establishments, in some field lying half-way between them. This has often occurred.

Every one must necessarily be acquainted with the ceremony of *barring out.* This took place at Easter and Christmas. The master was brought or sent out on some fool's errand, the door shut and barricadoed, and the pedagogue excluded, until a certain term of vacation was extorted. With this, however, the master never complied until all his efforts at forcing an entrance were found to be ineffectual; because if he succeeded in getting in, they not only had no claim to a long vacation, but were liable to be corrected. The schoolmaster had also generally the clerkship of the parish; an office, however, which in the country parts of Ireland is without any kind of salary, beyond what results from the patronage of the priest, a matter of serious moment to a teacher, who, should he incur his Reverence's displeasure, would be immediately driven out of the parish

The master, therefore, was always tyrannical and insolent to the people, in proportion as he stood high in the estimation of the priest. He was also the master of ceremonies at all wakes and funerals, and usually sat among a crowd of the village sages, engaged in exhibiting his own learning, and in recounting the number of his religious and literary disputations.

One day, soon after the visit of the gentlemen above mentioned, two strange men came into Mat's establishment—rather, as Mat thought, in an unceremonious manner.

"Is your name Matthew Kavanagh?" said one of them.

"That is indeed the name that's upon me," said Mat, with rather an infirm voice, whilst his face got as pale as ashes.

"Well, said the fellow, we'll jist trouble you to walk with us a bit."

"How far, with submission, are yees goin' to bring me?" said Mat.

"Do you know Johnny Short's hotel?"*

"My curse upon you, Findramore," exclaimed Mat, in a paroxism of anguish, "every day you rise! but your breath's unlucky to a schoolmasther; and it's no lie what was often said, that no

* The county gaol.

schoolmasther ever thruv in you, but something ill came over him."

"Don't curse the town, man alive," said the constable, "but curse your own ignorance and folly; any way, I wouldn't stand in your coat for the wealth of the three kingdoms. You'll undoubtedly swing, unless you turn king's evidence. It's about Moore's business, Mr. Kavanagh."

"Dang the that I'd do, even if I knew any thing about it; but, God be praised for it, I can set them all at defiance—that I'm sure of. Gintlemen, innocence is a jewel."

"But Barny Brady, that keeps the sheebeen house—you know *him*—is of another opinion. You and some of the Findramore boys took a sup in Barny's on a sartin night?"

"Ay, did we, on many a night, and will agin, plase Providence—no harm in takin' a sup, any how—by the same token, that maybe you and yer friend here would have a drop of rale stuff, as a thrate from me?"

"I know a thrick worth two of that," said the man; "I thank ye kindly, Mr. Kavanagh."

One Tuesday morning, about six weeks after this event, the largest crowd ever remembered in that neighbourhood was assembled at Findramore Hill, whereon had been erected a certain wooden machine, yclept—a gallows. A little after the hour of eleven o'clock, two carts were descried winding slowly down a slope in the southern side of the town and church, which I have already mentioned, as terminating the view along the level road north of the hill. As soon as they were observed, a low, suppressed ejaculation of horror ran through the crowd, painfully perceptible to the ear—in the expression of ten thousand murmurs all blending into one deep groan—and to the eye, by a simultaneous motion that ran through the crowd like an electric shock. The place of execution was surrounded by a strong detachment of military; and the carts that conveyed the convicts were also strongly guarded.

As the prisoners approached the fatal spot, which was within sight of the place where the outrage had been perpetrated, the shrieks and lamentations of their relations and acquaintances were appalling, indeed. Fathers, mothers, sisters, brothers, cousins, and all persons to the most remote degree of kindred and acquaintanceship, were present—all excited by the alternate expression of grief and low-breathed vows of retaliation; not only relations, but all who were connected with them by the bonds of their desperate and illegal oaths. Every eye, in fact, corruscated with a wild and savage fire, that shot from under brows knit in a spirit that seemed to cry out blood, vengeance—blood, vengeance. The expression was truly awful, and what rendered it more terrific, was the writhing reflection, that numbers and physical force were unavailing against a comparatively small body of armed troops. This condensed the fiery impulse of the moment into an expression of subdued rage, that really shot like livid gleams from their visages.

At length the carts stopped under the gallows; and, after a short interval spent in devotional exercise, three of the culprits ascended the platform, who, after recommending themselves to God, and avowing their innocence, although the clearest possible evidence of guilt had been brought against them, were launched into another life, among the shrieks and groans of the multitude. The other three then ascended, two of them either declined, or had not strength to address the assembly. The third advanced to the edge of the boards—*it was Mat.* After two or three efforts to speak, in which he was unsuccessful from bodily weakness, he at length addressed them as follows:—

" My friends and good people—In hopes that you may be all able to demonstrate the last proposition laid down by a dying man, I undertake to address you before I depart to that world where Euclid, De Carts, and many other larned men are gone before me. There is nothing in all philosophy more true, than that, as the multiplication-table says, 'two and two makes four;' but it is equally veracious and worthy of credit, that if you do not abnegate this system that you work the common rules of your proceedings by—if you don't become loyal men, and give up burnin' and murdherin', the solution of it will be found on the gallows. I acknowledge myself to be guilty, for not separatin' myself clane from yees; we have been all guilty, and may God forgive thim that jist now departed wid a lie in their mouth."

Here he was interrupted by a volley of execrations and curses, mingled with "stag, informer, thraithor to the thrue cause!" which, for some time, compelled him to be silent.

"You may curse," continued Mat; "but it's too late now to abscond the truth—the '*sum*' of my wickedness and folly is worked out, and you see the '*answer*.' God forgive me, many a young crathur I enticed into the *Ribbon* business, and now it's to ind in *Hemp!* Obey the law; or, if you don't, you'll find it a *lex talionis*—the construction of which is, that if a man burns or murdhers, he won't miss hanging; take warning by me—by us all; for, although I take God to witness that I was not at the perpetration of the crime that I'm to be suspinded for, yet I often connived, when I might have superseded the carrying of such intintions into effectuality. I die in pace wid all the world, save an' except the Findramore people, whom, may the maledictionary execration of a dying man follow into eternal infinity! My manuscription of conic sections—"

Here an extraordinary buz commenced among the crowd, which rose gradually into a shout of wild, astounding exultation. The sheriff followed the eyes of the multitude, and perceived a horseman dashing with breathless fury up towards the scene of execution. He carried and waved a white handkerchief on the end of a rod, and made signals with his hat to stop the execution. He arrived, and brought a full pardon for Mat, and a commutation of sentence to transportation for life, for the other two. What became of Mat I know not; but in Findramore he never dared to appear, as certain death would have been the consequence of his not dying *game*. With respect to Barny Brady, who kept the shebeen, and was the principal evidence against those who were concerned in this outrage, he was compelled to enact an *ex tempore* death in less than a month afterwards; having been found dead, with a slip of paper in his mouth, inscribed—"*This is the fate of all Informers.*

THE STATION.

Designed & Etched by W. H. Brooke, A.R.H.A.

The door was surrounded by Mendicants & strolling Impostors

page 50[illegible]

Dublin Published by Wm F Wakeman Oct.r 183[illegible]

THE STATION.

Our readers are to suppose the Reverend Philemy M'Guirk, parish priest of Tir-neer, to be standing upon the altar of the chapel, facing the congregation, after having gone through the canon of the Mass; and having nothing more of the service to perform, than the usual prayers with which he closes the ceremony.

"Take notice, that the Stations for the following week will be held as follows:—

"*On Monday, in Jack Gallagher's, of Corraghnamoddagh.* Are you there, Jack?"

"To the fore, yer Reverence."

"Why, then, Jack, there's something ominous—something auspicious—to happen, or we wouldn't have you here; for it's very seldom that you make part or parcel of this *present* congregation;

seldom are you here, Jack, it must be confessed: however, you know the old classical proverb, or if *you* don't, *I* do, which will just answer as well —*Non semper ridet Apollo*—it's not every day *Manus* kills a bullock: so, as you *are* here, be prepared for us on Monday."

"Never fear, yer Reverence, never fear; I think you ought to know that the grazin' at Corraghnamoddagh's not bad."

"To do you justice, Jack, the mutton was always good with you, only if you would get it better killed it would be an improvement."

"Very well, yer Rev'rence, I'll do it."

"*On Tuesday in Peter Murtagh's of the Crooked Commons.* Are you there, Peter?"

"Here, yer Reverence."

"Indeed, Peter, I might know you are here; and I wish that a great many of *my* flock would take example by you: if they did, I wouldn't be so far behind in getting in my *dues.* Well, Peter, I suppose you know that this is Michaelmas?"

"So fat, yer Reverence, that they're not able to wag; but, any way, Katty has them marked for you—two fine young crathurs, only last year's fowl, and the ducks isn't a taste behind them—she's crammin' them this month past."

"I believe you, Peter, and I would take your

word for more than the condition of the geese—remember me to Katty, Peter."

"*On Wednesday in Parrah More Slevin's, of Mullaghfadh.* Are you there, Parrah More?"—No answer. "Parrah More Slevin?"—Silence. "Parrah More Slevin, of Mullaghfadh?"—No reply. "Dan Fagan?"

"Present, Sir."

"Do you know what keeps that reprobate from mass?"

"I bleeve he's takin' advantage, Sir, of the frast, to get in his praties to-day, in respect of the bad footin', Sir, for the horses in the bog when there's not a frast. Any how, betune that and a bit of a sore head that he got, yer Reverence, on Thursday last in takin' part wid the O'Scallaghans agin the Bradys, I believe he had to stay away to-day."

"On the Sabbath day, too, without my leave! Well, tell him from me, that I'll make an example of him to the whole parish, if he doesn't attend mass better. Will the Bradys and the O'Scallaghans never be done with their quarrelling? I protest, if they don't live like Christians, I'll read them out from the altar. Will you tell Parrah More that I'll hold a station in his house on next Wednesday?"

"I will, Sir; I will, yer Reverence."

"*On Thursday in Phaddy Sheemus Phaddhy's of the Esker.* Are you there, Phaddy?"

"Wid the help of God, I'm here, Sir."

"Well, Phaddhy, how is yer son Briney, that's at the Latin? I hope he's coming on well at it?"

"Why, Sir, he's not more nor a year and a half at it yet, and he's got more books amost nor he can carry—he'll break me buying books for him."

"Well, that's a good sign, Phaddhy, but why don't you bring him to me till I examine him?"

"Why, never a one of me can get him to go, Sir, he's so much afeard of yer Reverence."

"Well Phaddhy, we were once modest and bashful ourselves, and I'm glad to hear that he's afraid of his *clargy;* but let him be prepared for me on Thursday, and maybe I'll let him know something he never heard before; I'll give him a Maynooth touch."

"Do you hear that Briney," said the father, aside to the son, who knelt at his knee--"ye must give up yer hurling and idling now, you see. Thank yer Reverence, thank you, docthor."

"*On Friday in Barny O'Darby's*, alias *Barny Butter's*. Are you there, Barny?"

"All that's left of me is here, Sir."

"Well, Barny, how is the butter trade this season?"

"It's a little on the rise now, Sir; in a month or so I'm expecting it will be brisk enough; *Boney*, Sir, is doing that much for us any way."

"Ay, and, Barny, he'll do more than that for us: God prosper *him* at all events—I only hope the time's coming, Barny, when every one will be able to eat his own butter, and his own beef, too."

"God send it, Sir."

"Well, Barny, I didn't hear from your brother Ned these two or three months; what has become of him?"

"Ah, yer Reverence, Pentland done him up."

"What! the gauger?"

"He did, the thief; but maybe he'll sup sorrow for it, afore he's much oulder."

"And who do you think informed, Barny?"

"Oh, I only wish we knew that, Sir."

"I wish *I* knew it, and if I thought any miscreant here would become an *informer*, I'd make an example of him. Well, Barny, on Friday next; but I suppose Ned has a drop still—eh, Barny?"

"Why, Sir, we'll be apt to have something stronger nor wather, any how."

"Very well, Barny: your family was always a dacent and spirited family, I'll say that for them: but tell me, Barny, did you begin to *dam* the river yet?* I think the trouts and eels are running by this time."

"The creels are made, yer Reverence, though we did not set them yet; but on Tuesday night, Sir, wid the help o' God, we'll be ready."

"You can *corn* the trouts, Barny, and the eels too; but, should you catch nothing, go to Pat Hartigan, Captain Sloethorn's game-keeper, and if you tell him it's for me, he'll drag you a batch out of the fish-pond."

"Ah! then, yer Reverence, it's 'imself that'ill do that wid a heart an' a half."

Such was the conversation which took place between the Reverend Philemy M'Guirk, and those of his parishioners in whose houses he had appointed to hold a series of stations, for the week ensuing the Sunday laid in this our account of that hitherto undescribed portion of the Romish discipline.

* It is usual among the peasantry to form, about Michaelmas, small artificial cascades, called *dams*, under which they place long deep wicker creels, shaped like inverted cones, for the purpose of securing the fish that are now on their return to the large rivers, after having deposited their spawn in the higher and remoter streams. It is surprising what a number of fish, particularly of eels, are caught in this manner—sometimes from one barrel to three in the course of a single night!

Now, the reader is to understand, that a station in this sense differs from a station made to any peculiar spot, remarkable for local sanctity. There, a station means the performance of a pilgrimage to a certain place, under peculiar circumstances, and the going through a stated number of prayers and other penitential ceremonies, for the purpose of wiping out sin in this life, or of relieving the soul of some relation from the pains of purgatory in the other; here, it simply means the coming of the parish priest and his curate to some house in the townland, on a day publicly announced from the altar for that purpose, on the preceding Sabbath.

This is done to give those who live within the district in which the station is held an opportunity of *coming to their duty*, as frequenting the ordinance of confession is emphatically called. Those who attend confession in this manner once a year, are considered *merely* to have done their duty; it is expected, however, that they should *approach the tribunal*, as it is termed. at least twice during that period, that is, at the two great feasts of Christmas and Easter. The observance or omission of this rite among Roman Catholics, establishes, in a great degree, the nature of individual character. The man who frequents his duty will seldom be pronounced a bad man, let his conduct and principles be what they may in other respects; and he who neglects it, is looked upon, by those who attend it, as in a state little short of reprobation, no matter how correct or religious he may be, either in public or private life.

When the "giving out" of the stations was over, and a few more jests were broken by his Reverence, to which the congregation paid the tribute of a general and uproarious laugh, he turned round on his heel, and with the greatest *sang froid* resumed the performance of the mass, whilst his "flock" began to finger their beads with faces as grave as if nothing of the kind had occurred. When mass was finished, and the holy water sprinkled upon the people, out of a tub carried by the mass-server through the chapel for that purpose, the priest gave them a fine Latin benediction, and they dispersed.

Now, of the four individuals in whose houses the "stations" were appointed to be held, we will select *Phaddhy Sheemus Phaddhy* for our purpose; and this we do, because it was the first time in which a station was ever kept in his house, and consequently *Phaddhy* and his wife had to undergo the initiatory ceremony of entertaining Father *Philemy* and his curate, the Reverend *Con M'Cool*, at dinner.

Phaddhy Sheemus Phaddhy had been, until a short time before the period in question, a very poor man; but a little previous to that event, a brother of his, who had no children, died very rich—that is, for a farmer—and left him his property, or, at least, the greater part of it. While Phaddhy was poor, it was surprising what little notice he excited from his Reverence; in fact, I have heard him acknowledge, that during all the days of his poverty, he never got a nod of recognition or kindness from Father Philemy, although he sometimes did, he said, from Father Con, his curate, who honoured him on two occasions so far as to challenge him to a bout at throwing the shoulder-stone, and once to a leaping match, at both of which exercises Father Con, but for the superior power of Phaddhy, had been unrivalled.

"It was an unlucky day to him," said Phaddhy, "that he went to challenge me, at all, at all; for I was the only man that ever bate him, and he wasn't able to hould up his head in the parish, for many a day afther."

As soon, however, as Phaddhy became a man of substance, one would almost think that there had been a secret relationship between his good fortune and Father Philemy's memory; for, on their first meeting, afther Phaddhy's getting the property, the latter shook him most cordially by the hand—a proof that, had not his recollection been as much improved as Phaddhy's circumstances, he could by no means have remembered him ; but this is a failing in the memory of many, as well as in that of Father Philemy. Phaddhy, however, *was no Donnell*, to use his own expression, and saw as far into a deal board as another man.

"And so, Phaddhy," said the priest, "how are all your family ?—six you have, I think ?"

"Four, yer Rev'rence, only four," said Phaddhy, winking at Tim Dillon, his neighbour, who happened to be present—"three boys an' one girl."

"Bless my soul, and so it is indeed, Phaddhy, and I ought to know it ; and how is your wife Sarah ?—I mean, I hope Mrs. Sheemus Phaddhy is well : by the bye, is that old complaint of her's gone yet ?—a pain in the stomach, I think it was, that used to trouble her—I hope in God, Phaddhy, she's getting over it, poor thing. Indeed, I remember telling her, last Easter, when she came to her duty, to eat oaten bread and butter with water-grass every morning, *fasting*, it cured myself of the same complaint."

"Why, thin, I'm very much obliged to your Rev'rence, for purscribin' for her," replied Phaddhy ;—" for, sure enough, she has neither pain nor ache, at the present time, for the best rason in the world, docthor, that she'll be dead jist seven years, if God spares yer Rev'rence an' myself till to-morrow fortnight, about five o'clock in the mornin'."

This was more than Father Philemy could stand with a good conscience, so after getting himself out of the dilemma as well as he could, he shook Phaddhy again very cordially by the hand, saying, " Well, good bye, Phaddhy, and God be good to poor Sarah's soul—I now remember her funeral, sure enough, and a dacent one it was, for indeed she was a woman that had every body's good word—and, between you and me, she made a happy death, that's as far as we can judge here; for, after all, there may be danger, Phaddhy, there may be danger, you understand—however, it's your own business, and your duty, too, to think of that; but I believe you're not the man that would be apt to forget her."

" Phaddhy, ye thief o' the world," said Tim Dillon, when Father Philemy was gone, " there's no comin' up to ye; how could you make sich a fool of his Rev'rence, as to tell 'im that Katty was dead, an' that you had ony four childher, an' you has eleven o' them, an' the wife in good health?"

" Why, jist, Tim," replied Phaddhy, with his

usual shrewdness, "to tache his Rev'rence himself to practice truth a little: if he didn't know that I got the stockin' of guineas and the Lisnaskey farm by my brother Barney's death, div ye think that he'd notish me at all at all?—not himself, avick; an' maybe he won't be afther comin' round to me for a sack of my best oats, instead of the bushel I used to give him, and houldin' a couple of stations wid me every year."

"But won't he go mad when he hears you tould him nothing but lies?"

"Not now, Tim," answered Phaddhy—"not now, thank God I'm not a poor man, an he'll keep his temper. I'll warrant you the horsewhip won't be up now, although, afore this, I wouldn't say but it might—though the poorest day I ever was, id's myself that wouldn't let a priest or friar lay a horsewhip to my back, an' that *you* know, Tim."

Phaddhy's sagacity, however, was correct; for, a short time after this conversation, Father Philemy, when collecting his oats, gave him a call, laughed heartily at the sham account of Katty's death, examined young Briney in his Latin, who was called after his uncle—pronounced him very *cute*, and likely to become a great scholar—promised his interest with the bishop to get him into Maynooth, and left the family, after having shaken hands with, and stroked down the heads of, all the children.

When Phaddhy, on the Sunday in question, heard the public notice given of the Station about to be held in his house, notwithstanding his correct knowledge of Father Philemy's character, on which he looked with a competent portion of contempt, he felt a warmth of pride about his heart, that arose from the honour of having a station, and of entertaining the clergy in their official capacity, under his own roof, and at his own expense; that gave him, he thought, a personal consequence, which even the "stockin' of guineas" and the Lisnaskey farm were unable, of themselves, to confer upon him. He did enjoy, 'tis true, a very fair portion of happiness on succeeding to his brother's property; but this would be a triumph over the envious and ill-natured remarks which several of his neighbours and distant relations had taken the liberty of indulging in against him, on the occasion of his good fortune. He left the chapel, therefore, in good spirits, whilst Briney, on the contrary, hung a lip of more melancholy pendency than usual, in dread apprehension of the examination that he expected to be inflicted on him by his Reverence at the Station.

Before I introduce the conversation which took

place between Phaddhy and Briney, as they went home, on the subject of this literary ordeal, I must observe, that there is a custom, hereditary in some Irish families, of calling fathers by their *Christian* names, instead of by the usual appellation of "father." This usage was observed, not only by Phaddhy and his son, but by all the Phaddhy's of that family, generally. Their surname was *Doran*, but in consequence of the great numbers in that part of the country who bore the same name, it was necessary, as of old, to distinguish the several branches of it by the Christian names of their fathers and grandfathers, and sometimes this distinction went as far back as the great.grandfather. For instance—Phaddhy Sheemus Phaddhy, meant Phaddhy, the son of Sheemus, the son of Phaddhy; and his son, Briney, was called, Brian Phaddhy Sheemus Phaddhy, or, *anglice*, Bernard the son of Patrick, the son of James, the son of Patrick. But the custom of children calling fathers, in a *viva voce* manner, by their Christian names, was independent of the other more general usage of the patronymic.

"Well, Briney," said Phaddhy, as the father and son returned home, cheek by jowl, from the chapel, "I suppose Father Philemy will go very deep in the Latin wid ye on Thursday; do ye think ye'll be able to answer him?"

"Why, Phaddhy," replied Briney, "how could *I* be able to answer a clargy?—doesn't he know all the languages, and I'm only in the *Fibulæ Æsiopii* yet."

"Is that Latin or Greek, Briney?"

"It's Latin, Phaddhy."

"And what's the translation of that?"

"It signifies the Fables of Æsiopius."

"Bliss my sowl! and Briney did ye consther that out of yer own head?"

"Hogh! that's little of it. If ye war to hear me consther *Gallus Gallinaceus*, a dunghill cock!"

"And, Briney, are ye in Greek at all yet?"

"No, Phaddhy, I'll not be in Greek till I'm in Virgil and Horace, and thin I'll be near finished."

"And how long will it be till that, Briney?"

"Why, Phaddhy, ye know I'm only a year and a half at the Latin, and in two years more I'll be in the Greek?"

"Do ye think will ye ever be as larned as Father Philemy, Briney?"

"Don't ye know whin I'm a clargy I will; but I'm only a *lignum sacerdotis* yet, Phaddhy."

"What's *ligdum saucerdoatis*, Briney?"

"A block of a priest, Phaddhy."

"Now, Briney, I suppose Father Philemy knows every thing."

"Ay, to be sure he does; all the languages that's spoken through the world, Phaddhy."

"And must all the priests know them, Briney? —how many are they?"

"Seven—sartinly, every priest must know them. or how could they lay the divil, if he'd spake to them in a tongue they couldn't understand, Phaddhy?"

"Ah, I declare, Briney, I see it now; ony for that, poor Father Philip, the heavens be his bed, wouldn't be able to lay ould Warnock, that haunted Squire Sloethorn's stables."

"Is that when the two horses was stole, Phaddhy?"

"The very time, Briney; but God be thanked, Father Philip settled him to the day of judgment."

"And where did he put him, Phaddhy?"

"Why, he wanted to be put anundher the hearth-stone; but Father Philip made him walk away with himself into a thumb-bottle, and tied a stone to it, and then sent him to where he got a cooling, the thief, at the bottom of the lough behind the house."

"Well, I'll tell you what I'm thinking I'll be apt to do, Phaddhy, when I'm a clargy."

"And what is that, Briney?"

"Why, I'll——but, Phaddhy, don't be talking of this, bekase, if it should come to be known, I might get my brains knocked out by some of the heretics."

"Never fear, Briney, there's no danger of *that* —but what is it?"

"Why, I'll translate all the Protestants into asses, and then we'll get our hands *red* of them altogether."

"Well, that flogs for cuteness, and it's a wondher the clargy* doesn't do it, and them has the power; for 'twould give us pace entirely. But, Briney, will you spake in Latin to Father Philemy on Thursday?"

"To tell you the thruth, Phaddhy, I would rather he wouldn't examine me this bout, at all at all."

"Ay, but you know we couldn't go agin him, Briney, bekase he promised to get you into the college. Will you spake some Latin now till I hear you?"

"Hem!—*Verbum personaley cohairit cum nomnatibo numbera at parsona at numquam sera yeast at bonis moras voia.*"

* I have no hesitation in asserting, that the bulk of the Irish peasantry really believe that the Romish priests have this power.

"Bless my heart!—and, Briney, where's that taken from?"

"From Syntax, Phaddhy."

"And who *was* Shintax—do you know, Briney?"

"He was a Roman, Phaddhy, bekase there's a Latin prayer in the beginning of the book."

"Ay, was he—a priest, I'll warrant him. Well, Briney, do you mind yer Latin, and get on wid yer larnin', and whin you grow up you'll have a pair of boots, and a horse of your own (and a good broadcloth black coat, too,) to ride on, every bit as good as Father Philemy's, and maybe betther nor Father Con's."

From this point, which usually wound up these colloquies between the father and son, the conversation usually diverged into the more spacious fields of science; so that, by the time they reached home, Briney had probably given the father a learned dissertation upon the elevation of the clouds above the earth, and told him within how many thousand miles they approached it, at their nearest point of approximation.

"Katty," said Phaddhy, when he got home, "we're to have a station here on Thursday next; 'twas given out from the altar to-day by Father Philemy."

"Oh, wurrah, wurrah!" exclaimed Katty, overwhelmed at the consciousness of her own incapacity to get up a dinner in sufficient style for such guests—" wurrah, wurrah! Phaddhy, ahagur, what on the livin' earth will we do, at all at all! Why, we'll never be able to manage it."

" Arrah why, Katty, woman; what do they want but their skinful to eat and dhrink, and I'm sure we're able to allow them that, any way?"

" Arrah, bad manners to me, but you're enough to vex a saint—' their skinful to eat and dhrink!' —you common crathur you, to spake that-a-way of the clargy, as if it was ourselves or the labourers you war spaking of."

" Ay, and aren't we every bit as good as they are, if you go to that?—haven't we sowls to be saved as well as themselves?"

" ' As good as they are!'—As good as the clargy!! *Manum a yea, agus a wurrah!**—listen to what he says! Phaddhy, take care of yourself, you've got rich, now; but, for all that, take care of yourself. You had betther not bring the priest's ill-will, or his bad heart upon us. You know they never thruv that had it; and maybe it's a short time your riches might stay wid you, or maybe it's a short time you might stay wid them: at any rate, God forgive you, and I hope

* My soul to God and the Virgin!

he will, for makin' use of sich unsanctified words to your lawful clargy."

"Well, but what do you intind to do?—or, what do you think of getting for them?" inquired Phaddhy.

"Indeed, it's very little matther what I get for them, or what I'll do either—sorrow one of myself cares almost: for a man in his senses, that ought to know better, to make use of such low language about the blessed and holy crathurs, that hasn't a stain of sin about them, no more than the child unborn!"

"So *you* think?"

"So *I* think! ay, and it would be betther for you that you thought so, too; but ye don't know what's before ye yet, Phaddhy; and now take warnin' in time, and mend your life."

"Why, what do you see wrong in my life? am I a drunkard? am I lazy? did ever I neglect my business? was I ever bad to you or to the childher? didn't I always give yees yer fill to ate? and kept yees as well clad as yer neighbours that was richer? don't I go on my knees, too, every night and morning?"

"That's true enough, but what signifies it all? When did ye cross a priest's foot, to go to your duty? not for the last five years, Phaddhy—not since poor Torly (God be good to him) died of the mazles, and that'ill be five years, a fortnight before Christmas."

"And what are you the betther of all yer confessions? did they ever mend yer temper, avourneen? no, indeed, Katty, but you're ten times worse tempered coming back from the priest than before ye go to him."

"Oh, Phaddhy! Phaddhy! God look down upon you this day, or any man that's in yer hardened state—I see there's no use in spaking to you, for you'll still be the ould cut."

"Ay, will I; so you may as well give up talking about it. Arrah, woman!" said Phaddhy, raising his voice, "who does it ever make betther—show me a man now in all the neighbourhood, that's a pin-point the holier of it? Isn't there Jemmy Shields, that goes to *his duty* wanst a month, malivogues his wife and family this minute, and then claps them to a Rosary the next; but the ould boy's a thrifle to him of a fast day, afther coming from the priest. Betune ourselves, Katty, you're not much behind him."

Katty made no reply to this, but turned up her eyes, and crossed herself, at the wickedness of her unmanageable husband.

"Well, Briney," said she, turning abruptly to the son, "don't take patthern by that man, if you expect to do any good; let him be a warning to you to mind yer duty, and respect yer clargy—and prepare yerself, now that I think of it, to go to Father Philemy or Father Con on Thursday: but don't be said or led by that man, for I'm sure I dunna how he intinds to face the man above when he laves this world—and to keep from his duty, and to spake of his clargy as he does!"

There are few men without their weak sides. Phaddhy, although the priests were never very much his favourites, was determined to give what he himself called *a let-out* on this occasion, simply to show his ill-natured neighbours that, notwithstanding their unfriendly remarks, he knew "what it was to be dacent," as well as his betters; and Katty seconded him in his resolution, from her profound veneration for the *clargy.*

Every preparation was accordingly entered into, and every plan adopted that could possibly be twisted into a capability of contributing to the entertainment of Fathers Philemy and Con.

One of these large round stercoraceous nosegays, that, like many other wholesome plants, make up by odour what is wanting in floral beauty, and which lay rather too *contagious,* as Phaddhy expressed it, to the door of his house, was transplanted by about half a dozen labourers, and as many barrows, in the course of a day or two, to a bed some yards distant from the spot of its first growth; because, without any reference whatsoever to the nasal sense, it was considered that it might be rather an *eye-sore* to their Reverences, on approaching the door. Several concave inequalities, which constant attrition had worn in the earthen floor of the kitchen, were filled up with blue clay, brought on a car from the bank of a neighbouring river, for the purpose. The dresser, chairs, tables, pots, and pans, all underwent a rigour of discipline, as if some remarkable event was about to occur; nothing less, it must be supposed, than a complete domestic revolution, and a new state of things. Phaddhy himself cut two or three large furze bushes, and, sticking them on the end of a pitchfork, attempted to sweep down the chimney. For this purpose he mounted on the back of a chair, that he might be able to reach the top with more ease; but, in order that his footing might be firm, he made one of the servant-men sit upon the chair, to keep it steady during the operation. Unfortunately, however, it so happened that this man was needed to assist in removing a meal chest to another part of the house; this was under Katty's superintendence, who, seeing the fellow sit rather more at his ease than she thought the hurry and importance of the occasion permitted, called him, with a little of her usual sharpness and energy, to assist in removing the chest. For some reason or other, which it is not necessary to mention here, the fellow bounced from his seat, in obedience to the shrill tones of Katty, and the next moment Phaddhy (who was in a state of abstraction in the chimney, and totally unconscious of what was going forward below) made a descent decidedly contrary to the nature of that which most aspirants would be inclined to relish. A severe stun, however, was the most serious injury he received on his own part, and several round oaths, with a good drubbing, fell to the servant; but unluckily he left the furze bush behind him in the highest and narrowest part of the chimney; and were it not that an active fellow succeeded in dragging it up from the outside of the roof, the chimney ran considerable risk, as Katty said, of being choaked.

But along with the lustration which every fixture within the house was obliged to undergo, it was necessary that all the youngsters should get new clothes; and for this purpose, Jemmy Lynch, the tailor, with his two journeymen and three apprentices, were sent for in all haste, that he might fit Phaddhy and each of his six sons, in suits, from a piece of home-made frize, which Katty did not intend to break up till "towarst Christmas."

A station is no common event, and accordingly

e web was cut up, and the tailor left a wedding-it half-made, belonging to Edy Dolan, a thin d bachelor, who took it into his head to try his ınd at becoming a husband ere he'd die. As ıon as Jemmy and his train arrived, a door was ken off the hinges, and laid on the floor, for mself to sit upon, and a new drugget quilt was ɪread beside it, for his journeymen and appren-ces. With nimble fingers they plied the needle ıd thread, and when night came, a turf was got, to which was stuck a piece of rod, pointed at ıe end and split at the other; the "white can-e," slipped into a shaving of the fringe that was aced in the cleft end of the stick, was then lit, hilst many a pleasant story, told by Jemmy, who ıd been once in Dublin for six weeks, delighted ıe circle of lookers-on that sat around them.

At length the day previous to the important ıe arrived. Hitherto, all hands had contributed ı make every thing in and about the house look dacent;"—scouring, washing, sweeping, pairing, ıd repairing, had been all disposed of. The ɔys got their hair cut to the quick with the tai-ɪr's scissors; and such of the girls as were not ıll grown, got only that which grew on the up-ɜr part of the head taken off, by a cut somewhat ɜsembling the clerical tonsure, so that they look-d extremely wild and unsettled, with their straight locks projecting over their ears; every thing, therefore, of the less important arrangements had been gone through—but the weighty and momentous concern was as yet unsettled.

This was the feast; and alas! never was the want of experience more strongly felt than here. Katty was a bad cook, even to a proverb; and bore so indifferent a character in the country for cleanliness, that very few would undertake to eat her butter. Indeed, she was called Katty *Sallagh** on this account: however, this prejudice, whether ill or well founded, was wearing fast away, since Phaddhy had succeeded to the stocking of guineas, and the Lisnaskey farm. It might be, indeed, that her former poverty helped her neighbours to see this blemish more clearly: but the world is so seldom in the habit of judging people's qualities or failings through this medium, that the supposition is rather doubtful. Be this as it may, the arrangements for the breakfast and dinner must be made. There was plenty of bacon, and abundance of cabbages—eggs, *ad infinitum*—oaten and wheaten bread in piles—turkeys, geese, pullets, as fat as aldermen—cream as rich as Crœsus—and three gallons of poteen, one sparkle of which, as Father Philemy said in the course of

* Dirty Katty.

the evening, would lay the hairs on St. Francis himself in his most self-negative mood, if he saw it. So far so good: every thing excellent and abundant in its way. Still the higher and more refined items—the *delicia epularum*—must be added. *White bread*, and tea, and sugar were yet to be got; and lump-sugar for the punch; and a tea-pot and cups and saucers to be borrowed—— and what else? Let me see. Yes; there was *boxty* bread to be made, to take, if they liked, with their tea; and for this purpose a number of raw-peeled potatoes was ground upon the rough side of a tin collinder, and afterwards put into a sheet, (for table-cloths they had none,) which was twisted in contrary directions by two of the stoutest men about the house, until it was shrunk up into a round hard lump in the middle, and made quite dry: it was then taken and (being mixed with a little flour, and some of Katty's questionable butter,) formed into flat cakes, and baked upon the griddle.

Well, suppose all things disposed for to-morrow's feast;—suppose Phaddhy himself to have butchered the fowl, because Katty, who was not able to bear the sight of blood, had not the heart to kill "the crathurs:" and imagine to yourself one of the servant men taking his red-hot tongs out of the fire, and squeezing a large lump of hog's lard, placed in a grisset, or *Kam*, on the hearth, to grease all their brogues; then see in your mind's eye those two fine, fresh-looking girls, slily taking their old rusty fork out of the fire, and going to a bit of three-cornered looking-glass, pasted into a board, or, perhaps, to a pail of water, there to curl up their rich-flowing locks, that had hitherto never known a curl but such as nature gave them.

On one side of the hob sit two striplings, "thryin' wan another in their catechise," that they may be able to answer, with some credit, to-morrow. On the other hob sits Briney, hard at his Syntax, with the *Fibulæ Æsiopii*, as he called it, placed open at a particular passage, on the seat under him, with a hope that, when Father Philemy will examine him, the book may open at his favourite fable of the "*Gallus Gallinaceus*—a dung-hill cock." Phaddhy himself is obliged to fast this day, there being one day of his penance yet unperformed, since the last time he was at his duty, which was, as aforesaid, about five years; and Katty, now that every thing is cleaned up and ready, kneels down in a corner to go over her beads, rocking herself in a placid silence that is only broken by an occasional malediction against the servants, or the cat, when it attempts the abduction of one of the dead fowl.

The next morning the family were up before the sun, who rubbed his eyes, and swore that he must have overslept himself, on seeing such a merry column of smoke dancing over Phaddhy's chimney A large wooden dish was placed upon the threshold of the kitchen door, filled with water, in which, with a trencher of oatmeal for soap, they successively scrubbed their faces and hands to some purpose. In a short time afterwards, Phaddhy and the sons were cased, stiff and awkward, in their new suits, with the tops of their fingers just peeping over the sleeve cuffs. The horses in the stable were turned out to the fields, being obliged to make room for their betters, that were soon expected under the reverend bodies of Father Philemy and his curate; whilst about half a bushel of oats was left in the manger, to regale them on their arrival. Little Richard Maguire was sent down to the *five-acres*, with the pigs, on purpose to keep them from about the house, they not being supposed fit company at a set-dinner. A roaring turf fire, which blazed two yards up the chimney, had been put down; on this was placed a large pot, filled with water for the tea, because they had no kettle.

By this time the morning was tolerably advanced, and the neighbours were beginning to arrive in twos and threes, to wipe out old scores.

Katty had sent several of the gorsoons "to see if they could see any sight of the clargy," but hitherto their Reverences were invisible. At length, after several fruitless embassies of this description, Father Con was seen jogging along, on his easy-going hack, engaged in the perusal of *his Office*, previous to his commencing the duties of the day. As soon as his approach was announced, a chair was immediately placed for him in a room off the kitchen—the parlour, such as it was, having been reserved for Father Philemy himself, as the place of greater honour. This was an arrangement, however, which went against the grain of Phaddhy, who, had he got his will, would have established Father Con in the most comfortable apartment of the house: but that old vagabond, human nature, is the same under all circumstances—or, as Katty would have (in her own phraseology) expressed it, "still the ould cut;" for even there the influence of rank and elevation was sufficient to throw merit into the shade; and the parlour-seat was allotted to Father Philemy, merely for being Parish Priest, although it was well known that he could not "*tare off*" mass in half the time that Father Con could; could not throw a sledge, or shoulder-stone, within a perch of him, nor scarcely clear a street channel, whilst the latter could jump one-and-twenty feet at a running leap. But these are rubs which men of merit must occasionally bear; and, when exposed to them, they must only rest satisfied in the consciousness of their own deserts.

From the moment that Father Con became visible, the conversation of those who were collected in Phaddhy's, dropped gradually, as he approached the house, into a silence which was only broken by an occasional short observation, made by one or two of those who were in habits of the greatest familiarity with the priest; but when they heard the noise of his horse's feet near the door, the silence became general and uninterrupted.

There can scarcely be a greater contrast in anything, than that presented by the beginning of a station-day and its close. In the morning, the faces of those who are about to confess, present an expression, in which terror, awe, guilt, and veneration, may be easily traced; but in the evening all is mirth and jollity. Before confession every man's memory is employed in running over the catalogue of crimes, as they are to be found in the prayer-books, under the ten commandments, the seven deadly sins, the *Commandments* of the Church! the four sins that cry to heaven for vengeance, and the seven sins against the Holy Ghost. How is it possible, therefore, that a man who is thus engaged in endeavouring to recollect and classify his individual offences, can possibly feel sincere sorrow, or the fear of God? According to the constitution of the human mind, it cannot be done.

It is wrong to say, that the Roman Catholic peasantry go *spontaneously* to comply with this unnatural rite: in many instances, it is true, they do; but they generally approach it with terror, and the most unequivocal reluctance; and nothing but the strange and superstitious belief, that the priests can absolve them from the guilt of their individual sins, how black and enormous soever they may be, induces them to go at all.

When Father Con arrived, Phaddhy and Katty were instantly at the door to welcome him.

"*Musha, cead milliah failtha ghud*, to our house, Father Con, avourneen!" said Katty, dropping him a low curtsey, and spreading her new, brown, quilted petticoat, as far out on each side of her as it would go—"musha, and it's you that's welcome from my heart out."

"I thank you," said honest Con, who, as he knew not her name, did not pretend to know it.

"Well, Father Con," said Phaddhy, "this is the first time you have ever come to us this a-way; but, plase God, it won't be the last, I hope."

"I hope not, Phaddhy," said Father Con, who,

notwithstanding his simplicity of character, loved a good dinner in the very core of his heart, "I hope not, *indeed*, Phaddhy."

He then threw his eye about the premises, to see what point he might set his temper to during the remainder of the day; for it is right to inform our readers, that a priest's temper, at a station, generally rises or falls, according to the prospect of his cheer.

Here, however, a little vista, or pantry, jutting out from the kitchen, and left ostentatiously open, presented him with a view which made his very nose curl with kindness. What it contained we do not pretend to say, not having seen it ourselves; we judge, therefore, only by its effects upon his physiognomy.

"Why, Phaddhy," he says, "this is a very fine house you've got over you;" throwing his eye again towards a wooden buttress which supported one of the rafters that was broken.

"Why then, your Riverence, it would not be a bad one," Phaddhy replied, "if it had a new roof, and new side-walls; and I intend to get both next summer, if God spares me till then."

"Then, upon my word, if it had new side-walls, a new roof, and new gavels, too," replied Father Con, "it would certainly look a grea deal the better for it;—and do you intend to get them next summer, Phaddhy?"

"If God spares me, Sir."

"Are all these fine gorsoons yours, Phaddhy?"

"Why, so Katty says, your Reverence," replied Phaddhy, with a good-humoured laugh.

"Havn't you got one of them for the Church, Phaddhy?"

"Yes, your Reverence, there's one of them that I hope will live to have the *robes* upon him.—Come over, Briney, and speak to Father Con.—He's not very far in his Latin yet, Sir; but his master tells me that he hasn't the likes of him in his school for brightness——Briney, will you come over, I say; come over, sirrah, and spake to the gintleman, and him wants to shake hands wid you - -come up man, what are you afeard of?—sure Father Con's not going to examine you now."

"No, no, Briney," said Father Con; "I'm not about to examine you at present."

"He's a little dashed, yer Reverence, bekase he thought you war going to put him through some of his Latin," said the father, bringing him up like a culprit to Father Con, who shook hands with him, and, after a few questions as to the books he read, and his progress, dismissed him.

"But, Father Con, wid submission," said Katty, "where's Father Philemy from us?—sure, we expected him along wid you, and he wouldn't go to disappoint us?"

"Oh, you needn't fear that, Katty," replied Father Con—"he'll be here presently—before breakfast, I'll engage for him, at any rate; but he had a touch of a head-ache this morning, and wasn't able to rise so early as I was."

During this conversation a little crowd collected about the door of the room in which he was to hear the confessions, each struggling and fighting to get the first turn; but here, as in the more important concerns of this world, the weakest went to the wall. He now went into the room, and, taking Katty herself first, the door was closed upon them, and he gave her absolution; and thus he continued to confess and absolve them, one by one, until breakfast.

Whenever a station occurs in Ireland, a crowd of mendicants and other strolling impostors seldom fail to attend it; on this occasion, at least, they did not. The day, though frosty, was fine; and the door was surrounded by a train of this description, including both sexes, some sitting on stones, some on stools, with their blankets rolled up under them; and others, more ostensibly devout, on their knees, hard at prayer; which, lest their piety might escape notice, our readers may be assured, they did not offer up in silence. On one side you might observe a sturdy fellow, with a pair of tattered urchins secured to his back by a sheet or blanket pinned across his breast with a long iron skewer, their heads just visible at his shoulders, munching a thick piece of wheaten bread, and the father on his knees, with a huge wooden cross in his hand, repeating his *padereens*, and occasionally throwing a jolly eye towards the door, or, through the window opposite which he knelt, into the kitchen, as often as any peculiar stir or commotion led him to suppose that breakfast, the loadstar of his devotion, was about to be produced.

Scattered about the door, were knots of these, men and women, occasionally chatting together; and when the subject of their conversation happened to be exhausted, resuming their beads until some new topic would occur, and so on alternately.

The interior of the kitchen where the neighbours were assembled, presented an appearance somewhat more decorous. Andy Lalor, the mass-server, in whom the priest had the greatest confidence, stood in a corner examining, in their catechism, those who intended to confess; and, if they were able to stand the test, he gave them a bit of twisted brown paper as a ticket, and they were received at the tribunal.

The first question the priest uniformly puts to the penitent is, "Can you repeat the *Confiteor?*" If the latter answers in the affirmative, he goes on until he comes to the words, *mea culpa, mea culpa, mea maxima culpa,* when he stops, it being improper to repeat the remainder until after he has confessed; but, if he is ignorant of the *Confiteor, the priest repeats it for him!* and he commences the rehearsal of his offences, specifically as they occurred; and not only does he reveal his individual crimes, but his very thoughts and intentions. By this wily regulation our readers may easily perceive, that the penitent is completely at the mercy of the priest—that all family feuds, quarrels, and secrets, are laid open to his eye—that the ruling passions of men's lives are held up before him, and all the weaknesses and propensities of a corrupt nature—all the unguarded avenues of the human heart and character are brought within his positive knowledge, and that too, as they exist in the young and the old, the married and the single, the male and the female. It has been often wondered at, why there is, and has been, such a deplorable prostration of reason and moral independence before the priesthood of the Church of Rome, in the persons of their followers; but, let me ask, would it not be a greater anomaly were it otherwise? How is it possible for any individual who throws open the secret corruptions and failings of his heart before the eye of a priest—who puts him in possession of all the crimes and delinquencies of his life, to stand in the confidence of a manly and erect independence before him? Is it possible that he should be able to look him in the face, or bear the force of his glance? Under these circumstances, without at all considering the influence produced by the spiritual power with which Roman Catholics believe the priests to be invested, let us not think it strange that such a melancholy debasement characterizes the laity of the Romish Church.

It was curious to remark the ludicrous expression of temporary sanctity which was apparent on the countenances of many young men and maidens who were remarkable in the neighbourhood for attending dances and wakes, but who, on the present occasion, were sobered down to a gravity which sat very awkwardly upon them; particularly in the eyes of those who knew the lightness and drollery of their characters. This, however, was observable only *before* confession; for, as soon as "the priest's blessed hand had been over them," their gloom and anxiety passed away, and the thoughtless buoyancy of their natural disposition resumed its influence over their minds. A good-humoured nod, or a sly wink, from a young man to his female acquaintance, would now be indulged in; or, perhaps, a small joke would escape, which seldom failed to produce a subdued laugh from such as *had* confessed, or an impatient rebuke from those who had *not*.

"Tim!" one would exclaim, "arn't ye ashamed or afeard to get an that-a-way, and his Reverence undher the wan roof wid ye?"

"Tim, you had betther dhrop your joking," a second would observe, "and not be putting us through other, wherein we have our offences to remimber; you have got your *job* over, and now you have nothing to trouble you."

"Indeed, it's fine behaviour," a third would say, "and you afther coming from the priest's knee; and what is more, didn't *resave* yet; but, wait till Father Con appears, and, I'll warrant, you'll be as grave as another, for all you're so stout now."

The conversation would then pass to the merits of Father Philemy and Father Con, as confessors.

"Well;" one would observe—"for my part, I'd rather go to Father Philemy, fifty times over, than wanst to Father Con, bekase he never axes questions; but whatever you like to tell him, he hears it, and forgives you at wanst."

"And so sign's an it," observed another; "he could confess more in a day, than Father Con could in a week."

"But for all that," observed Andy Lawlor, "it's still best to go to the man that puts the questions, you persave, and that won't let the turning of a straw escape him. Whin myself goes to Father Philemy, somehow or other, I totally disremember more nor wan half of what I intinded to tell him, but Father Con misses nothing, for he axes it."

When the last observation was finished, Father Con, finding that the usual hour for breakfast had arrived, came into the kitchen, to prepare for the celebration of mass. For this purpose, a table was cleared, and just in the nick of time arrived old Moll Brian, the vestment woman, or itinerant sacristan, whose usual occupation was to carry the priest's *robes* and other apparatus, from station to station. In a short time, Father Con was surpliced and robed; Andy Lawlor, whose face was charged with commensurate importance during the ceremony, *sarved* Mass, and answered the priest stoutly in Latin, although he had not the advantage of understanding that sacerdotal language. Those who had *confessed*, now *communi-*

ated; after which, each of them took a draught of water out of a small jug, which was handed round from one to another. The ceremony then closed, and those who had partaken of the sacrament, with the exception of such as were detained for breakfast, after filling their bottles with holy water, went home with a light heart. A little before the mass had been finished, Father Philemy arrived; but, as Phaddhy and Katty were then preparing to *receive*, they could not at that moment give him a formal reception. As soon, however, as communion was over, the *cead milliah failtah* was repeated, with the usual warmth, by both, and by all their immediate friends.

Breakfast was now laid in Katty's best style, and with an originality of arrangement that scorned all precedent. Two tables were placed, one after another, in the kitchen; for the other rooms were not sufficiently large to accommodate the company. Father Philemy filled the seat of honour at the head of the table, with his back to an immense fire. On his right hand sat Father Con; on his left, Phaddhy himself, "to keep the *clargy* in company;" and, in due succession after them, their friends and neighbours, each taking precedence according to the most scrupulous notions of respectability. Beside Father Con sat "Pether Malone," a "young collegian," who had been sent home from Maynooth to try his native air. for the recovery of his health, which was declining. He arrived only a few minutes after Father Philemy, and was a welcome reinforcement to Phaddhy, in the arduous task of sustaining the conversation with suitable credit.

With respect to the breakfast, I can only say, that it was superabundant—that the tea was as black as bog water—that there were hen, turkey, and geese eggs—plates of toast soaked, crust, and crumb, in butter, and lest there might be a deficiency, one of the daughters sat on a stool at the fire, with her open hand, by way of a fire-screen, across her red, half-scorched brows, toasting another plateful, and, to crown all, on each corner of the table was a bottle of whiskey. At the lower board sat the youngsters, under the *surveillance* of Katty's sister, who presided in that quarter. When they were commencing breakfast, "Father Philemy," said Katty, "won't yer Rev'rence bless the mate, if ye plase?"

"If I don't do it myself," said Father Philemy, who was just after sweeping the top off a turkey egg, "I'll get them that will.—Come," said he to the collegian, "give us grace, Peter, you'll never learn younger."

This, however, was an unexpected blow to Peter, who knew that an English grace would be incompatible with his "college breeding," yet was unprovided with any in Latin. The eyes of the company were now fixed upon him, and he blushed like scarlet on finding himself in a predicament so awkward and embarrassing. "*Aliquid, Petre, aliquid; 'de profundis'—si habes nihil aliud,*" said Father Philemy, feeling for his embarrassment, and giving him a hint. This was not lost, for Peter began, and gave them the *De profundis*, a Latin psalm which Roman Catholics repeat for the relief of the souls in purgatory. They forgot, however, that there was a person in company who considered himself as having an equal claim to the repetition of at least the one-half of it; and, accordingly, when Peter got up, and repeated the first verse, Andy Lawlor got also on his legs, and repeated the response.* This staggered Peter a little, who hesitated as uncertain how to act.

"*Perge, Petre, Perge,*" said Father Philemy, looking rather wistfully at his egg—"*Perge, stultus est et asinus quoque.*" Peter and Andy proceeded until it was finished, when they resumed their seats.

The conversation during breakfast was as sprightly, as full of fun and humour as such breakfasts usually are. The priest, Phaddhy, and the young

* This prayer is generally repeated by two persons.

collegian had a topic of their own, whilst the rest were engaged in a kind of bye-play until the meal was finished.

"Father Philemy," said Phaddhy, in his capacity of host, "before we begin we'll all take a dhrop of what's in the bottle, if its not displasing to yer Reverence; and, sure, I know, 'tis the same that doesn't come wrong at a station, any how."

This, *more majorum*, was complied with; and the glass, as usual, went round the table, beginning with their Reverences. They had not, however, been long at breakfast, when a circumstance occurred, which, that our readers may be enabled to form an opinion upon it, renders it necessary for us to go back a little in our narrative.

In the immediate vicinity of the scene of our present sketch, lived a man named Jack Shields, who was considered by his neighbours to be a person of an amiable benevolent disposition; moral and inoffensive in his conduct, as well as upright and honest in his principles and dealings—but looked upon to be somewhat eccentric in his general manners. Shields was a man very much addicted to reading, and had entertained, for years before the period in question, rather singular opinions upon several tenets of his own church. He read both the Douay and the Protestant Bibles, in defiance of the priest; gave mass up altogether, except when he understood that the priest was to preach, and then he was punctual in his attendance. He had also abandoned confession—having often been heard to say, that he did not think his brother sinner had any power to absolve his soul from the guilt which he incurred in relation to God. "I know," he would say, "*I am sure*, that *God can* forgive me; but I have not the same certainty as to the priest. God has commanded me to come to *Himself*, repenting, and has promised to pardon me: now this is enough for me, so I'll take the sure side."

When this came to the priest's ears, together with the account of his absenting himself from mass, he sent for him one day that he held a station in the neighbourhood, and Sheehis, with his Bible in his pocket, waited upon him without any reluctance.

"Jack," said the priest, "is all this true that I hear about you?"

"Now, doesn't yer Reverence know," replies Jack, "that that's more than I can say till I hear it?"

"I'm told," said the priest, addressing himself to what he considered to be the root of the evil—"I'm told, Jack, that you've got a Protestant Bible under your roof."

"I have," replied Sheehis, "and a Catholic one

to the back of that, which I suppose your Reverence didn't hear."

"I should think," said the other, "the Bible of your own church ought to be sufficient for you."

"The doctrines of our church are all just and true I suppose?" replied Jack, more skilfully than his Reverence was prepared for.

"You suppose!" replied the other; "Why, do you doubt it, Sir?"

"I'm not saying I do, your Reverence," responded Jack; "I suppose the Bible is equal to the church in soundness—I mean our *own* Bible."

"Undoubtedly," said the priest; "it is the written word of God."

"Well, now it's comfortable to hear your Reverence say so; because, as our church is true in all her doctrines and practices, and as our Bible is equally sound and uncorrupt, why, wid the help of God, I'll go home and examine both; and surely, as you have no fear that by doing so, I can find out any thing wrong in the church, you can't object against this."

"If you believe the church to be pure," said the priest, "what necessity is there for your entering upon such a task?"

"Why, I believe it to be so," replied the other;

"yet, some how, if you were to ax me why I believe this—may I never do harm, but your Reverence would puzzle me."

"Don't you believe, Sir," said Father Philemy, "whatever the church proposes for your belief?"

"I'll tell you what," replied Jack, "to make short work of it, I don't know the tythe of what the church proposes to my belief: no, nor the tythe of that again: and now, your Reverence, how can I believe what I don't know? How-an'-ever, I'm sartinly very willing that the church should give me proper instructions in what I'm to believe; but then, Docthor, on the other hand, where am I to go to look for the church?"

Father Philemy closed his eyes a little, and peered at Shields, as if he would have looked into his very spirit: "Shields," said he, dropping the subject, however, "I perceive clearly that you are verging into heresy, which is the result of your reading heretical books: you must send me that Bible—you must send me both Bibles; and, moreover, you must mind your business, and let theology alone."

"I don't neglect my business," said the other; "and I'm very willing to send you both back; but before I do, yer Reverence must tell me where I'm to find the church: may I never do harm, but I'm longing to have one meeting with her: some how or other, I think it would be pleasant to hear a few words upon the subject from her own lips, that is, if one *could* stumble on her; for, although it's said she's 'visible,' not a wan of myself ever was able to lay my two living eyes upon her yet."

"Sir," says Father Philemy, "you should have better breeding than to address me, or speak of the Church in that sneering, disrespectful manner—there is more reverence due to us both."

"I declare it, your Reverence," replied Shields, "I'm in the hoith of good humour with both of you; but I've got no answer to my question. Now, suppose I want the Church, where am I to find her, Docthor?"

"Jack, the doctrines of our Church are specified and promulgated in her own councils and decrees, and they are to be found there."

"Very good, Sir; there's some satisfaction in that; I like to come to the point: and may I ask yer Reverence, how many councils there were?"

"What's that to you, Sir, how many there were," replied Father Philemy: "it's not the number of councils you are to believe, but the doctrines contained in their decrees."

"Well, Sir, I don't object against that same, for there's rason in it; but will yer Reverence lend me the book they're in, until I run my eye over them—I'll not keep it more nor a day or two, and I'll take especial good care of it; for, to tell the truth, I think it ought to be in every body's hands."

"In the first place, Jack," replied Father Philemy, "I'll show you now the nature of *implicit* faith: the doctrines of our Church are contained in several large folio books, not one word of which you could understand, for you are not a classical scholar; you see, therefore, Jack, that it's not for an ignorant fellow like you to be turning your brain about what does not come under your line of duty; but, for all that, you're bound to believe them, under pain of excommunication. These doctrines are laid down and explained by the pastors of our Church, whose duty it is to enforce them; and in case of obstinacy or unbelief, to exercise the authority which the Church has delegated to them against the refractory and disobedient."

During this cogent argument of the priest's, Shields stood with a countenance on which astonishment was very strongly depicted. "The short and the long of it is this," he replied, "that the Church won't show herself to the poor and ignorant, at all at all—to none but the priests; and so we're to believe what we don't know, and what we can't know, and without having an opportunity of knowing whether it's true or not. That's not fair, I think; then, in the next place, the priest is all the Church we have to go to, whatever we want to know."

"And is not that sufficient?" said the priest.

"Yes; but how are we to know that the priest sticks to the Church, whin we can't see her rale doctrines? And agin, Docthor—how are we to know that all these doctrines are right, if we're not allowed to try and compare them with the word of God, which you grant *can't* be wrong? May I never sin, Docthor, but I think it's a little too hard to keep us from the Church and the word of God, both."

"Jack, my dear friend," said Father Philemy, in a softened conciliating tone, "you are bewildering yourself—indeed, you are; and I am sorry to see you in such a perplexed state of mind; but, as I said before, it is the consequence of your endeavouring to go beyond your depth, to understand more than you are bound to know. I'm sorry also to find that you neglect your duty of late, and that you are never seen at mass."

"I would rather, Sir," said Shields, "that you had brought about a meeting between me and the Church—but the truth is, that yer Reverence represints the Church."

"Ay, now, John, it's something about that; you are beginning to speak sense; I certainly stand in that capacity to every one of my parishioners, and, for that reason, they are bound to hear *me* as they would the Church."

"Yet," said Jack, with a sarcastic pertinacity that was by no means savoury to his Reverence, "the Church is *holy*, and *apostolical*, and *universal*?"

"She is," replied the priest.

"And yer Reverence represints her!" said the other. "Now, Father Philemy, do you remimber the day that you held the Station in my own house?"

"I do, about Easter last," replied the priest.

"Well, *so do I;*" said Shields, without adding another word.

Father Philemy now lost his temper; for, although he fairly exposed himself to the *argumentum ad hominem*, yet he was incapable of bearing it with patience. "Shields," said he, "I have borne your sneers with too much indulgence, because I have a regard for your family, and for yourself; but I tell you now, that I insist, Sir, on your depositing *both* your Bibles in my hands—I say, I *insist* on it; and if you do not come to your duty, and attend mass as usual, I will expose you from the altar; and if that doesn't do, I'll take other measures—so look to it.

"If yer Rev'rence," replied the other, "wishes to get any good of me, *convince me*—otherwise, Sir, you needn't resort to bullying, for that's the very thing would make me stiffer; and, in respect of denouncing me from the althar—if ye did, I wouldn't stay two days in yer Church."

"I see," said the priest, "you're nothing but a headstrong fool, and it is only a loss of time, and a waste of patience to speak to you."

"I know I'm very little that's good," says Shields; "but I know yer Rev'rence has given me no satisfaction concarning the Church. Now, Sir, before I lave you——."

"And that can't be a moment too soon, you blackguard you," interrupted Father Philemy.

"I say Sir, before I lave you, let me ask, did not the son of God himself spake and prache, and address himself to the poor?—didn't he instruct them in all things necessary for them to know? didn't he command them, with his own blessed lips, to sarche the Scriptures, for that they contained eternal life? You desire me to come to my duty: did ever the Lord himself tell us, that a fellow-crathur could forgive us our sins?—or, whether did he bid us come to you, or himself? Will yer Rev'rence answer me these questions? You say, *you* can forgive me my sins, and that I ought to come to you for that purpose. My Redeemer says, that HE can and WILL forgive me my sins, if I repent and go to HIM; which am I to follow—you or the Almighty? 'Come to ME,' he says, 'all ye that labour and are heavy laden, and I will give you rest; if your sins were like scarlet, they shall be as white as snow.' Your Rev'rence stands there as the Church, and you bid me close the Word of God, and not read it. The Lord desires me to search it; and, indeed, Docthor, I'm very far from going to obey you or the Church either, before God himself, when *you* and *He* command different things. And with respect of going to mass, did Christ or his Apostles spake to the people in an unknown tongue that they did not understand? Instead of that same, didn't the Apostles get the gift of tongues, that the strange nations might understand their prayers and instructions? No; as God has promised to forgive me, I'll go to God, and, with his blessing, I'll tache my childher to do the same."

"Get out, you reprobate," replied Father Philemy, wholly losing his temper; "out with you, and don't pollute the dacent man's house with your heretical breath, you vagabone you. I'll lay my horse-whip to your back."

"Ay, that's your strongest argument," replied

Jack. "That's your usual method of convincing —and a creditable one it is."

Shields then withdrew; and when he was gone, "That man's going straight to hell," observed his Reverence, "and, what is more, he'll bring his children along with him."

"The Lord be about us Father Philemy," observed those who were present, "don't prophesy sich a thing!—who would think it, and he so good and sensible a man?"

"Tom," said the priest, "after all, I believe there is but one way with him, and that's mildness—the fellow may lead but he won't drive; run after him and tell him to stop and eat his dinner with us; I suppose you'll have no objection to that, Phaddhy?"

"Is it me, yer Rev'rence?—och, och, and it's his father's son that would be welcome to a pratie and wather, if I had but that."

"Well, tell him to stop and spend the evening with us; say that I wish to have some conversation with him in a friendly way."

Shields, however, saw through this *finesse*, and was determined to disappoint his Reverence. "Tell him that I'll hear him some other time," said he, smiling. "I know that the argument his Rev'rence would bring against me might *lay me on my back*, but it couldn't convince me for all that. Didn't I give him a right hit about the station ?"

"I tell ye, Jack," replied the other, "it's a big shame for ye to be getting an as yc do; you should go to yer duty and to mass like another."

"Ah, Tom, " said Jack, "lave that to myself; do you think I'd do any thing that would go against my own salvation ? But ye may tell him this, that, excepting he goes to drive me out of it, I'll never lave the church I'm in, bekase I believe I can be saved in it as well as in any other, although my knee I'll never bend under him, or any other man by way of confession, while I live." So saying, he pursued his way home.

When the man returned, he repeated the conversation that passed between him and Shields, not omitting a word.

"Well," said the priest, "I'm not surprised that the Church interdicts the Word of God to the laiety; for, when one of them gets it for any length of time into his hands, he becomes as cunning as a bag fox: did you only hear that fellow just now? Nothing will do him, indeed, but *conviction !*—however, he is a stiff-necked animal, and must only be allowed to take his own swing, and be damned his own way."

Shields literally kept his word; for, true to his

views, he neither went to mass nor confession afterwards. In such tenets of his own church as he believed were true and scriptural, he educated and instructed his son and daughter, the only children he had. He also permitted both to attend mass, and the former to go to confession; but the daughter he would by no means allow to frequent that distressing rite.

His wife, however, who was as weak and as bigotted as the husband was firm and liberal, perpetually harrassed the daughter about the sin of neglecting confession; but the latter was intimately acquainted with the Bible, and without at all being aware of it, was considerably more attached to the Protestant, than to her own Church. For two or three years, that is, during the period in which the mere girl approximates to the full-grown woman, the mother's arguments to induce her to go to her duty were fruitless—for the father had drawn by no means a favourable character of confession, and the daughter possessing a pure and modest mind, entertained a rooted aversion against it. But a little before the time of Phaddhy's Station, the mother began to exhibit symptoms of a decline, and as she never ceased pressing the former on this point, the affection which was excited in the daughter's breast by the apprehension of losing her, induced a compliance on her part, which no other circumstances could have effected—for Mary (so she was called,) possessed much of her father's good sense, firmness, and independence.

The mother having, at length, prevailed, she and Mary attended at Phaddhy's early on the morning of the station in question. As soon as they entered the house, there was an especial welcome for both, particularly for the daughter, because the peculiar principles in which Shields had educated her, and her own firm adherence to them, were well known.

"Well, Katty, avourneen," said her mother—"blessed be the holy mother of God for it, she has come at long last; and it's well for her, ahagur, that she took my advice, I hope, for, indeed, Phaddhy," turning the discourse to *him*, "I won't be long with her—see how that bit of a walk up here has left me without a blast of breath in my body!"

The mother was certainly very much exhausted, and had every appearance of being in a deep and rapid decline. As she uttered these words, the daughter, who sat removed from the crowd that occupied the lower end of the house, fixed her eyes upon her, and, in an instant, her long, dark lashes were filled with tears. Mary, indeed, was a girl of uncommon personal beauty and fine figure, and, as she sat with her pocket handkerchief between her hands, and her dark eyes shining through her tears, she was certainly calculated to excite a strong interest in her favour. She wore no cap, but had a dark ribbon tied simply round her head, from which her brown clustering locks fell in thick luxuriant curls over her fair neck and shoulders. Her hair was divided before, and showed a white polished forehead, that would have graced a higher station in life. It might have been easily remarked, that her attendance here was involuntary, for there was a feverish anxiety about her amounting to a visible tremor. She was wrapped in thought, and sometimes appeared so pale, that one might almost feel apprehensive of her swooning away—at other times so flushed, that her face and neck were suffused with one glow of crimson. In this state of agitation she remained until the person who had been in with Father Con came out; her mother then said —"Mary, come now, acushla, there's nobody with Father Con: come and pluck up courage, alannah—you won't be long, and the best way for you is to get it over you, and then your mind will be aisy." Mary, however, got as pale as death, and her lips became white. She rose up, but was obliged to sit down again, until she regained more strength. In the meantime, her mother and Katty, and several other of the women then present, afforded her every assistance; as her lips were parched, she asked for a drink of water, but this she could not get.

"Mary, asthore," said the mother, "you know you couldn't get a dhrink of wather till afther you resave the sacrament.

"I wish, mother dear," said the modest girl, "my father was with me; if he was, I wouldn't be so weak, I think."

This she spoke in a very feeble voice, for all the moral instincts and delicate sensibilities of a modest disposition were up in arms against this profane violation—this daring intrusion into those recesses of the human heart, which are, and ought to be, visible only to that God to whom all things are known.

At last, by the force of flattery and persuasion, eked out with several melancholy allusions by the mother to her own state of health, Mary went in to comply with an ordinance which she felt to be revolting and indelicate in the highest degree; one which her soul detested and shrunk from, with mingled detestation and horror. On her return from the confessional, she walked up to the remote seat she had before occupied, which was instantly vacated on her approach to it; for the beauty of her person, and her modesty, commanded general admiration and respect. There was now a marked change visible in her countenance and demeanour; for although she sat as quiet as usual, there was on her complexion a flush of deeper hue than had mantled her cheek before; her eye, too, was lit with a spark, much more vivid than the mild and mellow light which usually shone there. Instead of appearing timid, her nerves were evidently strung to a high degree of firmness and tension, and her whole air betrayed marks of distress, indignation, and disgust. When she came out, her mother went in to confess, who was the last Father Con heard before mass From the time Mary left Father Con, until breakfast, she was certainly suffering intensely from her own feelings and reflections; for it was with much difficulty that she suppressed the tears which started to her eyes. Indeed, it was evident that if she had been alone, she would have relieved herself very much by weeping; but an apprehension of attracting notice restrained her tears, whilst it increased her distress. This state of prolonged excitement was more than she could bear; for a short time afterwards a powerful re-action in the state of her animal spirits and nerves took place. She became deadly and fearfully pale; and after many struggles against the weight which sank down her spirits so heavily, she at length fell into a fit of strong and alarming convulsions. This was an interruption to the harmony of the breakfast, which was by no means expected. She was now removed into another room; the women, with much difficulty, succeeded in restoring her to consciousness, or, at least, in assisting nature to restore herself. When she found herself among none but her own sex, she gave full vent to her tears, and wept long and bitterly. She then insisted on going home to her father, a determination which no force or entreaty could prevent her from putting into execution. She accordingly departed without noticing any one in the house, and the breakfast went on gloomily enough until it was finished.

Such was the effect which the unnatural and gross act of disclosing the frailties and weaknesses of a female to a man in private, had upon the natural modesty of a young woman. To make such an act a religious ceremony, when we consider the weakness of human passion, is probably the best clue to the complacency with which the Roman Catholic priesthood bear a life of celibacy. Of Mary it is only necessary to say, that ere many years passed, she and her father both embraced the Protestant faith.

Hitherto, Father Philemy had not had time to bestow any attention on the state of Katty's larder, as he was in the habit of doing, with a view to ascertain the several items contained therein for dinner. But as soon as the breakfast things were removed, and the coast clear, he took a peep into the pantry, and, after throwing his eye over its contents, sat down at the fire, making Phaddhy take a seat beside him, for the especial purpose of sounding him as to the practicability of effecting a certain design which was then snugly latent in his Reverence's fancy. The fact was, that on taking the survey of the premises aforesaid, he discovered that, although there was abundance of fowl, and fish, and bacon, and hung-beef—yet, by some unaccountable and disastrous omission, there was neither fresh mutton nor fresh beef. The priest, it must be confessed, was a man of considerable fortitude, but this was a blow for which he was scarcely prepared—particularly as a boiled leg of mutton was one of his fifteen favourite joints at dinner. He accordingly took two or three pinches of snuff in rapid succession, and a seat at the fire as I have said, placing Phaddhy, unconscious of his design, immediately beside him.

Now, the reader knows that Phaddhy was a man possessing a considerable portion of dry, sarcastic humour, along with that natural quickness of penetration and shrewdness for which most of the Irish peasantry are, in a very peculiar degree, remarkable; add to this that Father Philemy, in consequence of his contemptuous bearing to him before he came in for his brother's property, stood not very high in his estimation. The priest knew this, and consequently felt that the point in question would require to be managed, on his part, with suitable address.

"Phaddhy," says his Reverence, "sit down here till we chat a little, before I commence the duties of the day. I'm happy to see that you have such a fine thriving family: how many sons and daughters have you?"

"Six sons, yer Reverence," replied Phaddhy, "and five daughters: indeed, Sir, they're as well to be seen as their neighbours, considhering all things. Poor crathurs, they get fair play* now, thank God, compared to what they used to get—God rest their poor uncle's sowl for that. Only for him, your Reverence, there would be very few inquiring this or any other day about them."

"Did he die as rich as they said, Phaddhy?" enquired his Reverence.

"Hut, Sir," replied Phaddhy, determined to take what he afterwards called a *rise* out of the priest; "they knew little about it—as rich as

* By this is meant good food and clothing.

they said, Sir! no, but three times as rich, itself: but, any how, he was the man that could make the money."

"I'm very happy to hear it, Phaddhy, on your account, and that of your children. God be good to him—*requiescat animus ejus in pace, per omnia secula seculorum, Amen!*—he liked a drop in his time, Phaddhy, as well as ourselves, eh?"

"*Amen, amen*—the heavens be his bed!—he did, poor man! but he had it at first cost, your Reverence, for he *run* it all himself in the mountains: he could afford to take it."

"Yes, Phaddhy, the heavens be his bed, I pray; no Christmas or Easter ever passed, but he was sure to send me the little keg of stuff that never saw water; but, Phaddhy, there's one thing that concerns me about him, in regard of his love of drink—I'm afraid it's a throuble to him where he is at present; and I was sorry to find that, although he died full of money, he didn't think it worth his while to leave even the price of a mass to be said for the benefit of his own soul."

"Why, sure you know, Father Philemy, that he wasn't what they call a dhrinking man: once a quarther, or so, he sartinly did take a jorum; and except at these times, he was very sober But God look upon us both ver Reverence—or upon myself, any way; for I haven't yer excuse for dhrinking, seeing I'm *no* clargy; but if *he's* to suffer for his doings that-a-way, I'm afeard *we'll* have a troublesome reck'ning of it."

"Hem, a-hem!—Phaddhy," replied the priest, "he has raised you and your children from poverty, at all events, and you ought to consider *that*. If there is any thing in your power to contribute to the relief of his soul, you have a strong duty upon you to do it; and a number of masses, offered up devoutly, would ——"

"Why, he did, Sir, raise both myself and my childre from poverty," said Phaddhy, not willing to let that point go farther—"*that* I'll always own to; and I hope in God that whatever little trouble might be upon him for the dhrop of dhrink, will be wiped off by this kindness to us."

"He hadn't even a *month's mind!!*"

"And it's not but I spoke to him about both, yer Reverence."

"And what did he say, Phaddhy?"

"'Phaddhy,' said he, 'I have been giving Father M'Guirk, one way or another, between whiskey, oats, and dues, a great deal of money every year; and now, afther I'm dead,' says he, 'isn't it an ungrateful thing of him not to offer up one mass for my sowl, except I leave him payment for it.'"

"Did he say that, Phaddhy?"

"I'm giving you his very words, yer Reverence."

"Phaddhy, I deny it; it's a big lie—he could not make use of such words, and he going to face death. I say you could not listen to them; the hair would stand on your head if he did: but God forgive him!—that's the worst I wish him. Didn't the hair stand on your head, Phaddhy, to hear him?"

"Why, then, to tell yer Reverence God's truth, I can't say it did."

"You can't say it did! and if I was in your coat, I would be ashamed to say it did not. I was always troubled about the way the fellow died, but I hadn't the slightest notion that he went off such a reprobate. I fought *his* battle and *yours* hard enough yesterday; but I knew less about him then than I do now."

"And what, wid submission, did you fight our battles about, yer Reverence?" enquired Phaddhy.

"Yesterday evening, in Parrah More Slevin's, they had him a miser, and yourself they set down as very little better."

"Then I don't think I desarved that from Parrah More, any how, Father Philemy; I think

I can show myself as dacent as Parrah More or any of *his* faction."

"It was not Parrah More himself, or his family, that said any thing about you, Phaddhy," said the priest, "but others that were present. You must know that we were all to be *starred* here to-day."

"Oh! oh!" exclaimed Phaddhy, who was hit most palpably upon the weakest side—the very sorest spot about him, "they think bekase this is the first station that ever was held in *my* house, that you won't be thrated as you ought; but they'll be disappointed; and I hope, for so far, that yer Reverence and yer friends had no rason to complain."

"Not in the least, Phaddhy, considering that it was a first station; and if the dinner goes as well off as the breakfast, they'll be biting their nails: but I should not wish myself that they would have it in their power to sneer or throw any slur over you about it.——Go along, Dolan," exclaimed his Reverence to a countryman who came in from the street, where those stood who were for confession, to see if he had gone to his room—'Go along, you vagrant, don't you see I'm not gone to the *tribunal* yet?——But it's no matter about that, Phaddhy, it's of other things you ought to think: when were you at your duty?"

"This morning, Sir," replied the other—"but I'd have them to understand, that had the presumption to use my name in any such manner, that I know when and where to be dacint with any mother's son of Parrah More's faction; and *that* I'll be afther whispering to them some of these mornings, plase goodness."

"Well, well, Phaddhy, don't put yourself in a passion about it, particularly so soon after having been at confession—it's not right—I told them myself, that we'd have a leg of mutton and a bottle of wine at all events, for it was what *they* had; but that's not worth talking about: when were you with the priest before, Phaddhy?"

"If I wasn't able, it would be another thing, but, as long as I'm able, I'll let them know that I have the spirit"—said Phaddhy, smarting under the imputation of niggardliness—"when was I at confession before, Father Philemy? Why, then, dear forgive me, not these five years;—and I'd surely be the first of the family that would show a mane spirit, or a want of hospitality."

"A leg of mutton is a good dish, and a bottle of wine is fit for the first man in the land!" observed his Reverence—"five years!—why, is it possible you stayed away so long, Phaddhy!—how could you expect to prosper with five years' burden of sin upon your conscience—what would it cost you——?"

"Indeed, myself's no judge, your Rev'rence, as to that; but, cost what it will, I'll get both."

"I say, Phaddhy, what trouble would it cost you to come to your duty twice a year at the very least; and, indeed, I would advise you to become a monthly communicant. Parrah More was speaking of it as to himself, and you ought to go ——."

"And I will go and bring Parrah More here to his dinner, this very day, if it was only to let him see with his own eyes ——."

"You ought to go once a month, if it was only to set an example to your children, and to show the neighbours how a man of substance and respectability, and the head of a family, ought to carry himself."

"Where is the best wine, got, yer Rev'rence?"

"Alick M'Loughlin, *my nephew*, I believe, keeps the best wine and spirits in Ballyslantha.—You ought also, Phaddhy, to get a scapular, and become a scapularian; I wish your brother had thought of *that*, and he wouldn't have died in so hardened a state, nor neglected to make a provision for the benefit of his soul, as he did."

"Lave the rest to me, yer Rev'rence, I'll get

it—Mr. M'Loughlin will give me the right sort, if he has it betune him and death."

"M'Laughlin! what are you talking about?"

"Why, what is your Rev'rence talking about?"

"The scapular," said the priest.

"But I mane the wine and the mutton," says Phaddhy.

"And is that the way you treat me, you reprobate you?" replied his Reverence, in a passion: "is that the kind of attention you're paying me, and I advising you, all this time, *for the good of your soul?* Phaddhy, I tell you, you're enough to vex me to the core—five years!—only once at confession in five years! What do I care about your mutton and your wine!—you may get dozens of them if you wish; or, may be, it would be more like a Christian to never mind getting them, and let the neighbours *laugh* away. It would teach you humility, you hardened creature, and God knows you want it; for my part, I'm speaking to you about other things; but that's the way with the most of you—mention any spiritual subject that concerns your soul, and you turn a deaf ear to it—here, Dolan, come in to your duty. In the meantime, you may as well tell Katty not to boil the mutton too much; it's on your knees you ought to be at your rosary, or the seven penitential psalms."

"Thrue for you, Sir," said Phaddhy; but as to going wanst a month, I'm afeard, yer Rev'rence, if it would shorten my timper as it does Katty's, that we'd be bad company for one another; she comes home from confession, newly set, like a razor, every bit as sharp; and I'm sure that I'm within the truth when I say, there's no bearing her."

"That's because you have no relish for any thing spiritual yourself, you nager you," replied his Reverence, "or you wouldn't see her temper in that light—but, now that I think of it, where did you get that stuff we had at breakfast?"

"Ay, that's the sacret; but I knew yer Rev'rence would like it: did Parrah More equal it? No, nor one of his faction couldn't lay his finger on such a dhrop."

"I wish you could get me a few gallons of it," said the Priest; "but let us dhrop that; I say, Phaddhy, you're too worldly and careless about your duty."

"Well, Father Philemy, there's a good time coming; I'll mend yet."

"You want it, Phaddhy."

"Would three gallons do, Sir?"

"I would rather you would give me five, Phaddhy; but go to your rosary."

"It's the penitential psalm, first, Sir," said

Phaddhy, "and the rosary at night. I'll try, anyhow; and if I can make off five for you, I will."

"Thank you, Phaddhy; but I would recommend you to say the rosary *before* night."

"I believe yer Reverence is right." replied Phaddhy, looking somewhat slyly in the priest's face, "I think it's best to make sure of it now, in regard that in the evening your Reverence—do you persave?"

"Yes," said his Reverence, "you're in a better frame of mind at present, Phaddhy, being fresh from confession." So saying, his Reverence, for whom Phaddhy, with all his shrewdness in general was not a match, went into his room, that he might send home about four dozen of honest, good-humoured, thoughtless, jovial, swearing, drinking, fighting and murdering Hibernians, free from every possible stain of sin and wickedness!

"Are you all ready now?" said the priest to a crowd of country people who were standing about the kitchen door, pressing to get the "first turn" at the tribunal, which, on this occasion, consisted of a good oak chair, with his Reverence upon it.

"Why do you crush forward in that manner, you ill-bred spalpeens? Can't you stand back and behave yourselves like common Christians!—back with you, cr, if you make me get my whip, I'll soon clear you from about the dacent man's door. Hagarty, why do you crush them two girls there, you great Turk you? Look at the vagabonds!—Where's my whip?" said he, running in, and coming out in a fury, when he commenced cutting about him, until they dispersed in all directions. He then returned into the house; and, after calling in about two dozen, began to catechise them as follows, still holding the whip in his hand, whilst many of those individuals, who, at a party quarrel, in fair or market, or in the more inhuman crimes of murder or nightly depredations, were as callous and hardened specimens of humanity as ever set the laws of civilized society at defiance, stood trembling before him like slaves, absolutely pale and breathless with fear.

"Come, Kelly," said he to one of them, "are you fully prepared for the two blessed sacraments of Penance and the Eucharist, that you are about to receive? Can you read, Sir?"

"Can I read, is id?—my *brother Barney* can, yer Rev'rence," replied Kelly, sensible, amid all the disadvantages around him, of the degradation of his ignorance.

"What's that to me, Sir?" said the priest,

"what your brother Barney can do—can you not read yourself?—and, may be," he continued parenthetically, "your brother Barney's not much the holier for his knowledge."

"I cannot, yer Reverence," said Kelly in a tone of regret.

"I hope you have your Christian Doctrine; at all events," said the priest,—"Go on with the Confiteor."

Kelly went on—"*Confeetur Dimniportenti batchy Mary semplar virginy, batchy Mickletoe Archy Angelo batchy Johnny Bartisty, sanctris postlis—Petrum hit Paulum, omnium sanctris, et tabby, pasture quay a pixavit minus coglety ashy hony verbum et offer him smaxy quilta smaxy quilta smaxy maxin in quilta.*"*

"Very well, Kelly, right enough, all except the

* We subjoin the original for the information of our readers:—

"Confiteor Deo Omnipotenti, beatæ Mariæ, semper Virgini, beato Michaelo Archangelo, beato Johanni Baptistæ, sanctis Apostolis, Petro et Paulo, omnibus sanctis, et tibi, pater, quia, peccavi nimis cogitatione, verbo, et opera, mea culpa, mea culpa, mea maxima culpa." Let not our readers suppose, that the above version in the mouth of a totally illiterate peasant is overcharged, for we have the advantage of remembering how we ourselves used to hear it pronounced in our early days. We will back the version in the text against Edward Irving's new language for any money.

pronouncing, which wouldn't pass muster in Maynooth, however. How many kinds of commandments are there?"

"Two, Sir."

"What are they?"

"God's and the Church's."

"Repeat God's share of them."

He then repeated the first commandment according to *his* catechism.

"Very good, Kelly, very good. Now, you must know that the heretics split that into two, for no other reason in the world only to knock our blessed images on the head; but we needn't expect them to have much conscience. Well, now, repeat the commandments of the Church."

"First—Sundays and holidays, Mass thou shalt sartinly hear;
Second—All holidays sanctificate throughout all the whole year.
Third—Lent, Ember days, and Virgils, thou shalt be sartin to fast;
Fourth—Fridays and Saturdays flesh thou shalt not. good, bad, or indifferent, taste.
Fifth—In Lent and Advent, nuptial fastes gallantly forbear
Sixth—Confess your sins, at laste once dacently and soberly every year.
Seventh—Receive your God at confission about great Easter-day;
Eighth—And to his church and his own frolicsome clargy neglect not tides to pay.

"Well," said his Reverence, "now, the great point is, do you understand them?"

"Wid the help of God I hope so, yer Rev'rence—and I have also the three thriptological vartues."

"Theological, sirrah!"

"Theojollyological vartues; the four sins that cry to heaven for vingeance; the *five* carnal vartues—prudence, justice, timptation, and solitude;* the six holy Christian gifts; the seven deadly sins; the eight grey attitudes——"

"Grey attitudes! Oh, the Bæotian!" exclaimed his Reverence: "listen to the way in which he's playing havoc among them—stop, Sir," for Kelly was going on at full speed—"stop, Sir; I tell you it's not *grey* attitudes, but *bay* attitudes—doesn't every one know the eight beatitudes?"

"The eight *bay* attitudes; the nine ways of being guilty of another's sins; the ten commandments; the twelve fruits of a Christian; the fourteen stations of the cross; the fifteen mystheries of the passion——"

"Kelly," said his Reverence, interrupting him, and heralding the joke, for so it was intended, with a hearty chuckle, "you're getting fast out of your teens, ma bouchal!" and this was, of

* Temperance and fortitude.

course, honoured with a merry peal, extorted as much by an effort at softening the rigour of examination, as by the traditionary duty, which entails upon the Irish laity the necessity of laughing at a priest's jokes, without any reference at all to their quality. Nor was his Reverence's own voice the first to subside into that gravity which became the solemnity of the occasion; for, even whilst he continued the interrogatories, his eye was laughing at the conceit with which it was evident the inner man was not competent to grapple. "Well, Kelly, I can't say but you've answered very well, as far as the *repeating* of them goes: but, do you perfectly *understand* all the commandments of the church?"

"I do, Sir," replied Kelly, whose confidence kept pace with his Reverence's good humour.

"Well, what is meant by the fifth?"

"The fifth, Sir?" said the other, rather confounded—"I must begin agin, Sir, and go on till I come to it."

"Well," said the priest, "never mind that; but tell us what the eighth means?"

Kelly stared at him a second time, but was not able to advance. "First—Sundays and holidays, mass thou shalt hear;" but before he had proceeded to the second, a person who stood at his elbow began to whisper to him the proper reply, and, in the act of doing so, received a lash of the whip across the ear for his pains.

"You blackguard you!" exclaimed Father Philemy, "take that—how dare you attempt to prompt any person that *I*'m examining?"

Those who stood around Kelly now fell back to a safe distance, and all was silence, terror, and trepidation once more.

"Come, Kelly, go on—the eighth?"

Kelly was still silent.

"Why, you ninny you, didn't you repeat it just now. 'Eighth—And to his church neglect not tithes to pay.' Now that I have put the words in your mouth, what does it mean?"

Kelly having thus got the cue, replied in the words of the Catechism, "To pay *tides* to the lawful *pasterns* of the church, Sir."

"*Pasterns!* oh, you ass you, pasterns! You poor, base, contemptible, crawling reptile, as if we trampled you under our hooves—oh, you scruff of the earth! Stop, I say—it's *pastors*."

"Pasthors of the church."

"And tell me, do you fulfil that commandment?"

"I do, Sir."

"It's a lie, Sir," replied the priest, brandishing the whip over his head, whilst Kelly, instinctively, threw up his guard to protect himself from the blow; "It's a lie, Sir," repeated his Reverence, you don't fulfil it. What *is* the church?"

"The church is the congregation of the faithful that purfiss the true faith, and are obadient to the pope."

"And who do you pay your tithes to?"

"To the parson, Sir."

"And, you poor varmint you, is *he* obadient to the pope?"

Kelly only smiled at the want of comprehension which prevented him from seeing the thing according to the view which his Reverence took of it.

"Well, now," continued Father Philemy, "who are the *lawful* pastors of God's church?"

"You are, Sir, and all our own priests."

"And who ought you to pay your tithes to?"

"To you, Sir, in coorse; sure I always knew that, yer Rev'rence."

"And what's the reason, then, you don't pay them to me instead of the parson?"

This was a puzzler to Kelly, who only knew his own side of the question. "You have me there, Sir," he replied with a grin.

"Because," said his Reverence, "the Protestants, for the present, have the law of the land on their side, and power over you to compel the payment of tithes to themselves; but we have right, justice, and the law of God on ours; and, if every thing was in its proper place, it is not to the *parsons*, but to *us*, that you would pay them."

"Well, well, Sir," replied Kelly, who now experienced a community of feeling upon the subject with his Reverence, that instantly threw him into a familiarity of manner which he thought the point between them justified—"who knows, Sir?" said he with a knowing smile, "there's a good time coming, yer Rev'rence."

"Ay," said Father Philemy, "wait till we get once into the Big House, and if we don't turn the scales—if the Established Church doesn't go down, why, there's no truth in Scripture. Now, Kelly, all's right but the money—have you brought your dues?"

"Here it is, Sir," said Kelly, handing him his dues for the last year.

It is to be observed here, that, according as the penitents went to be examined, or to kneel down to confess, a certain sum was exacted from each, which varied according to the arrears that might have been due to the priest. Indeed, it is not unusual for the host and hostess, on these occasions, to be refused a participation in the sacrament, until they pay this money, notwithstanding the considerable expense they are put to in entertaining not only the clergy, but a certain number of their own friends and relations.

"Well, stand aside, I'll hear you first; and now come up here, you young gentleman, that laughed so heartily a while ago at my joke—ha, ha, ha!—come up here, child."

A lad now approached him, whose face, on a first view, had something simple and thoughtless in it, but in which, on a closer inspection, might be traced, a lurking, sarcastic humour, of which his Reverence never dreamt.

"You're for confession, of course," said the priest.

"*Of coorse*," said the lad, echoing him, and laying a stress upon the word, which did not much elevate the meaning of the blind compliance in general with the rite in question.

"Oh!" exclaimed the priest, recognizing him when he approached—"you are Dan Fegan's son, and designed for the church yourself; you are a good Latinist, for I remember examining you in Erasmus about two years ago—*Quomodo se habet corpus tuum Charum lignum sacerdotis?*"

"*Valde, Domine*," replied the lad, "*Quomodo se habet anima tua, charum exemplar sacer*dotage, *et fulcrum robustissimum Ecclesiæ sacrosanctæ.*"

"Very good, Harry," replied his Reverence,

laughing—" stand aside; I'll hear you after Kelly."

He then called up a man with a long melancholy face, which he noticed before to have been proof against his joke, and after making two or three additional fruitless experiments upon his gravity, he commenced a cross fire of peevish interrogatories, which would have excluded him from the "tribunal" on that occasion, were it not that the man was remarkably well prepared, and answered the priest's questions very pertinently.

This over, he repaired to his room, where the work of absolution commenced; and, as there was a considerable number to be rendered sinless before the hour of dinner, he contrived to unsin them with an alacrity that was really surprising.

Immediately after the conversation already detailed, between his Reverence and Phaddhy, the latter sought Katty, that he might communicate to her the unlucky oversight which they had committed, in neglecting to provide fresh meat and wine. "We'll be disgraced for ever," said Phaddhy, "without either a bit of mutton or a bottle of wine for the gintlemen, and that Parrah More Slevin had both."

"And I hope," replied Katty, "that you're not so mane as to let any of that faction out-do you in *dacency*, the nagerly set! It was enough for them to bate us in the law-shoot about the horse, and not to have the laugh agin at us about this."

"Well, that same law-shoot is not over with them yet," said Phaddhy; "wait till the spring fair comes, and if I don't have a faction gathered that'ill sweep them out of the town, why my name's not Phaddhy! But where is Mat. till we sind him off?"

"Arrah, Phaddhy," said Katty, "wasn't it friendly of Father Philemy to give us the *hard word* about the wine and mutton?"

"Very friendly," retorted Phaddhy, who, after all, appeared to have suspected the priest—"very friendly, indeed, when it's to put a good joint before himself, and a bottle of wine in his jacket. No, no, Katty! it's not altogether for the sake of Father Philemy, but I wouldn't have the neighbours say that I was near and undacent; and, above all things, I wouldn't be worse nor the Slevins—for the same set would keep it up agin us long enough."

Our readers will admire the tact with which Father Philemy worked upon the rival feeling between the factions; but, independently of this, there is a generous hospitality in an Irish peasant which would urge him to any stratagem, were it even the disposal of his only cow, sooner than incur the imputation of a narrow, or, as he himself terms it, "an undacent" or "nagerly" spirit.

In the course of a short time, Phaddhy dispatched two messengers, one for the wine, and another for the mutton; and, that they might not have cause for any unnecessary delay, he gave them the two Reverend gentlemen's horses, ordering them to spare neither whip nor spur until they returned. This was an agreeable command to the messengers, who, as soon as they found themselves mounted, made a bet of a "trate," to be paid on arriving in the town to which they were sent, to him who should first reach a little stream that crossed the road at the entrance of it, called the "pound burn." But I must not forget to state, that they not only were mounted on the priests' horses, but took their great coats, as the day had changed, and threatened to rain. Accordingly, on getting out upon the main road, they set off, whip and spur, at full speed, justling one another, and cutting each other's horses as if they had been intoxicated; and the fact is, that, owing to the liberal distribution of the bottle that morning, they were not far from it.

"Bliss us!" exclaimed the country people, as they passed, "what on airth can be the matther with Father Philemy and Father Con that they're abusing wan another at sich a rate!"

"Oh!" exclaimed another, "it's apt to be a sick call, and they're thrying to be there before the body grows cowld."

"Ay, or may be," a third conjectured, "it's to ould Magennis, that's on the point of death, and going to lave all his money behind him, and they're striving to see who'll get there first."

But their astonishment was not a whit lessened, when, in about an hour afterwards, they perceived them both return; the person who represented Father Con, having an overgrown leg of mutton slung behind his back like an Irish harp, reckless of its friction against his Reverence's coat, which it had completely saturated with grease, and the duplicate of Father Philemy with a sack over his shoulder, in the bottom of which was half a dozen of Mr. M'Laughlin's best port.

Phaddhy, in the meantime, being determined to mortify his rival Parrah More by a superior display of hospitality, waited upon that personage, and exacted a promise from him to come down and partake of the dinner—a promise which the other was not slack in fulfilling. Phaddhy's heart was now on the point of taking its rest, when it occurred to him that there yet remained one circumstance in which he might utterly eclipse his rival, and that was to ask Captain Wilson, his landlord, to meet their Reverences at dinner. He accordingly went over to him, for he only lived a few miles distant, having first communicated the thing privately to Katty, and requested that as their Reverences that day held a station in his house, and would dine there, he would have the kindness to dine along with them. To this the Captain, who was intimate with both the clergymen, gave a ready compliance, and Phaddhy returned home in high spirits.

In the meantime the two priests were busy in the work of absolution; the hour of three had arrived, and they had many to shrive; but, in the course of a short time, a Reverend auxiliary made his appearance, accompanied by one of Father Philemy's nephews, who was then about to enter Maynooth. This clerical gentleman had been appointed to a parish, but owing to some circumstances which were known only in the distant part of the diocese where he had resided, he was deprived of it, and had, at the period I am writing of, no appointment in the church, though he was in full orders. If I mistake not, he incurred his bishop's displeasure by being too warm an advocate for domestic nomination, a piece of discipline, the re-establishment of which was then attempted by the junior clergymen of the diocese wherein the scene of this station is laid. Be this as it may, he came in time to assist the gentlemen in absolving those penitents (as we must call them so) who still remained unconfessed.

During all this time Katty was in the plenitude of her authority, and her sense of importance manifested itself in a manner that was by no means softened by having been that morning at her duty. Her tones were not so shrill, nor so loud as they would have been, had not their Reverences been within hearing; but what was wanting in loudness, was displayed in a firm and decided energy, that vented itself frequently in the course of the day upon the backs and heads of her sons, daughters, and servants, as they crossed her path in the impatience and bustle of her employment. It was truly ludicrous to see her, on encountering one of them in these fretful moments, give him a drive head foremost against the wall, exclaiming, as she shook her fist at him, "Ho, you may bless your stars, that *they're* under the roof, or it wouldn't go so asy wid you; for if goodness hasn't said it, you'll make me lose my sowl this blessed and holy day: but this is still the case—the very time I go to my duty, the devil (between us and harm) is sure to throw fifty temptations acrass me, and to help him, you must come in my way—but wait till to-morrow, and if I don't pay you for this, I'm not here."

That a station is an expensive ordinance to the peasant who is honoured by having one held in his house, no one who knows the characteristic hospitality of the Irish people can doubt. I have reason, however, to think, that since the Church of Rome and her discipline have undergone so rigorous a scrutiny by the advocates of scriptural truth, she has been much more cautious in the manner in which they have been conducted. The policy of Romanism has uniformly been, to adapt herself to the circumstances by which she may be surrounded; and as the unbecoming licentiousness, which about twenty, or even so late as fifteen years ago, trod so closely upon the heels of a ceremony which the worship of God and the administration of sacramental rites, should have in a peculiar manner solemnized, was utterly disgraceful and shocking—she felt that it was expedient, as knowledge advanced around her, to practice a greater degree of external decorum and circumspection, lest her *little ones* should be scandalized. This, however, did not render it necessary that she should effect much reformation on this point in those parts of the kingdom which are exclusively Catholic; and accordingly stations, with some exceptions in a certain diocese, go on much in the old manner, as to the expense which they occasion the people to incur, and the jolly convivial spirit which winds them up.

About four o'clock the penitents were at length all dispatched; and those who were to be detained for dinner, many of whom had not eaten any thing until then, in consequence of the necessity of receiving the Eucharist fasting, were taken aside to taste some of Phaddhy's poteen. Of course, no remorse was felt at the impiety of mingling it so soon with the sacrament they had just received, believing, as they did, the latter to contain the immaculate Deity; but, indeed, their Reverences at breakfast had set them a pretty example on that point. At length the hour of dinner arrived, and along with it the redoubtable Parrah More Slevin, Captain Wilson, and another nephew of Father Philemy's, who had come to know what detained his brother who had conducted the auxiliary priest to Phaddhy's. It is surprising, on these occasions, to think how many uncles, and nephews, and cousins, to the forty-second degree, find it needful to follow their Reverences on messages of various kinds; and it is equally surprising to observe with what exactness they drop in during the hour of dinner. Of course, any blood-relation or friend of the priest's must be received with cordiality; and consequently they do not return without solid proofs of the good-natured hospitality of poor Paddy, who feels no greater pleasure than in showing his "dacency" to any belonging to his Reverence.

I dare say it would be difficult to find a more motley and diversified company than sat down to the ungarnished fare which Katty laid before them. There were first, Fathers Philemy, Con, and the Auxiliary from the far part of the diocese; next followed Captain Wilson, Peter Malone, and Father Philemy's two nephews; after these came Phaddhy himself, Parrah More Slevin, with about two dozen more of the most remarkable and uncouth personages that could sit down to table. There were besides about a dozen of females, most of whom by this time, owing to Katty's private kindness, and a slight thirst occasioned by the long fast, were in a most independent and placid state of feeling. Father Philemy, *ex officio*, filled the chair—he was a small man, with cherub cheeks as red as roses, black twinkling eyes, and double chin; was of the fat-headed genus, and, if phrenologists be correct, must have given indications of early piety, for he was bald before his time, and had the organ of veneration standing visible on his crown; his hair, from having once been black, had become an iron-grey, and hung down behind his ears, resting on the collar of his coat according to the old school, to which, I must remark, he belonged, having been educated on the Continent. His coat had large double breasts, the lappels of which hung down loosely on each side, being the prototype of his waistcoat, whose double breasts fell downwards in the same manner—his black small-clothes had silver buckles at the knees, and the gaiters, which did not reach up so far, discovered a pair of white lamb's-wool stockings, somewhat retreating from their original colour.

Father Con was a tall, muscular, able-bodied young man, with an immensely broad pair of shoulders, of which he was vain; his black hair was cropped close, except a thin portion of it which was trimmed quite evenly across his eyebrows; he was rather bow-limbed, and when walking looked upwards, holding out his elbows from his body, and letting the lower parts of his arms fall down, so that he went as if he carried a keg under each; his coat, though not well made, was of the best glossy broad cloth—and his long clerical boots went up about his knees like a dragoon's; there was an awkward stiffness about him, in very good keeping with a dark melancholy cast of countenance, in which, however, a man might discover an air of simplicity not to be found in the visage of his superior, Father Philemy.

The latter gentleman filled the chair, as I said, and carved the goose; on his right sat Captain Wilson; on his left, the Auxiliary—next to them Father Con, the nephews, Peter Malone, *et cetera.* To enumerate the items of the dinner is unnecessary, as our readers have a pretty accurate notion of them from what we have already said. We can only observe, that when Phaddhy saw it laid, and all the wheels of the system fairly set a-going, he looked at Parrah More with an air of triumph which he could not conceal. It is also unnecessary for us to give the conversation in full; nor, indeed, would we attempt giving any portion of it, seeing it was not very edifying, except for the purpose of showing the spirit in which a religious ceremony, looked upon by its advocates as one of particular solemnity, is too frequently closed.

The talk in the beginning was altogether confined to the clergymen and Mr. Wilson, including a few diffident contributions from "Pether Malone," and the "two nephews."

"Mr. M'Guirk," observed Captain Wilson, after the conversation had taken several turns, "I'm sure that in the course of your professional duties, Sir, you must have had occasion to make many observations upon human nature, from the circumstance of seeing it in every condition and state of feeling possible; from the baptism of the infant, until the aged man receives the last rites of your church, and the sweet consolations of religion from your hand."

"Not a doubt of it, Phaddhy," said Father Philemy to Phaddhy, whom he had been addressing at the time, "not a doubt of it; and I'll do every thing in my power to get him in too, and I am told he is bright."

"Uncle," said one of the nephews, "this gentleman is speaking to you."

"And why not?" continued his Reverence, who was so closely engaged with Phaddhy, that he did not hear even the nephew's appeal—"a bishop—and why not? Has he not as good a chance of being a bishop as any of them? though, God knows, it is not always merit that gets a bishoprick in any church, or I myself might—— But let *that* pass," said he, fixing his eyes on the bottle.

"Father Philemy," said Father Con, "Captain Wilson was addressing himself to you in a most especial manner."

"Oh! Captain, I beg ten thousand pardons, I was engaged talking with Phaddhy here about his son, who is a young shaving of our cloth, Sir; he is intended for the *mission*.——Phaddhy, I will either examine him myself, or make Father Con examine him, by-and-by.——Well, Captain?"

The Captain now repeated what he had said.

"Very true, Captain, and we do see it in as many shapes as ever—Con, what do you call him?—put on him."

"Proteus," subjoined Con, who was famous at the classics.

"Father Philemy nodded for the assistance, and continued—"but as for human nature, Captain, give it to me at a good roasting christening; or, what is better again, at a jovial wedding between two of my own parishioners—say this pretty, fair-haired daughter of Phaddhy Sheemus Phaddhy's here, and long Ned Slevin, Parrah More's son there—eh, Phaddhy, will it be a match?—what do you say, Parrah More? Upon my veracity I must bring that about."

"Why, then, yer Reverence," replied Phaddhy, who was now a little softened, and forgot his enmity against Parrah More for the present, "unlikelier things might happen."

"It won't be my fault," said Parrah More, "if my son Ned has no objection."

"*He* object!" replied Father Philemy, "if *I* take it in hands, let me see who'll dare to object; doesn't the Scripture say it? and sure we can't go against the Scripture."

"By the by," said Captain Wilson, who was a dry humourist, "I am happy to be able to infer from what you say, Father Philemy, that you are not, as the clergymen of your church are supposed to be, inimical to the Bible."

"Me an enemy to the Bible! no such thing, Sir; but, Captain, begging your pardon, we'll have nothing more about the Bible: you see we are met here, as friends and good fellows, to enjoy ourselves after the severity of our spiritual duties, and we must relax a little; we can't always carry long faces like Methodist parsons—come, Parrah More, let the Bible take a nap, and give us a song."

His Reverence was now seconded in his motion by the most of all present, and Parrah More, accordingly gave them a song. After a few songs more, the conversation went on as before.

"Now, Parrah More," said Phaddhy, you must try *my wine;* I hope it' as good as what *you* gave his Reverence yesterday."

The words, however, had scarcely passed his lips, when Father Philemy burst out into a fit of laughter, clapping and rubbing his hands in a manner the most astonishing. "Oh, Phaddhy, Phaddhy!" shouted his Reverence, laughing heartily, "I *done* you for once—I done you, my man, *cute* as you thought yourself: why, you nager you, did you think to put us off with punch, and you have a stocking of hard guineas hid in a hole in the wall?"

"What does yer Rev'rence mane," said Phaddhy; "for myself can make no undherstanding out of it, at all at all?"

To this his Reverence only replied by another laugh.

"*I* gave his Reverence no wine," said Parrah More, in reply to Phaddhy's question.

"What!" said Phaddhy, "none yesterday, at the station held with you?"

"Not a bit of me ever thought of it."

"Nor no mutton?"

"Why, then, devil a morsel of mutton, Phaddhy; but we had a rib of beef."

Phaddhy now looked over to his Reverence rather sheepishly, with the smile of a man on his face who felt himself foiled. "Well, yer Reverence has *done* me, sure enough," he replied, rubbing his head—"I give it up to you, Father Philemy; but, any how, I'm glad I got it, and you're all welcome from the core of my heart. I'm only sorry I haven't as much more now to thrate you all like gintlemen; but there's some yet, and as much punch as will make all our heads come round."

Our readers must assist us with their own imaginations, and suppose the conversation to have passed very pleasantly, and the night, as well as the guests, to be somewhat *far gone*. The principal part of the conversation was borne by the three clergymen, Captain Wilson, and Phaddhy; that of the two nephews and Peter Malone ran in an under current of its own; and in the preceding part of the night, those who occupied the bottom of the table, spoke to each other rather in whispers, being too much restrained by that rustic bashfulness which ties up the tongues of those who feel that their consequence is overlooked among their superiors. According as the punch circulated, however, their diffidence began to wear off; and occasionally an odd laugh or so might be heard to break the monotony of their silence. The youngsters, too, though at first almost in a state of terror, soon commenced plucking each other; and a titter, or a suppressed burst of laughter, would break forth from one of the more waggish, who was put to a severe task in afterwards composing his countenance into sufficient gravity to escape detection, and a competent portion of chastisement the next day, for not being able to "behave himself with betther manners."

During these juvenile breaches of decorum, Katty would raise her arm in a threatening attitude, shake her head at them, and look up at the clergy, intimating more by her earnestness of gesticulation than met the ear. Several songs again went round, of which, truth to tell, Father Philemy's were by far the best; for he possessed a rich, comic expression of eye, which, added to suitable ludicrousness of gesture, and a good voice, rendered him highly amusing to the company. Father Con declined singing, as being decidedly serious, though he was often solicited.

"He!" said Father Philemy, "he's no more voice than a wool-pack; but Con's a cunning fellow. What do you think, Captain Wilson, but he pretends to be too pious to sing, and gets credit for piety—not because he is devout, but because he has a bad voice: now, Con, you can't deny it, for there's not a man in the three kingdoms knows it better than myself; you sit there with a face upon you that might go before the lamentations of Jeremiah the Prophet, when you ought to be as jovial as another."

"Well, Father Philemy," said Phaddhy, "as he won't sing, may be, wid submission, he'd examine Briney in his Latin, till his mother and I hear how he's doing at it."

"Ay, he's fond of dabbling at Latin, so he may try him—I'm sure I have no objection——: so, Captain, as I was telling you——"

"Silence there below!" said Phaddhy to those at the lower end of the table, who were now talkative enough; will yees whisht there till Father Con hears Briney a lesson in his Latin. Where are you, Briney? come here, ma bouchal."

But Briney had absconded when he saw that the tug of war was about to commence. In a few minutes, however, the father returned, pushing the boy before him, who, in his reluctance to encounter the ordeal of examination, clung to every chair, table, and person in his way, hoping that his restiveness might induce them to postpone the examination till another occasion. The father, however, was inexorable, and by main force dragged him from all his holds, and placed him beside Father Con.

"What's come over you, at all at all, you insignified *shingawn* you, to affront the gintleman in this way, and he kind enough to go for to give you an *examination?*—come now, you had betther not vex me, I tell you, but hould up your head, and spake out loud, that we can all hear you: now, Father Con, achora, you'll not be too hard upon him in the beginning, till he gets into it, for he's aisy dashed."

"Here, Briney," said Father Philemy, handing him his tumbler, "take a pull of this, and if you have any courage at all in you it will raise it;—take a good pull."

Briney hesitated.

"Why but you take the glass out of his Reverence's hand, sarrah," said the father—"what! is it without dhrinking his Reverence's health first!"

Briney gave a most melancholy nod at his Reverence, as he put the tumbler to his mouth, which he nearly emptied, notwithstanding his shyness.

"For my part," said his Reverence, looking at the almost empty tumbler, "I am pretty sure that that same chap will be able to take care of himself through life. And so, Captain,———" said he, resuming the conversation with Captain Wilson—for his notice of Briney was only parenthetical.

Father Con now took the book, which was Æsop's Fables, and, in accordance with Briney's intention, it opened exactly at the favourite fable of Gallus Gallinaceus. He was not aware, however, that Briney had kept that place open during the preceding part of the week, in order to effect this point. Father Philemy, however, was now beginning to relate another anecdote to the Cap-

tain, and the thread of his narrative twined rather ludicrously with that of the examination.

Briney, after a few hems, at length proceeded —" *Gallus Gallinaceus*, a dunghill cock——"

" So, Captain, I was just after coming out of Widow Moylan's—it was in the Lammas fair—and a large one, by the by, it was—so, Sir, who should come up to me but Branagan. 'Well, Branagan,' said I 'how does the world go now with you?'——"

" *Gallus Gallinaceus*, a dunghill cock——"

——" Says he. 'And how is that?' says I,——"

" *Gallus Gallinaceus*——"

——" Says he, 'Hut tut, Branagan,' says I—'you're drunk.' 'That's the thing, Sir,' says Branagan, 'and I want to explain it all to your Reverence.' 'Well,' said I, 'go on.'——"

" *Gallus Gallinaceus*, a dunghill cock——"

——" Says he,——Let your *Gallus Gallinaceus* go to roost for this night, Con," said Father Philemy, who did not relish the interruption of his story; "I say, Phaddhy, send the boy to bed, and bring him down in your hand to my house on Saturday morning, and we will both examine him, but this is no time for it, and me engaged in conversation with Captain Wilson.—So, Captain——'Well, Sir,' says Branagan, and he staggering, 'I took an oath against liquor, and I want your Reverence to break it,' says he. 'What do you mean?' I enquired. 'Why, please your Reverence,' said he, 'I took an oath against liquor, as I told you, not to drink more nor a pint of whiskey in one day, and I want your Reverence to break it for me, and make it only half a pint; for I find that a pint is too much for me; by the same token, that when I get that far, your Reverence, I disremember the oath entirely.'"

The influence of the bottle now began to be felt, and the conversation absolutely blew a gale, wherein hearty laughter, good strong singing, loud argument, and general good-humour blended into one uproarious peal of hilarity, accompanied by some smart flashes of wit and humour, which would not disgrace a prouder banquet. Phaddhy, in particular, melted into a spirit of the most unbounded benevolence—a spirit that would (if by any possible means he could effect it) embrace the whole human race; that is to say, he would raise them, man, woman, and child, to the same elevated state of happiness which he enjoyed himself. That, indeed, was happiness in perfection, as pure and as unadulterated as the poteen which created it. How could he be otherwise than happy?—he had succeeded to a good property, and a stocking of hard guineas, without the hard labour of acquiring them; he had the "clargy" under his roof at last, partaking of a hospitality which he felt himself well able to afford them; he had settled with his Reverence for five years' arrears of sin, all of which had been wiped out of his conscience by the blessed absolving hand of the priest; he was training up Briney for the Mission, and, though last, not least, he was——far gone in his seventh tumbler!

"Come, jinteels," said he, "spare nothing here—there's lashings of every thing; thrate yourselves dacent, and don't be saying to-morrow or next day, that ever my father's son was nagerly. Death alive, Father Con, what are you doin'? Why, then, bad manners to me if that'ill sarve, any how."

"Phaddhy," replied Father Con, "I assure you I have done my duty."

"Very well, Father Con, granting all that, it's no sin to repate a good turn, you know. Not a word I'll hear, yer Reverence—one tumbler along with myself, if it was only for ould times." He then filled Father Con's tumbler, with his own hand, in a truly liberal spirit. "Arrah Father Con, do you remember the day we had the leapin'-match, and the bout at the shoulder-stone?"

"Indeed, I'll not forget it, Phaddhy."

"And it's yourself that may say that; but I bleeve I rubbed the consate off of your Reverence —only that's betune ourselves, you persave."

"You did win the palm, Phaddhy, I'll not deny it; but you are the only man that ever *bet* me at either of the athletics."

"And I'll say this for yer Reverence, that you are one of the best and most able-bodied gintlemen I ever engaged with. Ah! Father Con, I'm past all that now—but no matter, here's yer Reverence's health, and a shake hands; Father Philemy, yer health, docthor: yer strange Reverence's health—Captain Wilson, not forgetting you, Sir: Mr. Pether, yours; and I hope to see you soon with the robes upon you, and to be able to prache us a good sarmon. Parrah More—*wus dha lauv** give me yer hand, you steeple you; and I hav'nt the smallest taste of objection to what Father Philemy hinted at—ye'll obsarve. Katty, you thief o' the world, where are you? Your health, avourneen; come here, and give us your fist, Katty: bad manners to me if I could forget you afther all;—the best crathur, your Reverence, undher the sun, except when yer Reverence puts yer *comedher* on her at confession, and then she's a little sharp or so, not a doubt of it: but no mat-

* The translation follows it.

ther, Katty ahagur, you do it all for the best. And Father Philemy, maybe it's myself didn't put the thrick upon you in the Maragy More, about Katty's death—ha, ha, ha! Jack M'Cramer, yer health—all yer healths, and yer welcome here, if you war seven times as many. Briney, where are you, ma bouchal? Come up and shake hands wid yer father, as well as another—come up, acushla, and kiss me. Ah, Briney, my poor fellow, ye'll never be the cut of a man yer father was; but no matther, avourneen, ye'll be a betther man, I hope; and God knows you may asy be that, for Father Philemy, I'm not what I ought to be, yer Reverence; however, I may mend, and will, maybe, before a month of Sundays goes over me: but, for all that, Briney, I hope to see the day when you'll be siting an ordained priest, at my own table; if I once saw that, I could die contented—so mind yer larning, acushla, and his Reverence here will back you, and make interest to get you into the college. Musha, God pity them crathurs at the door—aren't they gone yet? Listen to them coughin', for fraid we'd forget them: and throth and they won't be forgot this bout, any how—Katty, avourneen, give them every one, big and little, young and ould, their skinfull—don't lave a wrinkle in them; and see, take one of them bottles—the crathurs, they're starved sitting there all night in the could—and give them a couple of glasses a-piece—it's good, yer Reverence, to have the poor body's blessing at all times; and now, as I was saying, Here's all yer healths! *and from the very veins of my heart yer welcome here.*"

Our readers may perceive that Phaddhy

> "Was not only blest, but glorious,
> O'er a' the ills o' life victorious;"

for, like the generality of our peasantry, the native drew to the surface of his character those warm, hospitable, and benevolent virtues, which a purer system of morals and education would most certainly keep in full action, without running the risk, as in the present instance, of mixing bad habits with frank, manly, and generous qualities.

* * * * * *

* * * * * *

"I'll not go, Con—I tell you I'll not go, till I sing another song. Phaddhy, you're a prince—but where's the use of lighting more candles now, man, than you had in the beginning of the night? Is Captain Wilson gone? Then, peace be with him; it's a pity he wasn't on the right side, for he's not the worst of them. Phaddhy, where are you?

"Why, yer Reverence," replied Katty, "he's

got a little unwell, and jist laid down his head a bit."

"Katty," said Father Con, "you had better get a couple of the men to accompany Father Philemy home; for, though the night's clear, he doesn't see his way very well in the dark—poor man, his eye-sight's failing him fast."

"Then, the more's the pity, Father Con. Here, Denis, let yourself and Mat go home wid Father Philemy."

"Good night, Katty," said Father Con—"Good night: and may our blessing *sanctify* you all!"

"Good night, Father Con, ahagur," replied Katty; "and for goodness' sake see that they take care of Father Philemy, for it's himself that's the blessed and holy crathur, and the pleasant gintleman, out and out."

"Good night, Katty," again repeated Father Con, as the cavalcade proceeded in a body—"Good night!" And so ended the Station.

GALLUS
Gallinaceus

CPSIA information can be obtained at www.ICGtesting.com
Printed in the USA
LVOW11s1852230913

353733LV00019B/944/P